828562 L4·95

GW00724528

COMPUTER LOGIC:
Principles and Technology

ELLIS HORWOOD BOOKS IN COMPUTING SCIENCE

General Editors: Professor JOHN CAMPBELL, University College London, and BRIAN L. MEEK, King's College London (KQC), University of London

Series in Computers and Their Applications

Series Editor: BRIAN L. MEEK, Computer Centre, King's College London (KQC), University of London

Series continued at end of book

COMPUTER LOGIC:
Principles and Technology

DAVID HUTCHISON, Ph.D., M.B.C.S., C.Eng., M.I.E.E.
Department of Computing

and

PETER SILVESTER, B.Sc., Dipl.El., C.Eng., M.I.E.E.
Department of Engineering

University of Lancaster

ELLIS HORWOOD LIMITED
Publishers · Chichester

Halsted Press: a division of
JOHN WILEY & SONS
New York · Chichester · Brisbane · Toronto

First published in 1987 by
ELLIS HORWOOD LIMITED
Market Cross House, Cooper Street,
Chichester, West Sussex, PO19 1EB, England
The publisher's colophon is reproduced from James Gillison's drawing of the ancient Market Cross, Chichester.

Distributors:

Australia and New Zealand:
JACARANDA WILEY LIMITED
GPO Box 859, Brisbane, Queensland 4001, Australia

Canada:
JOHN WILEY & SONS CANADA LIMITED
22 Worcester Road, Rexdale, Ontario, Canada

Europe and Africa:
JOHN WILEY & SONS LIMITED
Baffins Lane, Chichester, West Sussex, England

North and South America and the rest of the world:
Halsted Press: a division of
JOHN WILEY & SONS
605 Third Avenue, New York, NY 10158, USA

© **1987 D. Hutchison and P. Silvester/Ellis Horwood Limited**

British Library Cataloguing in Publication Data
Hutchison, David *1949–*
Computer logic: principles and techniques. — [Rev. ed.] —
(Ellis Horwood series in computers and their applications)
1. Logic circuits
2. Electronic digital computers — Circuits
I. Title   II. Silvester, Peter
III. Hutchison, David *1949* Fundamentals of computer logic
621.395   TK7888.4

Library of Congress Card No. 87–21356

ISBN 0–7458–0316–4 (Ellis Horwood Limited — Library Edn.)
ISBN 0–7458–0317–2 (Ellis Horwood Limited — Student Edn.)
ISBN 0–470–20988–7 (Halsted Press)

Phototypeset in Times by Ellis Horwood Limited
Printed in Great Britain by R. J. Acford, Chichester

COPYRIGHT NOTICE
All Rights Reserved. No part of this publication may be reproduced, stored in a retrieval system, or transmitted, in any form or by any means, electronic, mechanical, photocopying, recording or otherwise, without the permission of Ellis Horwood Limited, Market Cross House, Cooper Street, Chichester, West Sussex, England.

Contents

Authors' preface

This book is an updated version of *Fundamentals of Computer Logic* by David Hutchison previously issued in 1981 in the Ellis Horwood series in Computers and Their Applications. Much of the material in the earlier text has been revised in the light of developments in the subject over the last five years, and two entirely new chapters have been added: Chapter 5 on VLSI circuit design and Chapter 8 on new computer architectures. The approach used in the original text has been preserved. Material is introduced in a bottom-up way, starting with a description of the basic building blocks of logic circuits and proceeding in a series of layers to build a picture of how computers are designed and constructed. Although the material is principally concerned with computer hardware, some attention is paid to the mutual dependence of hardware and software requirements in computer design.

While the book is aimed primarily at first- and second-year undergraduate students at universities and polytechnics—in computer science, microprocessor studies and related engineering subjects—the approach is intended also to benefit those with an interest in computers from a mainly hardware point of view. Those who wish to learn about logic building blocks and their use in designing logic circuits (on printed circuit boards or VLSI chips), but not necessarily their application in computers, are also catered for, since these topics—the core of the book—are essentially self-standing. A little background knowledge is required: a familiarity with binary numbers and an acquaintance with the notion of programming. The reader who has attended a short course on computer appreciation will be well enough prepared.

Chapter 1 sets the scene of the book by presenting a brief history of computers and outlining the structural layers of a modern 'von Neumann' computer. In Chapter 2 the building blocks of logic are introduced from both an abstract and a physical point of view: the theory of Boolean algebra and the implementation tools of integrated circuits ('chips') are brought together. The TTL circuit which has 'set the standard' for many years is described in detail, together with the MOS structures which are now widely used in VLSI design. Chapter 3 classifies logic circuits into combinational and sequential varieties, and describes techniques for designing both types of circuit, with worked examples in each case. Further worked design examples are presented in Chapter 4, along with other aspects of the uses of logic circuits in practice. Several logic circuits which form the basic building blocks of computers are introduced. Chapter 5 is an introduction to VLSI circuit design, covering both software design aids (CAD) and hardware realisation and testing of silicon chips. Chapter 6 illustrates how circuits introduced in earlier chapters fit together to implement the major functional units in a computer. Particular attention is paid to the design of arithmetic and control units. The interdependence of hardware and software design is discussed in Chapter 7. Computer architectures other than the familiar von Neumann one are described in Chapter 8.

Appendix 1 contains a sample of typical literature available from a semiconductor manufacturer, describing some of the small-scale integrated circuits with which logic circuits and computers can be constructed. In the book the importance of referring to, and understanding, such data sheets is emphasised. Appendix 2 is an example of the kind of data sheet available to designers using programmable logic devices. Appendix 3 gives brief details of four typical examples of VLSI design systems together with addresses from which further information about them can be obtained. The Reading List contains chapter-by-chapter recommendations for further reading. Few references are included in the text, but the annotations with each title in the List direct the reader to suitable sources for specific topics.

Students using this book as a course text will greatly benefit from practical courses illustrating both the use of integrated circuits in logic design and the way in which computers can be used to aid this design process. Both the practical work and the choice of any design problems for students are left to the discretion, and ingenuity, of the course lecturer. The computer aided design (CAD) system used will depend on what is available at the reader's place of learning.

Thanks are due to students of Computer Science in the Universities of Strathclyde and Lancaster and to Engineering students at Lancaster who have helped, wittingly or otherwise, to evolve the approach used in this book by their participation in courses in logic design and computer appreciation at the two establishments. Our thanks in general go to our colleagues for helpful comments and advice and to Miss Agnes Wisley and Mrs Judith Haxby for their help in typing the manuscript. Brian Meek (the Series Editor) and Michael Horwood and Melanie Leggett for the publishers have helped give the book shape and direction and have been very patient during the several stages of its revision. We are most grateful to them.

Lancaster, *July 1987*

1

The structure of computers

1.1 INTRODUCTION

Computers have two major ingredients: hardware and software. *Hardware* is the collective term used to describe the physical units of the computer—the processor, memory and peripheral devices, including all mechanical and electronic components. *Software,* on the other hand, refers in general to the programs which cause the computer hardware to obey specific sequences of instructions. The physical realisation of software is either a set of instructions, written in a particular language, on a piece of paper or a pattern of binary digits (*bits*) in the memory hardware of a computer.

Very often a distinction is made between system software and applications software. *System software,* sometimes referred to confusingly as simply software, is a set of programs written by the manufacturer or supplier of the hardware (or in some cases by the users themselves). This software consists of an *operating system* which controls the basic functions of the hardware, and a set of utility programs such as language translators, editors and debugging aids. Depending on the intended application area of the computer its operating system may provide more or less extensive facilities: in a large multi-access machine the operating system may have to service the widely-different needs of its many concurrent users and support a complex file system held on magnetic discs and tape. At the opposite extreme a small single-user computer may require an operating system which simply allows single programs to be loaded and started, and memory locations to be inspected and their contents altered. All computers require some system software which enables users to operate them easily. The extent to which utility programs are provided also depends on how the computer is used: systems on which programs are constantly being developed would typically have available a variety of high-level language compilers and a file editor, whereas dedicated systems in which the programs are fixed and proven may provide no such utilities along with the operating system.

Applications software, usually written by users or software houses, tailors a computer system (already provided with system software) to a particular task or application. Typically applications software is written in a high-level programming language such as COBOL, FORTRAN or Pascal, and in this way the hardware features of the computer are hidden from the programmer. The compiler translates the user program into machine-code instructions, the form in which the computer can understand the programmer's intentions. Interaction with the outside world, via the peripheral devices, is handled on behalf of the programmer by the operating system; the programmer simply indicates the need for input or output by means of a high-level statement such as read(X) or print(X) in the program text. In special circumstances, such as cases in which the speed of operation of programs is critical, applications may be programmed in assembly language, a symbolic form of the machine-code which computers understand. The central part, or kernel, of an operating system is often written in this machine-oriented form. Applications written in assembly language also rely on the presence of an operating system to control the resources of the computer hardware and to provide a machine-independent user interface.

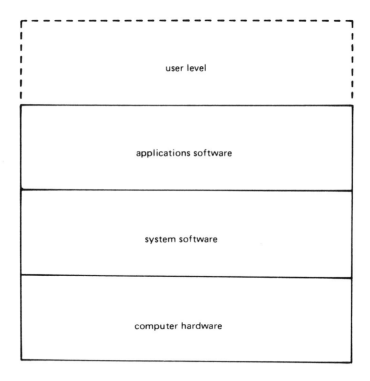

Fig. 1.1 — The broad layers of a computer system.

In very general terms the structure of a computer system can be illustrated as in Fig. 1.1. This shows the three components introduced above—hardware, system software, and applications software—ordered in a hierarchy or a set of *layers*. The computer hardware is the lowest, or most basic, of the layers, while the highest layer in the computer hierarchy is the user level. Strictly speaking the user level is not a part of the computer as such; this is indicated by the dashed lines in the diagram.

Each layer provides a set of facilities for the one above. The architecture of the computer hardware determines the nature of the machine features which the system software has to handle; the type of use of the computer system influences the facilities which the system software offers to the applications programmer; and lastly, but very importantly, the applications level should provide a friendly set of facilities to the users. The boundary between one layer and the next is termed an *interface*: as we go from the hardware to the user level the interface facilities offered are more and more high-level, in other words further from the low-level machine features and somewhat closer to a form which people can easily understand. The *man-machine interface,* as the highest-level interface is called, is increasingly important with computer systems finding their way into every office and factory, where non-expert users are called upon to operate them.

* * *

The scope of this book falls well short of the man-machine interface, and short also of applications software. It deals with computer hardware, and to some extent with the interface between hardware and system software. More specifically the book is about *computer logic,* the electronic rather than the mechanical aspects of computer hardware—the logic circuits as opposed to the moving parts such as magnetic discs or line printers. The remainder of this chapter outlines the context in which the main material of the text is set.

1.2   COMPUTER LOGIC

To explain the meaning of computer logic let us look a little more deeply into the hardware layer of the computer system. It should be borne in mind that in this book we are dealing exclusively with *digital* as opposed to *analogue* computers. Analogue computers represent information in the form of continuously varying voltages or currents and are used in special-purpose applications like the design of automobile suspension systems where the physical system can be modelled or simulated by the computer.

A brief history
Digital computers represent information in discrete binary (two-valued) form and have evolved from the calculating machines of the last century, including Charles Babbage's design for an Analytical Engine (1837) and Hollerith's Electric Tabulating System (1889). The first electronic computer was the ENIAC (1946), inspired by a memorandum of J. W. Mauchly in 1942 within the Moore School of Electrical Engineering at the University of Pennsylvania. The ENIAC (Electronic Numerical Integrator and Calculator) took three years to build and was large-scale in every way. It contained

some 19,000 valves, weighed 30 tons and consumed 200 kilowatts of electricity. It was also extremely fast by the standards of the day, being able to multiply two 10-digit decimal numbers in 3 milliseconds. However, the effort of programming the ENIAC was such as to discourage its use for any other than extensive computational problems, since it had to be programmed manually by plugging and unplugging sets of connecting wires. Data could be entered using a punched card reader, and results output on punched cards or on an electric typewriter. A large team was responsible for the design and construction of the ENIAC, most notably J. P. Eckert and J. W. Mauchly who in 1947 jointly founded a company to produce computers commercially. One of their first products was called the UNIVAC (Universal Automatic Computer). Later their company became the UNIVAC division of the Sperry-Rand Corporation, which along with IBM began selling computers successfully in the early 1950s.

Another member of the Moore School team, John von Neumann (1903–1957), is credited with the idea now seen as the final step in the development of the general-purpose computer. This is the idea of a *stored-program* machine in which program and data share a common memory. The most important consequence is that programming is made very much easier; thus the computer possesses a generalised instruction set, fixed into its hardware, and the program—consisting of a sequence of appropriately chosen instructions—can be read in via a punched-card reader in the same way as the data. An additional consequence, one that has had less lasting significance, is that programs can be made to modify their own instructions.

There is evidence to suggest that others before von Neumann had the notion of a stored-program computer, notably Konrad Zuse (in his 1936 paper), who produced in Germany in the 1930s a series of mechanical and electro-mechanical computers called Z1, Z2 and Z3; A. M. Turing, whose 1936 abstract model of a computer—called a Turing machine—formed the basis for much of the present-day knowledge of the theory of computation; and even Charles Babbage, although in his case perhaps the suggestion is closer to speculation than in the others. However, it is certain that von Neumann's draft report on the EDVAC (Electronic Discrete Variable Computer) written in 1945 contains the earliest documented presentation of the stored-program idea. The EDVAC was the successor to ENIAC and contained several design changes which originated during the ENIAC project. The main differences were that it was a binary rather than a decimal machine and that it had a much larger memory: 1K (or 1024) 40-bit words of mercury delay-line main store, plus a secondary, slower magnetic store 20K words in size. This machine did not become operational until 1951.

Meantime a report written for the U.S. Army Ordnance Department in 1946 by Burks, Goldstine and von Neumann proposed a methodology for designing computers. This report was the first of a series which led to yet another machine called the IAS. In effect its proposals summarise the characteristics of *first-generation* digital computers. Burks, Goldstine and von Neumann suggest the following features:

—main units: control
                 arithmetic
                 memory
                 input/output communication
—program and data sharing the memory
—binary internal forms
—a synchronous clock system
—the use of subroutines
—possible adder hardware, but multiplier software
—the use of an accumulator register
—parallel operation for memory accessing
—diagnostic/single-step provision.

All these features are to be found in the majority of present-day computers. They characterise what has become known as the *von Neumann machine*. A schematic diagram of such a machine is shown in Fig. 1.2. This gives us an outline description of the typical hardware structure of a computer.

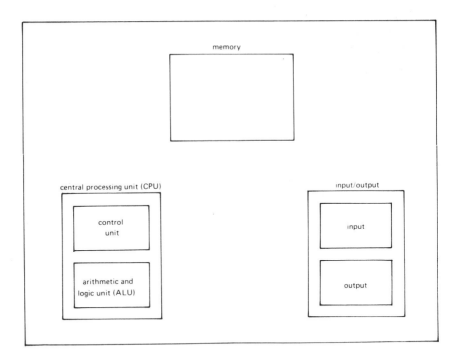

Fig. 1.2 — Outline computer structure.

There are three main parts:
(1) the memory, in which program and data co-reside.
(2) the central processing unit (CPU) which in turn has two components—the arithmetic and logic unit (ALU) in which all calculations are

performed, the results being held in the associated accumulator register; the control unit, whose job it is to fetch and obey program instructions from the memory, and to co-ordinate the activities of the other units.

(3) input and output units, which respectively read information into the computer and print it out.

In the late 1940s and early 1950s many computers were built. In Britain there was notable work at Manchester and at Cambridge. Probably the first working stored-program computer was a small experimental machine built at Manchester University in 1948 by F. C. Williams and T. Kilburn. The range of machines produced at Manchester culminated (much later, around 1961) in the famous ATLAS computer which had a *one-level store,* the forerunner of the present-day virtual memory systems in which the (fast) main memory and the (slow) magnetic backing store are seen by the programmer as effectively a single large memory. At Cambridge M. V. Wilkes and others designed and built the EDSAC (Electronic Delay Storage Automatic Calculator), a machine modelled on the lines of the EDVAC. It was completed in 1949 and had a fixed program which could nowadays be described as an assembler and loader, an early contribution to programming aids.

Following on from the early days of computer design, from about the mid 1950s, we can identify the emergence of the *second-generation* machine. These were characterised by improvements in both hardware and programmability. Perhaps the most important hardware innovation was the replacement of the vacuum tube by the *transistor,* a semiconductor device invented at Bell Telephone Labs. by J. Bardeen and W. H. Brattain. This permitted computers to be built which were smaller and more reliable, and consumed less power. Not until the surface-barrier transistor was developed in 1954 by Philco did the operating speed of computers improve significantly, however. Thereafter the development of discrete transistor technology continued with the introduction of *logic families* called direct-coupled transistor logic (DCTL), diode-transistor logic (DTL), and resistor-transistor logic (RTL). These represented efforts continually being made by the manufacturers to improve the performance of the basic elements of computer hardware. A key aim was to reduce the cost of the elements, while nevertheless also improving their speed and reliability.

Alongside the new technology of transistors in characterising second-generation machines stands the introduction of *high-level programming languages* as a major aid to speeding up the process of computer programming. The intention of the high-level language was to permit programming to be problem-oriented and machine-independent. A *compiler* (or translator program) converts the high-level language programs into machine-code specific to the computer which will run the program. FORTRAN (Formula Translation) was the first widely-used high-level programming language. It was developed by a group at IBM under the direction of John Backus between 1954 and 1957. COBOL (Common Business Oriented Language) followed in 1959, intended mainly for business applications, in contrast to

Fortran which was designed specifically to be used in scientific work. ALGOL (Algorithmic Language), specified in 1960 and revised in 1962 by an international committee including, amongst others, John Backus and Peter Naur, was another important language designed during the second generation of computers. Other languages, now obsolete, were being designed and compilers implemented. The first system software was now beginning to be produced by computer manufacturers and was supplied as part of a package along with the computers themselves. This early system software tended to consist of compilers and rudimentary operating systems.

Apart from changes in technology and software, the architecture and logical design of computers were developing too. Second-generation machines tended to have a floating-point arithmetic unit; index registers and indirect addressing became standard; with magnetic core main memory the design of the CPU tended to be strongly influenced by the timing of memory accesses; and synchronous operations (that is linked to a common timing source) became very widely used.

Previously, asynchronous operations dominated: in this scheme the component parts of an operation (some slow, others fast) were allowed to proceed at their own pace, and job completion signals indicated that the next phase could begin. In computers of the second generation onwards the cycle of events within the machine was controlled by a central clock, both CPU and memory operations being synchronised from its timing pulses. The use of index registers was pioneered by the Manchester University team: these fast-access storage locations in the CPU allowed modification of memory addresses and were particularly intended to help improve the efficiency of machine-code programs produced by compilers. Together with indirect addressing, the presence of index registers extended the memory addressing capabilities of computers in line with the requirements dictated by high-level languages. Experience with software was influencing the design of computers considerably. Applications, too, influenced their design. The requirement for very powerful computational facilities was satisfied by the widespread use of floating-point arithmetic units.

Details apart, the general structure of computers as specified by von Neumann and his colleagues was still the same—the three main parts, CPU, memory and input/output—and has remained so ever since. Moving on beyond 1960 the trend was still to improve the speed, size (and inevitably cost) and programmability of computers.

As with the previous generation, *third-generation* computers are most strongly characterised by a technological innovation, in this case the use of *integrated circuits* (ICs). Instead of the former discrete components, the semiconductor industry began producing monolithic ICs on which the equivalent of several transistors were fabricated. This newest advance took place in the early 1960s, with Fairchild and Texas Instruments well to the fore amongst the semiconductor manufacturers. It was, however, the Sylvania Corporation which first produced the logic family which has remained popularly in use up to the present day: transistor-transistor logic (TTL). With higher packing density of components and improved switching speeds, ICs enabled computers (and other digital logic devices) to be much smaller and faster. It is alternatively suggested that third-generation machines are mainly characterised, from the programmer's point of view, by multiprogramming operating systems based on large capacity magnetic drum and disc stores. Certainly all of the major computer manufacturers set out to implement such operating systems, although it cannot be claimed that many had success until much later in the 1960s. One of the most successful third-generation machines was IBM's System/360, which was available in a variety of different configurations to meet the needs of the individual customer. These machines, in common with the majority being produced at the time, were very large, powerful *mainframe computers.*

About the middle of the 1960s a somewhat different type of machine began to appear on the market. This was the *minicomputer,* characterised by short word lengths (of some 12 to 24 bits) and modest hardware and software facilities. These machines were built to satisfy a new, but soon growing demand for dedicated computers in industrial applications. Digital Equipment Corporation (DEC) was one of the first manufacturers, with its PDP series, to sell minicomputers.

Although more powerful computers continued to be designed, the trend towards smaller machines accelerated as whole new applications areas in industry and commerce revealed themselves. This trend was helped along considerably by the increasing performance/cost ratio of integrated circuit technology. In 1964 Texas Instruments introduced a standard TTL product line called semiconductor network (SN) series 54. Although this was intended primarily for the military market, Texas Instruments soon produced a lower-cost, lower-specification version called series 74. This logic family originally packaged up to about twelve transistor equivalents on one IC: this *level of integration* is called small-scale integration (SSI). In 1969 medium-scale integration (MSI) was introduced, packing from twelve up to a hundred transistors onto an IC.

Large-scale integration (LSI) soon enabled thousands of transistors to be packaged together on one monolithic structure. With this level of integration manufacturers saw that they could produce an IC containing enough logic to implement a small CPU. In 1971 Intel brought the first *microprocessor* into the marketplace, the 4-bit 4004. Soon 8-bit microprocessors, notably Intel's 8080 and the Motorola 6800, became very widely used products.

The development of very large-scale integration (VLSI) in the late 1970s meant that tens then hundreds of thousands of individual components could be produced on a single silicon chip. This led to the development, not only of complete 'single-chip computers', but also of much more powerful single-chip processors, 32-bit architectures and devices for use in parallel-processing systems soon becoming readily available.

The increasing levels of integration and the lowering of IC component costs brought changes to computer memories as well as to CPUs. Semiconductor memories began to displace magnetic core as the standard memory product. These various innovations—LSI, microprocessors and semiconductor memories—led us into the fourth generation of computers.

In the mid-1980s, research in computer architectures progressed towards a fifth generation computer. Chapter 8 discusses work in non-von Neumann architectures which form the basis of this generation.

Fig. 1.3 summarises the main characteristics of the computer generations. The dates are by no means universally agreed.

Generation	Characteristics
First (1945–1955)	vacuum tubes, delay line memory, paper-tape/cards backing store, fixed-point arithmetic, machine-language programming
Second (1955–1965)	transistors, magnetic core memory, magnetic drum and disc backing store, floating-point arithmetic, high-level language programming
Third (1965–1971)	integrated circuits, magnetic core memory, magnetic disc and tape backing store, multiprogramming operating systems
Fourth (1971–1986)	large-scale integrated circuits, semiconductor memory, VSLI processes
Fifth (1986–)	non-von Neumann architectures, . . .

Fig. 1.3 — Computer generations.

Computer architecture

We have seen briefly how computer systems—hardware and software—have been developing up to the present day. Three broad classes of computers have been identified: mainframes, minicomputers and microcomputers (computers based round microprocessor CPUs). The distinction between these classes has traditionally been made by their application areas and also by what can loosely be termed their 'power'. This term reflects the number of program instructions a machine is capable of obeying per unit time; in addition, power is related to the hardware configuration—the number and the size of backing store and other peripheral units—which a machine is capable of supporting. Mainframes are traditionally powerful, whereas minicomputers are only moderately so. Microcomputers, up till now, have always been regarded as least powerful of all. We should perhaps no longer speak in such clear-cut terms about the three classes. The most recent 32-bit microprocessors are more powerful than many minicomputers, and strongly challenge some of the mainframes. It seems likely, however, that the size of a computer configuration will continue to determine its classification: a large, multi-access system will still be a mainframe.

The *architecture* of a computer is the structure and the inter-relationships of the various logical hardware units: the CPU, memory and peripheral units. This excludes the physical hardware construction of the surrounding machine like the power supply, the processor cabinet or any of the peripheral hardware. The physical construction and layout of the electronic circuits which make up the logical units may, however, be important in describing an architecture.

There are very many different computer architectures, but fundamentally most are von Neumann machines. It is not the purpose of this book to discuss architectures, nor even any specific architecture, but rather to describe the fundamental building bricks—both logically and physically—of computers, and to show how they are used in the design and implementation of the units inside a generalised von Neumann machine. This is what is implied by *computer logic.* At the same time it must be stressed that although the treatment of logic elements and logic design is placed in the context of computers, the material is applicable in digital systems of all kinds.

To conclude this section let us outline a generalised von Neumann machine which reflects a typical modern computer architecture. This will be used as a basis for discussing the design of logical units within computers later in the book. Fig. 1.4 illustrates such a machine. Basically there are only three units—CPU, memory and input/output (I/O) as previously described. In this diagram the units are shown connected by an *address bus* and a *data bus,* and the sub-units within the CPU (control unit and ALU) are shown with their associated *registers,* connected by the *CPU bus.*

The address bus is uni-directional: addressing information can be sent only from the CPU to one of the memory or input/output units. The data bus is bi-directional, meaning that data can pass in either direction, to or from the CPU. Inside the CPU information is transferred on the bi-directional CPU bus between registers—fast-access storage locations—as the CPU obeys program instructions. These registers require a little more explanation.

Associated with the address and data buses are the (memory) address register or MAR and the (memory) data register or MDR. In this generalised machine it is assumed that input/output units are addressed and data transferred to and from them in the way that applies to the memory unit. Such a system is called *memory-mapped I/O.*

The length of or number of bits in these registers is important to note. Whereas the MDR length is the same as the basic *word length* of the computer—that is the number of bits in parallel which the machine processes at once—the length of the MAR is related to the *addressing capability*

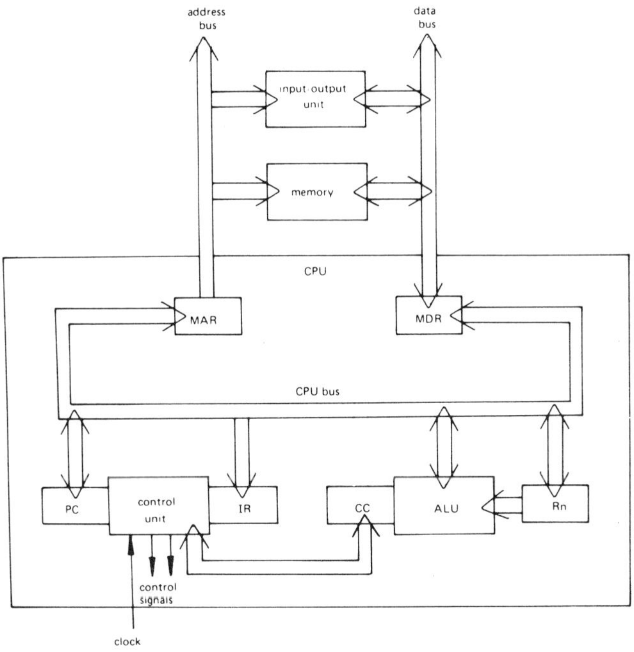

Fig. 1.4 — A generalised von Neumann machine.

of the computer. It is quite common for a microprocessor to have a word length of 8 bits but an addressing capability of 64K, meaning that it is capable of reading or writing any of 64K different 8-bit storage locations. A MAR length of 16 bits gives an addressing capability of 64K. In general the relationship between MAR length and addressing capability is that

$$\text{addressing capability} = 2^{\text{MAR length}}$$

(independent of the basic computer word length).

The ALU has associated registers called Rn and CC. Rn stand for (any number of) general purpose registers, used for storing or accumulating information during the course of a program. These registers can also be used as index registers. CC is a condition codes register which records information about operations in the ALU, for example whether the result of an addition gave a positive, negative or zero result, or very importantly whether in an arithmetic operation the results register (one of the Rn) was not capable of holding the result—this is called overflow.

Lastly, the control unit has two registers PC and IR linked to it. These have a central role in the operation of the von Neumann machine, and to understand them it is necessary to describe how the computer runs programs. Every computer program, whether written in a high-level language or not, is eventually stored in the memory as a sequence of *machine-code instructions*. Each machine-code instruction implies a set of actions to be carried out by the computer to achieve the required goal. A typical instruction at this level is:

ADD Rn, X

meaning 'add the contents of memory location X to register Rn'. The binary form of this instruction (produced by the compiler or machine-code programmer) will occupy i consecutive memory locations. The number i depends on the type of instruction and also on the architecture of the computer. Each machine-code instruction in the sequence follows in successive memory locations.

The purpose of the PC or program counter is to hold the memory address of the current instruction as the program proceeds. Basically a computer fetches, decodes and obeys each machine-code instruction in a program. Each instruction, when fetched from the memory, has to be decoded by the control unit: the purpose of the IR or instruction register is to hold the current instruction while it is obeyed. As well as obeying the current instruction, the control unit has to alter the contents of the PC to point to the next instruction in sequence. For most instructions (such as ADD) the 'next' instruction is the one immediately following the current one. However, JUMP or BRANCH instructions are intended to cause the program to continue with a different part of its sequence (in conditional BRANCH cases, only if a specific condition, recorded in the CC register, is satisfied) and their only action in fact is to alter the contents of the PC to point to the 'next' location specified in the instruction.

The actions implied by a machine-code instruction are generally called *micro-operations*, small steps which the hardware can perform as a result of signals from the control unit. Most micro-operations correspond to the transfer of data from one register to another within the CPU. These micro-operations are called *register transfers* and are very important in the design and specification of computer architectures. A simple but effective notation for representing register transfers is shown in the example

PC → MAR

meaning that the contents of the PC are copied into the MAR. This implies that the contents of the PC are not lost. Sometimes it is necessary to indicate indirect addressing, so for example

(MAR) → MDR

means that the contents of the location pointed to by the MAR are copied into the MDR. In this case the MAR contents specify a memory location, and it is the contents of this memory location which are transferred into the MDR. The above operation is used every time a word of program or data is fetched from the memory. There is a corresponding register transfer for storing values into memory, namely

MDR → (MAR)

where again the MAR specifies which location in memory is to be involved in the transfer.

To illustrate how a computer processes a single machine-code instruction let us consider the micro-operations required to implement the instruction ADD Rn, X ('add the contents of memory location X to register Rn'). It is assumed that the PC is already pointing to this instruction, and that in this case the instruction occupies two memory words, the first for the instruction code and the identity of the register, Rn, and the second containing the address X. Fig. 1.5 illustrates a micro-instruction implementation using the

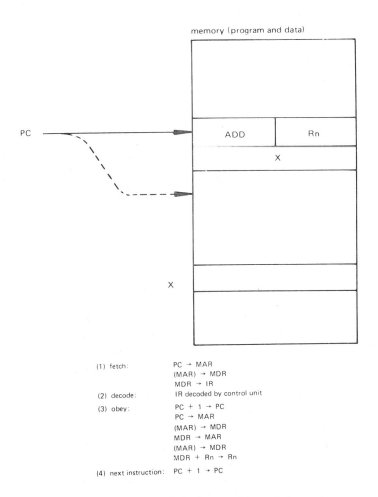

Fig. 1.5 — Fetching and obeying a machine-code instruction.

generalised von Neumann machine in Fig. 1.4. Note that the only micro-operation shown which is not a register transfer is (2), the decode step.

The operation

$$MDR + Rn \rightarrow Rn$$

involves not only a register transfer, but also an addition within the ALU. Each micro-operation is initiated by signals from the control unit which, in the case of register transfers, open and close appropriate data paths, to connect the registers involved in the transfer. The fetch step fetches the first instruction word from memory. If, as in this example, an operand address is specified in the instruction it is fetched in the obey step. Steps (1) and (2) are identical for all instructions but (3) and (4) depend on the nature of the instruction. In the example ADD Rn, X there are altogether three memory fetches.

The control unit in turn is actioned by a *clock* or source of timing signals (usually external to the CPU) which determines the basic time for a micro-operation. Roughly speaking, each clock 'tick' causes the next micro-instruction to begin. The time increment between ticks (the *machine cycle* time) is chosen to allow the logic circuits to complete their operation: since micro-operations may take different lengths of time, the clock frequency or rate of ticking depends on the slowest operation. Obviously the faster the circuits operate, the faster the clock frequency can be and ultimately the more powerful the computer. Some machine-code instructions will take more, and others fewer, machine cycles in direct correspondence to the number of micro-operations required to implement them.

1.3 STRUCTURAL LAYERS

Computer logic is a subject which, in common with other topics in computing, can perhaps best be viewed as a series of layers which represent its essential structure. Computers can be viewed as logical units which themselves comprise more fundamental logical units. These basic logical units have a structure which the student of this subject should know about.

In Fig. 1.6 the structural layers of computer logic are illustrated. Three layers are identified, along with the roots of computer logic in mathematical theory and the physics and technology of circuit implementations.

The structure of this book reflects the layers in the diagram. Chapter 2 deals with logic building blocks and the background material of Boolean algebra and physical realisations, Chapters 3 and 4 with combinational and sequential logic, and Chapter 5 shows how all these ideas are required to produce a system as a VLSI chip. Chapter 6 deals, fairly briefly, with von Neumann computer architecture whilst Chapter 7 takes the discussion a little way into the software part of the computer spectrum, to emphasise that hardware design and software requirements are closely interdependent. Recent developments in computer architectures which differ from the von Neumann model are described in Chapter 8.

Finally, the three layers can be seen to correspond roughly to what we may call the bit, word and processor levels of computer logic. In many

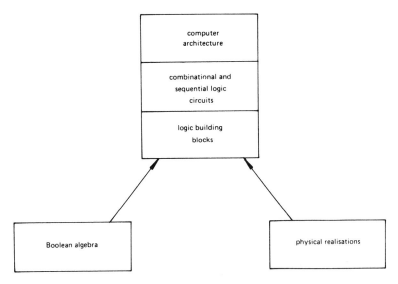

Fig. 1.6 — The structural layers of computer logic.

computers in use today the layers may also be associated with SSI, MSI and LSI respectively. With the advent of VLSI, these distinctions are very largely being lost at the device level but provide a very useful frame of reference at the design level. These two sets of equivalences may on the one hand be regarded simply as alternative shorthand names for the layers but, on the other hand, should both be remembered because they reflect the presence of the abstract and physical streams which run through computer logic.

2

Logic builidng blocks

2.1 LOGIC SYMBOLISM

Computer hardware, and digital systems of all kinds, are made of logic circuits. In practice there are many levels of complexity of logic circuits, although for the present it will be convenient to regard them as being all at the *word* level. Logic circuits in turn are built from more basic units at the *bit* level. This chapter is about the bit-level logic units which are the building blocks of digital logic circuits.

There are two distinct streams leading up to a full appreciation of logic building blocks, the abstract and the physical. These correspond to the *design* and *implementation* stages in which logic circuits are produced. The design process may be carried out in terms of abstract logic units without regard to the physical details of implementation. Of course the design must then be realised in hardware, using available components. It is always desirable to cut the cost and physical size of circuits to a minimum, while also ensuring that the speed of their operation is as high as possible. These *minimisation criteria* generally conflict with one another because of natural physical limitations, so a suitable balance has to be struck between the various criteria in the designer's mind. The choice must be made at the design stage so that the circuit structure may be manipulated appropriately. Because of the minimisation requirement, and also for the reason that circuit implementations depend on the availability of components, design and implementation must be closely linked in practice. Let us consider these two streams together.

A logic unit may conveniently be viewed as a *black box* as illustrated in Fig. 2.1. A black box is characterised by the fact that nothing is known, nor

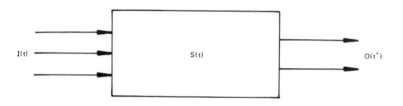

Fig. 2.1 — A black-box logic unit.

need be known, of its internal structure. At any time t, $I(t)$ represents the set if input values and $S(t)$ the *internal state* of the unit. A little time later, at t', the outputs become $O(t')$ and the internal state changes to $S(t')$. The outputs are derived from the inputs and internal state according to the transformation:

$$O(t') = f(I(t), S(t)) \qquad (2.1)$$

Similarly the new internal state is a function of the inputs and previous internal state:

$$S(t') = g(I(t), S(t)) \qquad (2.2)$$

Each input and output has a finite number of possible values, and the unit a finite number of internal states. It is more generally known as a *finite state machine* (FSM). Although formal FSM theory is beyond the scope of this book, it is important to point out the close relationship between computer logic and the well-established work on FSMs (otherwise known as automata). The theory describes the structure and behaviour of FSMs in general, including the necessary and sufficient properties which enable them to be used as universal computing machines. Computer logic makes exclusive use of a class of FSMs in which individual inputs and outputs may have only two possible values.

The (simplified) FSM shown in Fig. 2.1 represents a general type of logic unit called a *sequential logic element*. Its characteristic is that its outputs depend on the present input values, and also on the past history of the inputs which are summarised by the present internal state. Although both equations (2.1) and (2.2) are important in describing the behaviour of the sequential element, only the inputs and outputs are actually observable. Note that because of the possibility that the element can be in one of a number of possible internal states at any one time, and because the outputs depend (partly) on the present state, the same input values applied at different times may produce different output results. An important special case of the sequential logic element is the one in which there is only a single internal state. This type is called a *combinational logic element*. The characteristic feature of a combinational element is that a given set of input values always produces the same output results. It can be described by a modified version of equation (2.1) in which no internal state is specified:

$$O(t') = f(I(t)) \qquad (2.3)$$

In this case there is no equivalent of equation (2.2) since the element has no alternative states to sequence through. Note that equation (2.3) implies a *delay* in producing new outputs whenever a new set of input values is applied to the element. Although for most of the purposes of designing logic circuits this delay can be ignored, it is a realistic factor which must be taken into account in some circumstances. This point will be discussed more fully in Section 4.2 ('Circuit problems in practice').

Another special case of the general sequential element is one with only two possible internal states. These are called *bistables* or, more colourfully, *flip-flops*. They are very important in computer logic, because the two states can be used to represent the 1s and 0s of the binary number system, the basis of the method by which information is handled and represented inside computers. Flip-flops are fundamentally easy to implement because of the many two-state representations achievable using natural phenomena: hole/no hole, current/no current, high voltage/low voltage. They are most importantly used as *memory elements*.

There are many possible combinational logic elements, each distinguished by the function f which maps inputs to outputs as in Fig. 2.1, and by the number of inputs and outputs themselves. The most fundamental combinational elements are called AND, OR, NOT *gates*. The first two, AND and OR, are single-output elements but may be defined for any number of inputs, from two upwards. The third, NOT, is a single-output, single-input element. The NOT gate and two-input versions of AND and OR are defined in Fig. 2.2 alongside the black-box equivalent of each.

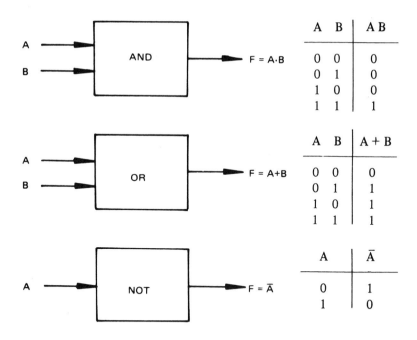

A	B	A B
0	0	0
0	1	0
1	0	0
1	1	1

A	B	A + B
0	0	0
0	1	1
1	0	1
1	1	1

A	$\bar{A}$
0	1
1	0

Fig. 2.2 — The fundamental combinational logic gates.

The inputs and outputs of all logic functions can take only two possible values — the binary digits 0 and 1 — and thus it is particularly easy to describe these functions by tabulating all possible combinations of input values and writing down the corresponding output value in each case. The definitions of AND, OR, NOT in Fig. 2.2 are in this form which is generally known as the *truth table*. The term 'truth' drives from the origins of the theory of computer logic in which the two values of inputs and outputs are TRUE or FALSE. This will be elaborated in Section 2.2 following.

Fig. 2.2 shows the usual form of writing AND, OR, NOT operations: AND is represented by · ('dot'); OR by + ('plus'), both of these operators being placed between their two operands; and NOT by ⁻ ('bar') placed over the top of its single operand. It is important not to confuse the logical + as defined for OR with the usual arithmetical +. Operations AND, OR, NOT can also usefully be defined in plain words:

A·B has the value 1 only if A *and* B both have value 1; otherwise the result is 0.

A+B has the value 1 if either A *or* B has value 1; if both are 0 the result is 0.

$\overline{A}$ negates the value of A: if A is 0 then $\overline{A}$ is *not* 0 (that is, 1); if A is 1 then $\overline{A}$ is *not* 1 (but 0).

The OR operation + is more precisely called *inclusive-OR* to distinguish it from another operation called *exclusive-OR*. This is defined, and its operator symbol shown, in Fig. 2.3.

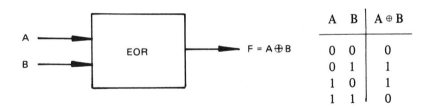

A	B	A ⊕ B
0	0	0
0	1	1
1	0	1
1	1	0

Fig. 2.3 — The exclusive-OR gate.

In plain words:

A ⊕ B has the value 1 if either A *or* B has value 1, but not both; if both are 0 or both are 1 the result is 0.

Although EOR is not fundamental (in the sense that it *can* be synthesised from AND, OR, NOT gates) it is nevertheless a commonly-used logic element and will be referred to again.

Two other very important functions related to AND, OR, NOT are NAND and NOR. Basically these are concatenations of AND — NOT and OR — NOT respectively, and are much used in practice. They are conveniently fabricated in integrated circuit form and are more readily available components than AND and OR. The definitions of NAND and NOR are shown in Fig. 2.4. Note that the ⁻ 'bar' covers the entire function in each case, that is the NOT is applied to the output of the functions, not to their inputs.

We have identified the various combinational logic gates — AND, OR, NOT, EOR, NAND, NOR — and sequential elements called flip-flops which are all logic building blocks. The fundamental operations AND, OR, NOT are used mainly in the abstract design of logic circuits, while NAND, NOR and NOT are widely available in small-scale integrated (SSI) form (EOR in MSI) and tend to be used for implementation. There are three main types of flip-flop — S–R, D and J–K — which will be more fully explained in Section 3.3 ('Sequential logic design'). These, too, are available as SSI components.

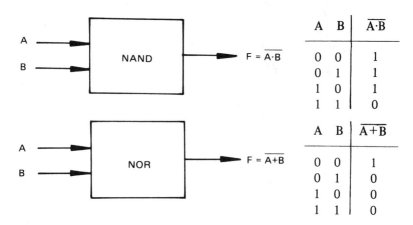

Fig. 2.4 — The 2-input NAND and NOR gates.

In the remainder of the book a standard symbolic form will be adopted for these logic elements. The black-box outlines used so far will be replaced by *distinctive shapes* which clearly identify the logic functions. There are several standards but the one used in this book is perhaps the most common. It conforms to the recommendations in 'IEEE Standard Graphic Symbols for Logic Diagrams' (IEEE Std. 91–1973, ANSI Y 32.14–1973). Drawing templates containing the recommended shapes are available commercially. Fig. 2.5 shows the distinctive shapes for all the combinational logic gates and one flip-flop, the S–R. All flip-flop symbols have the same basic rectangular shape but there are extra distinguishing features for other types which will be described in Section 3.3.

The basic logic building blocks have been introduced and their symbols illustrated. To be able to use them in designing and implementing logic circuits requires further development of their abstract and physical background. These two areas are explored further in the following sections of this chapter.

2.2 BOOLEAN ALGEBRA

The fundamental building blocks of digital logic are the AND, OR and NOT gates. Although circuits are implemented using other types of elements — particularly NAND gates — the logic design phase is most easily expressed

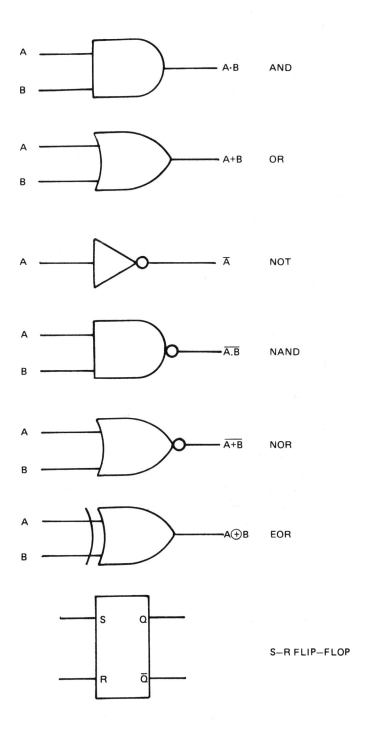

Fig. 2.5 — Distinctive logic symbol shapes used in this book.

in terms of the fundamental gates. The set of rules which governs the way AND, OR and NOT are used in designing and manipulating logic functions forms the basis of this section.

George Boole was a nineteenth-century mathematician who devised an *algebra of propositions*. His work, published in 1854, showed that any proposition, no matter how complex, could be expressed as a combination of simpler propositions linked by the logical operators *and, or* and *not*. The propositions themselves are logical expressions with two possible values, either *true* or *false*. Boole's algebra is a mathematical expression of the rules by which propositions can be analysed, manipulated and simplified, but it is not in a form which is palatable to the prospective logic designer. The property by which the set {*and, or* and *not*} can be used to synthesis any logical expression whatever is called *completeness*. It is important to note that there exist other sets of operators with the same property, particularly {*nand*} and {*nor*} themselves.

Boole's work is, however, the basis of the modern techniques of digital logic design. Claude Shannon, in 1938, published a paper in which he demonstrtated how Boole's algebra could be used to help design electromechanical relay circuits systematically. Up to that time such switching circuits were designed by ad hoc methods. Shannon expressed Boole's results in a more suitable form which is referred to as *switching algebra* or more commonly *Boolean algebra*. The basic usefulness of Boolean algebra as suggested by Shannon lies in its ability to enable complex switching systems to be expressed then optimised in terms of the basic *and, or* and *not* operators, and finally implemented using their physical realisations. The techniques used for modern logic design are just the same, even though the physical realisations may not be in the same form.

The rules of Boolean algebra

Boolean algebra, like any other algebra, consists of a *set of elements*, *operators* which act on the elements, and a number of *rules* which define the properties of both elements and operations.

There are two classes of rules: basic rules (or *postulates*) which are stated without proof, and *theorems* which are proved using postulates and/or previously proved theorems. In Fig. 2.6 the postulates of Boolean algebra are listed, in a form due to Huntington (1904).

A, B and C are the names of arbitrary elements of the set. In logic design our interest is a Boolean algebra in which the set of elements contains only the identity elements namely {0, 1}. This is the simplest possible Boolean algebra. Any *variable* such as A, B or C and therefore take only the values 0 or 1.

The postulates state the basic properties by which we shall be able to manipulate logic expressions. A number of theorems which will also be found useful for this purpose are listed in Fig. 2.7. Two theorems in particular are very important: T9 and T10, the so-called *de Morgan's laws* named after their originator. These tell us how the *inverse* of arbitrary logic expressions can be rewritten in terms of the inverted variables in the

P1 There are two operations $\cdot$ and $+$ on pairs of elements in the set which produce a result also belonging to the set of elements: this is the *closure rule.*

P2 The operations $\cdot$ and $+$ are *commutative:*

$$A \cdot B = B \cdot A$$
$$A + B = B + A$$

P3 The operations $\cdot$ and $+$ are *distributive:*

$$A \cdot (B+C) = (A \cdot B) + (A \cdot C)$$
$$A + (B \cdot C) = (A+B) \cdot (A+C)$$

P4 Two elements 1 and 0 called *identity* elements exist such that:

$$1 \cdot A = A$$
$$0 + A = A$$

P5 For each element A in the set there is an *inverse* $\overline{A}$ such that:

$$A \cdot \overline{A} = 0$$
$$A + \overline{A} = 1$$

Fig. 2.6 — The postulates of Boolean algebra.

T1	$A \cdot 0 = 0$
T2	$A + 1 = 1$
T3	$A \cdot A = A$
T4	$A + A = A$
T5	$A + (A \cdot B) = A$
T6	$A + (\overline{A} \cdot B) = A + B$
T7	$A \cdot B \cdot C = (A \cdot B) \cdot C = A \cdot (B \cdot C)$
T8	$A + B + C = (A+B) + C = A + (B+C)$
T9	$\overline{A \cdot B} = \overline{A} + \overline{B}$
T10	$\overline{A + B} = \overline{A} \cdot \overline{B}$
T11	$\overline{(\overline{A})} = A$

Fig. 2.7 — The theorems of Boolean algebra.

expression. Although T9 and T10 show a two-variable case the theorems apply also to expressions containing any number of variables greater than two. For example

$$\overline{A \cdot B \cdot C} \quad = \overline{A} + \overline{B} + \overline{C}$$

and

$$\overline{A + B + C + D} = \overline{A} \cdot \overline{B} \cdot \overline{C} \cdot \overline{D}$$

demonstrate the 3-variable form of T9 and the 4-variable form of T10. De Morgan's laws also provide a means by which · operations can be changed to +, or vice versa, by forming the inverse of an expression. This can be useful for manipulating logic expressions into a form suitable for implementation: in particular it is often required to implement circuits entirely using NAND gates, so basically any + operations in the original expression of the circuit to be changed to · operations.

Theorems T7 and T8 are called the *associative laws*. Together with the commutative and distributive laws (postulates P2 and P3) they describe properties of · and + which are very similar to the properties of the arithmetic operators in the everyday algebra of real numbers. For this reason we find · and + convenient operators to work with in abstract logic design (rather than, say, the NAND and NOR operators). The + operator, pronounced 'plus', is also called the *sum* operation, while · ('dot') has the alternative title *product*. Resemblances to the arithmetic operators are rather superficial and the parallel must not be taken too seriously. An abbreviation arising out of the resemblances, however, is widely used: the · operator may be omitted altogether in logic expressions. For example theorem T7 may be written as

$$ABC = (AB)C = A(BC)$$

The + operator always appears explicitly. Note the use of brackets in theorems T5 and T6. Bracketed expressions show explicitly how the expression is to be evaluated — the expressions in brackets first. However, brackets may be omitted from expressions, in which case the *implicit strengths* of the operators determine the order of evaluation. The important rule is that · is stronger than +. Thus theorem T5 can equally well be written:

$$A + A \cdot B = A$$

or indeed

$$A + AB = A$$

Proving the theorems
Two methods may be used for proving the theorems of Boolean algebra. The first, *perfect induction,* involves evaluating the expressions we are trying to prove equal for all possible values of the variables, and comparing

the results in each case. This method is particularly easy for Boolean expressions because each variable has only two possible values. Fig. 2.8 gives an example of this type of proof for theorem T5.

A	B	A·B	LHS: A + A·B	RHS: A
0	0	0	0	0
0	1	0	0	0
1	0	0	1	1
1	1	1	1	1

Fig. 2.8 — Proof of theorem T5 by perfect induction.

The second method is by *algebraic manipulation* whereby the postulates (and previously proved theorems) are employed in re-writing the expressions on one or both sides until they are identical. An example of the algebraic proof for theorem T6 is given in Fig. 2.9. Each re-writing of an expression should be justified by quoting the identity of the postulate or theorem used.

$$
\begin{aligned}
\text{LHS:} &= A + (\bar{A}B) \\
&= (A + \bar{A}) \cdot (A + B) & \text{by P3} \\
&= 1 \cdot (A + B) & \text{by P5} \\
&= (A + B) & \text{by P4} \\
&= \underline{\text{RHS}}
\end{aligned}
$$

Fig. 2.9 — Proof of theorem T6 by algebraic manipulation.

Duality

The postulates (apart from the closure rule P1) consist of pairs of expressions. These are called *dual forms* and reflect the symmetry of the · and + operators. Every Boolean expression has a dual which may be derived by replacing each occurrence of · by +, each + by ·, 0 by 1 and 1 by 0. Inversion is not affected. Notice that in Fig. 2.7 the dual forms are paired consecutively: T1 and T2 are duals, also T3 and T4, T5 and T6, followed by the associative laws (T7 and T8), and de Morgan's laws (T9 and T10). For obvious reasons T11 appears on its own.

A note on Boolean expressions

The Boolean expression

AB + CD

is said to be in a *sum-of-products* form, where AB and CD are product terms linked by the sum operator. The expression has a dual form

$$(A+B)(C+D)$$

known as a *product-of-sums* form. In logic design it is usual to adhere to one or other of the two forms throughout the process of expressing and manipulating Boolean expressions. In this book we shall use the sum-of-products form for writing down logic functions.

A general Boolean function of n variables may be expressed in a sum-of-products form as follows:

$$\begin{aligned}
f(A_1,A_2,\ldots,A_{n-1},A_n) &= \overline{A_1}\overline{A_2}\ldots\ldots\overline{A_{n-1}}\overline{A_n}\,f(0,0,\ldots\ldots,0,0) \\
&+ \overline{A_1}\,\overline{A_2}\ldots\ldots\overline{A_{n-1}}\,A_n\,f(0,0,\ldots\ldots,0,1)+ \\
&+ \overline{A_1}\,\overline{A_2}\ldots\ldots A_{n-1}\,\overline{A_n}\,f(0,0,\ldots\ldots,1,0)+\ldots\ldots \\
&+ A_1\,A_2\ldots\ldots A_{n-1}\,A_n\,f(1,1,\ldots\ldots,1,1)
\end{aligned}$$

(giving $2\uparrow(2\uparrow n)$ n-variable Boolean functions).

For $n=2$ we have:

$$f(A,B)=\overline{A}\overline{B}f(0,0)+\overline{A}Bf(0,1)+A\overline{B}f(1,0)+ABf(1,1)$$

The values of $f(0,0)$, $f(0,1)$, $f(1,0)$ and $f(1,1)$ can be either 0 or 1, giving a total of 16 different Boolean functions of two variables as shown in Fig. 2.10.

B	0	1	0	1	
A	0	0	1	1	
$f0$	0	0	0	0	
$f1$	0	0	0	1	AND
$f2$	0	0	1	0	
$f3$	0	0	1	1	
$f4$	0	1	0	0	
$f5$	0	1	0	1	
$f6$	0	1	1	0	EOR
$f7$	0	1	1	1	OR
$f8$	1	0	0	0	NOR
$f9$	1	0	0	1	
$f10$	1	0	1	0	
$f11$	1	0	1	1	
$f12$	1	1	0	0	
$f13$	1	1	0	1	
$f14$	1	1	1	0	NAND
$f15$	1	1	1	1	
	$f(0,0)$	$f(0,1)$	$f(1,0)$	$f(1,1)$	

Fig. 2.10 — The Boolean functions of two variables.

The familiar functions are identified by their names.

The specific case of the exclusive-OR function EOR can be written as:

$$f6 = A \oplus B = \overline{A}\overline{B} \cdot 0 + \overline{A}B \cdot 1 + A\overline{B} \cdot 1 + AB \cdot 0$$

but since by the rules of Boolean algebra

$$A \cdot 0 = 0 \text{ (T1) and } A \cdot 1 = A \text{ (P4 and P2)}$$

the expression reduces to $A \oplus B = \overline{A}B + A\overline{B}$.

This sum-of-products form can be derived more simply from the truth table (see Fig. 2.10 or Fig. 2.3) by identifying the combination of input variables which produces each 1 output. The combinations are expressed as product terms and summed together. The final expression for EOR may be interpreted in words: the output is 1 if (*not* A) *and* B is 1 *or* A *and* (*not* B) is 1.

2.3 LOGIC FAMILIES

Boolean algebra provides the tools by which abstract logic functions can be expressed and manipulated. Paper designs are not an end in themselves and must be closely linked to the implementation stage in which logic circuits take their final physical form. The implementer is faced with choosing from the available physical building blocks, of which there are increasingly many. This section, and the one following, are concerned with the physical realisations of abstract logic elements and aim to provide a background of knowledge about their characteristics which will aid the implementer in his choice.

Several alternative ranges of electronic components with which to build computers, and other digital devices, have been developed since the first-generation machines. All computers since then have been binary (two-valued) in principle, working in terms of high or low voltages, current flow or lack of current, and (for the memory) the two opposite directions of magnetisation. At the very lowest level of operation is the basic *electronic switching element* which allows the implementation of two-valued quantities. Since 1948 this switch has been, in one form or another, the *transistor*. Corresponding to the abstract design level, the fundamental building block for implementation is the *gate,* a circuit based round transistors which provides one of the logical operations previously described (AND, NOR, etc). It is the form of the basic gate which distinguishes each of the range of components or *logic families*.

The early logic families, including diode transistor logic (DTL) and resistor transistor logic (RTL), provided gates which were individually packaged. These families are now of mainly historical interest. Development of the transistor-transistor logic (TTL) gate in the 1960s enabled a number of gates of the same type to be packaged together in one integrated circuit (IC) for a cost little greater than that of the previous, discrete gate. The gates were fabricated on a monolithic structure, that is a single chip of semiconductor material (hence the popular name 'chip' for a packaged IC). Since the early 1970s developments in metal oxide semiconductor (MOS) technology have led to the production of a range of devices based on MOS transistors or MOSTs. In their most recent forms they offer both size and power advantages over TTL and are now the most widely used devices in the manufacture of ICs.

From the early 1960s to the mid 1980s, during which time digital systems have been designed and constructed using standard 'off-the-shelf' components, several levels of integration have been established to describe the ranges of components available. Small-scale integration, SSI, which dates from the earliest days when only a small number of gates could reliably and economically be produced on a single chip, is the name given to packages containing of the order of 10 gates. Such packages typically contain several circuits of the same kind, and until the mid 1980s, were used to provide the 'random logic' which inevitably forms part of any digital system. Such devices still have their uses and most students will carry out their first logic design exercises using them. Medium-scale integration, MSI, describes packages containing of the order of 100 gates and allows the production of widely used standard circuits such as adders, registers, counters, etc. Since most of the unreliability of electronic systems lies in the joints and interconnections made outside the packages, these devices were welcomed as they became available and widely used since they provided cheaper, more reliable systems. Large-scale integration, LSI, describes packages which began to become available in the early 1970s and contain a thousand or so gates, so interconnected as to produce such circuits as multiplier units, memory chips or small microprocessors. Very large-scale integration, VLSI, is the name used for chips containing from several thousand gates upwards — chips containing a million devices have been designed experimentally. Included in this category are the larger microprocessors and memory chips now available (also standard, off-the-shelf devices) together with special purpose or application specific integrated circuits (ASICs) which can now be produced by IC manufacturers to a customer's requirements. Because of the advantages of using as few ICs as possible in a system the current trend, if enough systems are being built to make it economically viable, is to use the largest available standard ICs for most of the system and to 'mop up' the remaining random logic with some form of 'customised' VLSI device. In some cases, in fact, complete systems will be built with customised devices. The whole of Chapter 5 is devoted to a discussion of VLSI design and construction techniques. The next step up the complexity ladder is to wafer-scale integration, WSI, in which a whole silicon slice or wafer is devoted to a single system. Experimental devices have been produced but the organisational problems of designing, checking and testing such devices are immense.

Physical realisation of gates

At the heart of every logic family is the fundamental electronic switching element, the transistor. Some of the families are based on the *bipolar transistor* invented in 1948 by Bardeen and Brattain, and others on the *unipolar transistor* first described by William Shockley in 1952. The difference between the two types lies in their detailed structure and semiconductor action — giving the associated logic families characteristic properties. Broadly speaking the transistor structure and action are the same for both transistor types, and may adequately be described as follows by using the bipolar transistor as an example.

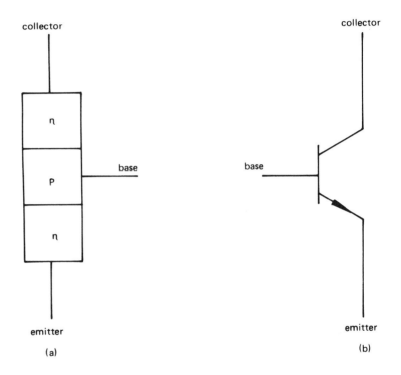

Fig. 2.11 — The bipolar transistor: (a) structure, (b) symbol.

Transistors are made from semiconductor material such as germanium or silicon which have an intrinsic electrical conductivity between that of conductors and insulators. Their conducting properties may be altered by doping the material with either n-type or p-type impurities. The result of n-type doping is that a suitable voltage applied to the material causes *electrons* (negative charge carriers) to flow whereas p-type doping results in a flow of positive charge carriers called *holes*. The bipolar transistor — or junction transistor as it is sometimes called — is formed by diffusing n-type and p-type impurities into the same piece of semi-conductor material so that two *p-n junctions* are formed, as illustrated in Fig. 2.11. This shows an n-p-n transistor structure together with its circuit symbol. Alternatively a p-n-p transistor, with similar properties, may be made from one n-type and two p-type regions. The arrow on the symbol indicates the direction of conventional current flow: electrons flow in the opposite direction, originating from the emitter. They travel to the base from which most make their way to the collector. Holes produced at the base terminal are attracted to the emitter, although some combine with electrons inside the base region. The name bipolar reflects the fact that both types of charge carriers are active.

To explain the transistor action consider the *common emitter* configuration of Fig. 2.12. The circuit INPUT is the base, its OUTPUT the

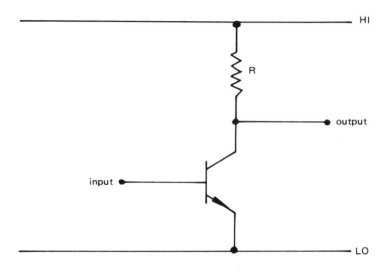

Fig. 2.12 — Common-emitter transistor configuration.

collector. This arrangement, in which the emitter is common to both INPUT and OUTPUT, is used in many switching applications. The collector is connected via a resistor R of suitable value to the positive voltage supply (HI) while the emitter is at zero voltage (LO). The operation of the transistor is summarised by the output characteristic graph shown in Fig. 2.13. This is a plot of the collector current I_c as a function of collector-emitter voltage V_{ce} and base current I_b. When there is zero base current — INPUT at ground potential — I_c is very nearly zero (a small *leakage* current flows between collector and emitter). Under these conditions the transistor is said to be OFF. By applying an increasing potential at the INPUT, at constant V_{ce}, the value of I_c increases in proportion to the increasing base current according to the relationship

$$I_c = hI_b$$

where typically h is 10 or more. The transistor *amplifies* the input current. When the INPUT voltage is increased to a suitably high value the collector-emitter potential drops to nearly zero and a large collector current flows.

The transistor is then said to be *saturated* or in the ON state. Thus the transistor appears as a switch controlled by the base current (or voltage). In the OFF state the collector current is effectively zero and the OUTPUT potential is at HI; when ON the collector current is large and the OUTPUT is almost at LO.

Note that the circuit in Fig. 2.12 has an *inverting* action: INPUT at LO gives OUTPUT at HI, but INPUT at HI produces OUTPUT at LO. This circuit basically implements a NOT gate. Its amplification properties (sometimes called *gain*) enable the output of the gate to control the inputs of several other, similar gates, an important requirement in logic circuits. The number of inputs which may be so connected to one output is called the *fanout* capability of the gate.

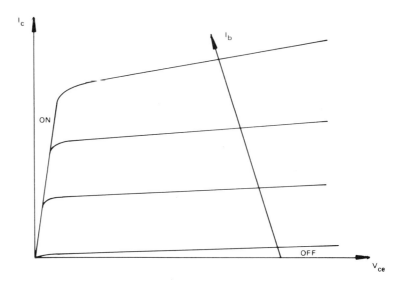

Fig. 2.13 — Transistor output characteristic.

Although Fig. 2.13 demonstrates that the bipolar transistor, working in saturated mode, may be switched between the OFF and ON states, it gives no indication of the *switching time*. Of all the properties of transistor circuits this is perhaps the most important, since it determines the *speed* of the logic family. The time taken by a logic gate to switch output states when the input is changed from OFF to ON (or vice versa) is called the *propagation delay* of the gate. Many of the developments in IC technology have resulted from a desire to reduce gate delay. As a simple example, the switching speed of the circuit in Fig. 2.12 can be improved by using two transistors as illustrated in Fig. 2.14. This shows the output stage common to TTL gates, called an

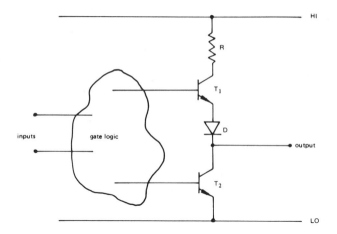

Fig. 2.14 — TTL gate output stage.

active pull-up or *totem-pole* output. The gate logic is specific to the type of gate but in each case ensures that one of two conditions applies at the output stage: either T1 is OFF and T2 is ON, in which case the OUTPUT is (almost) at HI (+3.5 volts for TTL logic), or T1 is ON and T2 is OFF giving a LO (0 volts) at the OUTPUT. The typical gate delay for this TTL configuration is 10 ns (ns=nanosecond$=10^{-9}$ second). D is a diode which helps keep the switching time low and also improves the electrical *noise immunity* of the device.

An important characteristic of TTL logic is the use of a multiple-emitter transistor for inputs (Fig. 2.15). This type of transistor is easily fabricated in

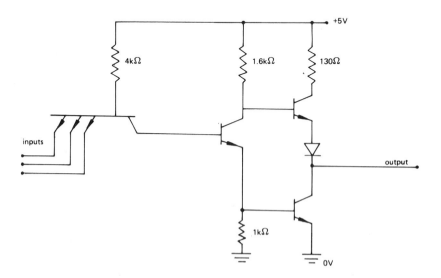

Fig. 2.15 — A 3-input TTL NAND gate.

monolithic form and gives a compact input stage. Fig. 2.15 shows the
original series 54/74 TTL gate. It performs the NAND operation — a three-
input version is shown but there are also 2-, 4- and 8-input versions. Because
of its wide availability and because the NAND is itself a logically complete
set, as explained in Section 2.2, many logic designers work entirely in terms
of NAND elements. We shall do the same in this book (apart from making
convenient use of NOT gates).

Various forms of TTL logic have now been developed, all belonging
basically to the same family. These are the standard (N) type as described
above, and the low-power (L), high-speed (H), Schottky-clamped (S) and
low-power-Schottky (LS) versions, each with its own special advantages
(and complementary disadvantages). The Schottky varieties are examples
of *non-saturated* mode devices. Diodes are added to the transistors in such a
way as not to become saturated when ON and this improves the device
switching speed.

Other logic families which use the bipolar transistor are available.
Emitter-coupled logic (ECL), which also operates in a non-saturated mode,
is currently the fastest logic family, but is particularly susceptible to noise
and has a relatively high power consumption. Unfortunately, high speed and
low power consumption, the two most desirable logic family properties, are
in general achieved each at the expense of the other. Their product, the so-
called speed-power product, is often used to compare and classify logic
families, as we shall see later in this section. Both TTL and ECL are used in
making SSI and MSI building blocks, although the use of TTL is now finding
less favour since the speed-power product it offers (see Fig. 2.22) can now be
matched by other technologies at lower cost. Because of its very widespread
use in the 1970s, however, it has left a very important legacy to the
semiconductor industry: the majority of logic circuits now being designed
have inputs and outputs which are *TTL compatible* — a logic HI voltage
which is nominally 3.5 volts and a logic LO which is within a few hundred
millivolts of zero. These levels can readily be derived from a single 5 V
power supply and offer acceptable noise immunity. Many LSI and VLSI
circuits, whatever their internal construction, have 'peripheral circuits'
which ensure that connections to the pins of the package may be made at
TTL voltage levels.

Integrated injection logic (I^2L) is a bipolar family, principally used in LSI
components because of its small space requirements: thus chips with a high
circuit density can be manufactured in this technology. The name derives
from the use of a p-n-p transistor to inject current into the base of several
active n-p-n transistors. I^2L combines its low packing density with moderately high speed operation and moderately low power consumption.

The other logic families of interest are based on the unipolar or field
effect transistor (FET) reported in 1952 but not available in IC form until the
mid 1960s. The most widely used devices are those made from MOSTs.
Their main advantages are that they are simple and economical to fabricate
— requiring fewer process steps than bipolar devices — and, particularly in
one circuit configuration, consume little power. This latter property is

particularly important in VLSI circuit design when many thousands of circuits are produced on a silicon chip less than a centimetre square and power dissipation problems can be significant. There is a variety of types of MOST: broadly speaking they fall into two classes, called *depletion mode* and *enhancement mode*. The depletion-mode devices have current flowing in them in the absence of an input control voltage, whereas conduction in enhancement-mode MOSTs is absent under these conditions and requires an input control voltage to start current flow. The basic structure of a MOST is shown in Fig. 2.16(a). A substrate is doped in a particular way — y in the

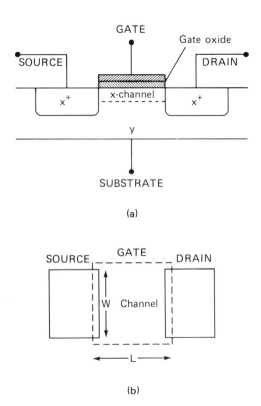

(a)

(b)

Fig. 2.16 — (a) The basic structure of a MOS transistor. (b) Plan view of a MOS transistor.

figure is either p or n. In this substrate two wells are produced heavily doped in the opposite way — x is either n or p, the + implies heavy doping. A thin oxide is formed over the region between the two wells and covered by a layer of ohmic material — the *gate,* which is either metal or polysilicon. If a potential difference is applied between the two wells, designated *source* and *drain,* conduction in the channel between them is controlled by the potential on the gate due to the field produced below it — hence field effect transistor. A set of characteristics very like those of Fig. 2.13 may be produced for a MOST. Values of the drain to source voltage V_{ds} are plotted on the horizontal axis, values of the drain to source current I_{ds} on the vertical axis whilst the gate to source voltage V_{gs} is the parameter which changes to give different curves in the family.

The most noticeable difference between MOST characteristics and bipolar transistor characteristics is that with MOSTs the characteristics are much more nearly horizontal towards the right-hand side of the diagram indicating that the devices have much higher output resistances when used in linear mode. The kind of doping determines the kind of device made. They are usually called n-channel or NMOS devices and p-channel or PMOS devices. One device type is the dual or complement of the other, voltage polarities which would turn one type of device on would turn the other off and vice versa. This feature is made use of in a circuit configuration called CMOS (C for complementary) which is discussed more fully below. As may be seen in Fig. 2.16(a) there is no direct connection between the gate of the device and either the source or the drain. Signals connected to the gate of a MOST will therefore see a capacitance in parallel with a very large resistance. In switching applications the value of this capacitance has a significant effect on the switching speed of the circuit.

Several different circuit symbols are used to depict MOSTs in circuit diagrams, as shown in Fig. 2.17. The most explicit is 2.17(a) which shows an

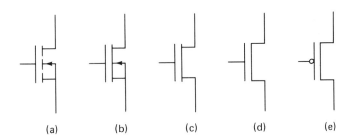

(a)   (b)   (c)   (d)   (e)

Fig. 2.17 — Symbols commonly used to depict MOS transistors.

enhancement mode NMOS device. All important device terminals are shown separately and connections to and between them clearly indicated. The arrow, representing a connection to the substrate, is the other way round for a PMOS device. However, this symbol often degenerates to Fig. 2.17(b) (which, according to the British Standard, strictly repesents a depletion mode device) and, more commonly, to 2.17(c) or (d). Symbols 2.17(c) and (d) are often used to represent both NMOS and PMOS devices even in the same circuit diagram (e.g. a CMOS gate) although some authors use 2.17(e) for a PMOS device when 2.17(d) represents an NMOS device. Where no clear indication of the device type is given in the circuit diagram this must be deduced from the context in which the circuit is discussed. In circuits using both enhancement and depletion mode devices the latter are sometimes indicated by a modification to Fig. 2.17(c) or (d) in which the line joining the source to the drain is made thicker.

Two types of MOST circuits have found wide favour particularly in LSI and VLSI design. These are circuits based on NMOS technology and those using the CMOS configuration.

NMOS circuits

A basic NMOS inverter could be made as shown in Fig. 2.18(a) using an NMOS enhancement mode transistor and a resistor. This would operate in much the same way as the bipolar transistor described earlier with reference to Figs 2.12 and 2.13. If the inverter input voltage V_{in} were less than the transistor threshold voltage V_{th} (a voltage in excess of the threshold is necessary to establish the field which produces the conducting path between source and drain) the transistor would be 'off' and the output 'pulled up' to the supply rail V_{DD}. If V_{in} were greater than the threshold voltage (typically a few volts) the transistor would conduct and current would flow through the resistor and transistor to earth. The output voltage level V_o could be set lower than the threshold voltage by suitable choice of the resistor and the transistor geometry — the width-length ratio shown in Fig. 2.16(b). Input and output voltage levels could thus be chosen so that the output always complemented the input. In this technology, however, implementing a large enough resistor would require a very large area of silicon compared to that used by the transistor. To overcome this problem a depletion mode NMOS transistor may be used as an active load, configured as shown in Fig. 2.18(b).

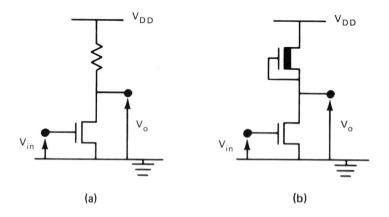

(a)   (b)

Fig. 2.18 — NMOS inverters. (a) Resistor as load (b) Depletion mode NMOS transistor as load.

For a depletion mode NMOS transistor to turn off, its gate must be negative with respect to its source by an amount in excess of its negative threshold voltage. Since the gate and source of the active load in this configuration are connected, the device is always on. When the input is low, therefore, and the enhancement mode device turned off, the output will be connected through the depletion mode device to V_{DD}. When the input is high, both devices will be on and the output will be determined by their relative geometries. These can be so chosen that inputs and outputs again complement each other. Reference 1 (see Reading List for Chapter 2) provides a good description of circuit design details.

NOR gates and NAND gates can be made by adding extra enhancement transistors as shown in Fig. 2.19. The number of devices added, i.e. the

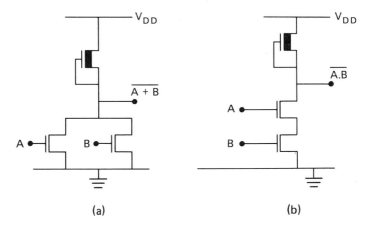

Fig. 2.19 — NMOS logic gates. (a) A 2-input NOR gate. (b) A 2-input NAND gate.

number of gate inputs required, will determine the relative geometries of enhancement and depletion mode devices if consistent output voltage levels are to be maintained throughout a family of devices. Since, when both devices are 'on' they have a given 'on-resistance' for a given geometry, adding extra devices is the same as adding extra resistors in series (NAND gates) or parallel (NOR gates). To produce the same LO output level for a two-input NAND gate as an inverter, both having the same-sized active load, would require that the enhancement devices in the NAND gate were twice the width of that in the inverter thus preserving the overall width/length ratio of the 'on' devices. In a NOR gate the enhancement devices are in parallel but, since only one device needs to be 'on' to define the logic LO level, all such devices can be the same size as in the inverter. Multi-input NOR gates thus take up much less space than multi-input NAND gates. It will be shown later that multilevel logic functions can be formed from either NAND gates alone or NOR gates alone. For reasons of economy of silicon area the NOR implementation is preferred whenever it can be used.

CMOS circuits

Whenever the output of an NMOS gate is low there is a direct current path from power supply to ground through the active load and the on transistor or transistors. In a complex circuit employing multilevel logic approximately half the active loads will thus be connected to ground at any instant even if the circuit is in a quiescent state, i.e. not passing any switching signals. There is thus a consequent standing power supply current drain and associated power dissipation problem in the circuit. The CMOS circuit configuration shown in Fig. 2.20 uses the complementary properties of NMOS and PMOS transistors to overcome this.

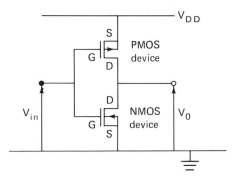

Fig. 2.20 — A CMOS inverter showing substrate connections and using device-specific symbols.

All transistors used in this circuit are enhancement mode types. The NMOS transistor requires a gate voltage which is higher than its source in order to turn on whereas the PMOS device requires a gate voltage less than its source in order to turn on. Both these voltages must exceed the appropriate threshold voltage for the device concerned. With suitable choice of V_{DD} and V_{in} HI and LO levels the circuit works in the following way. When V_{in} is LO the PMOS device is turned on and the NMOS device turned off. The output is therefore connected to V_{DD} through the on resistance of the PMOS device. Current can thus be supplied through this device and will normally be used to charge the gate capacitance of the next stage. When V_{in} is HI the opposite set of circumstances exists: the NMOS device is turned on, the PMOS device turned off and the output connected to earth through the on resistance of the NMOS device. Current through this path can thus be used to discharge the gate capacitance of a connected stage. The great advantage of this circuit is that standing power supply current drain is very small indeed and that, when currents do flow, they are used mainly to charge gate capacitances. Since these capacitances are very small, average total power dissipation is also very low. This feature is particularly useful in VLSI design, for example in applications such as digital watches which are required to keep going for long periods with a very small power source.

CMOS NAND and NOR gates can be made by adding extra transistors as shown in Fig. 2.21.

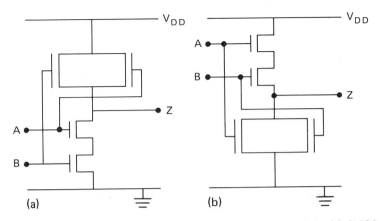

Fig. 2.21 — CMOS NAND and NOR gates using simplified symbols. (a) CMOS
NAND gate (positive logic). (b) CMOS NOR gate (positive logic).

The CMOS fabrication process is the most complicated of the MOS
technologies since both kinds of device must be constructed on a single
silicon chip. Several processes have been developed and are well described
in Reference 2. In essence, to produce for example a PMOS transistor in a p-
type substrate one first diffuses in a (relatively) large well of n-type material
and then diffuses smaller p+ type regions into this. NMOS devices can be
produced in the p-type substrate in the usual way. In early CMOS processes
problems were encountered with parasitic bipolar transistors which were
produced incidentally as part of the process. These problems have now been
overcome by process innovations and well-understood circuit techniques.

A feature of CMOS circuit design is that complex multi-level functions
can be realised in what, by conventional SSI design methods, are quite
unusual circuit structures. Fig. 2.22 shows a possible CMOS implementation

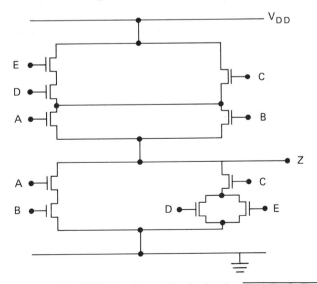

Fig. 2.22 — A complex CMOS circuit to realise the function $\overline{Z=A.B+C.\,(D+E)}$.

of the function $\overline{Z=A.B+C.(D+E)}$ which could equally well be realised in other ways but, in this configuration, produces a very economical circuit. The reader is advised to study Chapter 3 before attempting a full understanding of this circuit.

The basic design of the CMOS circuit makes it very easy to produce a version which is directly TTL compatible and CMOS replacements can now be obtained off-the-shelf for many TTL SSI and MSI circuits. The real use of CMOS, however, is in VLSI, the SSI and MSI circuits being of use to designers in allowing them to gain confidence in the technology by producing SSI and MSI models of potential VLSI systems. Software design aids are, however, rendering this step unnecessary.

A comparison of logic families

As previously mentioned the two most important aims for any logic family are high speed (that is low gate propagation delay) and low power consumption. To a great extent each of these tends to be achieved at the expense of the other. In comparing logic families it is useful to plot their speed-power products: this is done in Fig. 2.23.

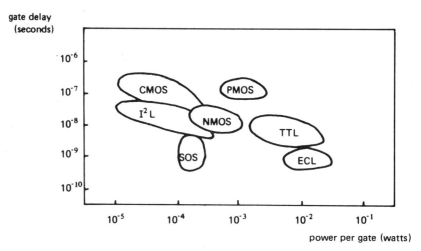

Fig. 2.23 — Comparison of logic families.

Essentially the product of gate delay and power per gate gives the amount of energy required for a switching operation. The lower the figure is, the better. On this basis, SOS would appear to be best all round, CMOS and I^2L best for power consumption and ECL the fastest. It is, however, worth keeping in mind the other factors which contribute to the merit of a logic family including packing density, fanout capability and the cost of fabrication.

The TTL family

Let us return briefly to the TTL family; despite the fact that other families have been developed in competition, TTL remains the most popular technology for SSI and MSI components. Any given logic family has a fairly small range within which its speed-power product can be varied, but either property can be improved at the expense of the other rather more easily. This has been exploited in TTL to produce five different types as mentioned earlier. Their characteristics are listed in Fig. 2.24.

Type	Power Per Gate (mw)	Gate Delays (ns)
Standard (N)	10	10
Low power (L)	1	33
High speed (H)	20	6
Schottky (S)	20	3
Low-power Schottky (LS)	2	10

Fig. 2.24 — The five types of TTL logic.

Their speed-power products are all within an order of magnitude of each other. Low-power Schottky is rapidly displacing the standard variety as the most popular of the TTL family.

Lastly there are three output configurations for each of the above logic types: *totem-pole* (already described — see Fig. 2.15), *open-collector* and *tri-state*. The open-collector arrangement is designed to overcome the inability of totem-pole outputs to be directly connected together in an AND operation (called the *wired-AND*). Tri-state gates are provided to permit circuits to communicate with each other over common buses. A third output state (not LO, not HI, but a *high impedance* condition) disables the gate and prevents undesirable currents from flowing: at any time only one of the tri-state outputs connected to the bus will be enabled.

2.4 INTEGRATED CIRCUIT BUILDING BLOCKS

The growth of semiconductor industries has been very rapid since integrated circuits were first produced in the early 1960s. There has been an enormous demand for ICs particularly for the computer and computer-related markets. From the first SSI chips containing the basic gates the range of available ICs has exploded, so that now there are several logic families, between them offering components at all levels of integration to meet a variety of needs. The very variety of ICs is somewhat overwhelming, but they may be classified into two broad areas: *digital and linear*. Linear ICs include operational amplifiers, voltage regulators, analogue-to-digital (A/D) and digital-to-analogue (D/A) converters, phase-locked loops and consumer devices for radio and television. The operational amplifier is the predominant linear device. Although these ICs are used in computer systems, particularly in A/D and D/A interfaces, they are not our concern here.

Digital devices, by far the larger of the two classes, may be further subdivided into the following categories:

> logic
> memory
> interface

Not all the literature available from semiconductor manufacturers and their appointed distributors uses these classifications — for example 'logic' is sometimes called 'digital', implying that memory and interfacing components do not belong to this class. What do the three categories listed above include? They are chosen to correspond roughly with the three main areas of computer hardware — CPU, memory and I/O.

Integrated circuit packages

From the logic implementer's point of view the form in which ICs are packaged is very important. Part of the task in implementing a circuit design is to ensure that the circuit diagram can be easily translated into physical connections. Circuits are built on boards specially made for the purpose, with an array of holes drilled through them so that the components can be mounted and soldered directly, or instead sockets into which the components will be inserted later. The designer chooses a board of sufficient dimensions for the circuit and makes a plan showing the locations of various ICs, resistors, capacitors and so on. When the necessary components and sockets have been soldered into place all that remains to be done is to connect their inputs and outputs according to the circuit diagram. Connections are made either by wire and solder or by the method of wire-wrapping, for which special pins have to be inserted in the board (these may be part of the IC sockets already mentioned).

Whichever inter-connection technique is used it cannot be done without a *point-to-point wiring diagram*. Usually it is possible to incorporate this on the designer's circuit diagram, although for more complex circuits it may have to be made separately.

IC packages traditionally come in three forms:

> TO
> flat
> dual-in-line (DIL)

The TO are cylindrical metal packages which have been developed from transistor cases. They come in a variety of sizes. Flat packages are useful in applications where the product must be as two-dimensional as possible, such as in wrist-watch manufacture. Most used in computer applications are DIL packages, which have the basic outline shown in Fig. 2.25.

The body of the package is either ceramic (hermetically sealed for demanding environments) or more usually the cheaper plastic form (suit-

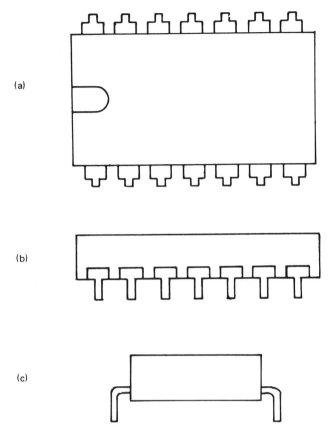

Fig. 2.25 — A DIL integrated circuit package: (a) top, (b) side, (c) end view.

able for most applications). The metal leads or *pins* are connected to the chip itself which is enclosed inside the package body. Each pin has a function which is specified on the *data sheet* provided by the manufacturer. Two of the pins (at least) are reserved for connection to the power supply: these are usually indicated by the names V_{cc} and GND. The pin configuration shown in the data sheet conventionally uses the top view of the package (as in Fig. 25(a)).

Various sizes of DIL package are produced, the number of pins depending on the type of IC — although note that the pin spacing is always the same: 0.1 inches. SSI packages generally have 14 or 16 pins, but MSI and LSI types tend to be larger, with 20-, 24- and 40-pin packages. The newest microprocessors may have larger packages still, 48 pins or more. Packaging is very costly, so manufacturers tend to minimise the pin count for new designs of IC (even though more standardisation of pin positions, another desirable aim, can be achieved with larger packages, leaving some pins unused). The 40-pin microprocessors, for example, would be larger still had this minimisation not been applied.

Fig. 2.26 shows the pin configuration for a 2-input NAND gate (SSI) package. This package has 14 pins, of which two are used for the power supply lines. There are four identical gates in this package.

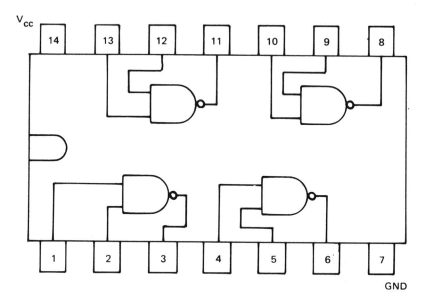

Fig. 2.26 — Pin configuration for 2-input NAND gate (SSI) package.

Note that the notch at the left hand end of the package in the diagram is present on the package body itself: the pin numbers are not. Pin 1 is always in the position shown, relative to the notch (see also Fig. 2.25(a)). For SSI, and some MSI, ICs the function of each pin is pictorially described on the data sheet. In the case of larger-scale integration chips the pins are identified by name (simply a label beside each, with an annotated explanation).

For 3- and 4-input gates the package size stays the same but the number of gates in each is reduced. NAND gates are available as follows:

4×2-input
3×3-input
2×4-input.

The jargon in the literature calls these *quad, triple* and *dual* configurations respectively. The package of 6 NOT gates is referred to as *hex,* while there is an MSI package containing 8 flip-flops called *octal.*

All IC packages are identified by a unique *designator* or reference number. There is a fairly good standardisation between manufacturers, so that the same type of package is likely to bear the same reference number, with the manufacturer's symbol or name beside it. The IC in Fig. 2.26 is a 7400, in fact the first in the 54/74 TTL series produced by Texas Instruments.

As new packages are marketed so they are given a higher number, but still starting with 74 to identify the logic family. When ordering or specifying ICs it is important to add to the designator a suffix specifying which type of packaging is required. For example N and J indicate plastic and ceramic DILs respectively, while W refers to a flat package.

Appendix 1 shows a selection of typical literature and data sheets available from a manufacturer or distributor.

Digital integrated circuits

Interface ICs are intended for connecting peripheral devices to computers. Some devices are for local interfacing, others for remote connection over transmission lines. In general the devices are for *line driving* or *receiving* where high power is required (compared to the power capabilities of logic ICs, inadequate for that purpose), and the environment can be very noisy. They tend to be mixtures of linear and digital circuits. Recently general-purpose interface chips have been produced in conjunction with microprocessor chips (and memory units) to provide a kit of parts from which microcomputer systems can be built in a standard way. Both serial and parallel devices are available, which go by the names of ACIA (asynchronous communications interface adapter) and PIA (parallel interface adapter) respectively. These are both memory-mapped devices, meaning that they are addressed as if they are memory locations but actually allow the transmission of data to and from peripheral units connected to them. In these two cases the drive capability of the chips is limited so for heavy-load or remote interfacing other more suitable chips have to be selected.

An increasingly important area in computing is that of *distributed* systems, networks of computers and other devices connected together by data transmission lines. Interface devices are likely to increase in variety and importance as these systems become more widespread. They will normally be designed to adhere to the interfacing standards being set up by the telecommunications and computing communities so that difficulties in connecting equipment from different manufacturers will be minimised. As the international X-series recommendations for data communications become fixed then adopted, so complex interfacing chips to implement them will be manufactured.

Memory ICs consist of arrays of semiconductor memory cells, each cell capable of storing one bit of information. There is an enormous variety of memory chips of different capacities, speeds and configurations. The constant decline in the price of computer hardware has been very largely due to the falling cost per bit of memory. Semiconductor manufacturers have always been keen to pack more bits onto a single chip, and there is fierce competition to be the first to produce commercial quantities of yet more densely packed ICs.

The two main classes of IC technology are used in fabricating memory technology. Bipolar memories are faster but cannot be so densely packed: MOS (predominantly NMOS) memories yield large packing densities but do not operate so fast. For low-power applications CMOS memories are available.

Computer memories consist of groups of bits called *words*, each word being identified by a unique numerical *address*. The dimensions of the memory depend on the number of bits in the address and data paths of the CPU (as described in Section 1.2). A memory space with addressing capability m, and n-bit word length (an $m \times n$ memory), is illustrated in Fig. 2.27.

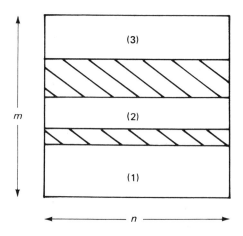

Fig. 2.27 — A fragmented $m \times n$ memory space.

The actual memory size may be any value up to m. It is increasingly common for the memory to be *fragmented* within the address space, as the diagram indicates. Areas (1), (2) and (3) are the occupied regions; the shaded areas are empty. It is now quite common to find different types of memory sharing the same address space, as will be explained below.

Common word lengths n used in computers range from 8 to 32 bits (and sometimes more) The majority of computers use either 8-, 16-, 24- or 32-bit words. This fact is reflected in the *organisation* of available memory chips (their dimensions in terms of m and n), the most common n values being 1, 4 and 8 bits: chips are often quoted only by their total storage capacity, for example '4K' (=4096) bits, but it is important also to known how the cells are organised internally. A 4K chip might be a 4K×1, or 1K×4, or even 512×8. Even though these three configurations represent the same total number of bits they are quite distinct from the designer's point of view. Each requires an IC package with a different arrangement of address and data lines, for example in the first case 12 lines for address and 2 for data (1 input, 1 output) while in the second only 10 address lines but either 8 or 4 for data (4 if bi-directional lines are used). The pin configuration of a typical 1K×4 memory chip is shown in Fig. 2.28. A_0 to A_9 are the address lines, D_0 to D_3

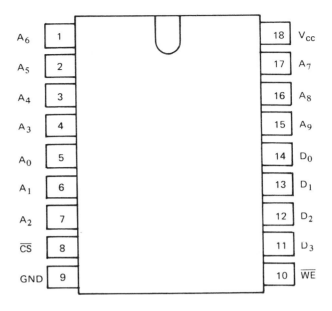

Fig. 2.28 — Pin configuration for a typical 1K×4 memory IC.

the (bi-directional) data inputs and outputs, and $\overline{\text{WE}}$ (*write enable*) selects the reading or writing of data.

Each memory chip in a system represents a part of the address space. The *chip select* input $\overline{\text{CS}}$ is used to enable the data inputs and outputs. Suitable *address decoding logic* would arrange their values to be set appropriately whenever the address of a word within its address space is generated by the CPU. Inputs with a 'bar' over their symbols are called *active-LO* since it is a low voltage which causes the required action (the normal state of the input would be HI, or high voltage). If an input has no 'bar' it is *active-HI* (its normal, inactive state being LO).

A variety of types of memory is available. They are briefly described as follows:

Random access memory (RAM) should really be called read-write memory since it is the type which allows cells to be read from or written to. This is the type of memory used most commonly in computer systems for programs and data. The name RAM should apply also to the older technology magnetic core memory, which also allows reading and writing, but has come to be associated only with semiconductor memories. RAM is *volatile*, meaning that it loses its stored information should the electrical supply be switched off. In some computer applications loss of information cannot be tolerated, so their memory is equipped with battery back-up in case of an accidental loss of power.

Read-only memory (ROM), as the name implies, cannot be written to. This type of memory is used in systems where fixed programs or read-only data are required. ROMs are *non-volatile*. Most microcomputer systems have a minimum of one ROM area in their address space, containing a small fixed program called the *monitor* which allows the progress of programs in RAM to be controlled. *Bootstrap* programs which will be obeyed immediately when a computer is switched on can also be implemented in ROM. Various sub-divisions of ROM exist, distinguished by the way in which the information in the ROM is put there.

Mask-programmable ROMs are programmed by the manufacturer. A mask representing a pattern of 1s and 0s is used in the production process to set up the electrical connections which determine the ROM contents. The mask pattern is specified by the customer in advance. There is a masking charge which is such that it may be uneconomical to buy small quantities of mask-programmed ROMs.

Programmable ROMs (PROMs) are more accurately named field-programmable devices. They can be programmed by the user to his own requirements. Each memory cell is like a tiny fuse wire which when intact represents a 1. The 0 state is produced by passing a heavy electric current which breaks the fuse wire. A suitable *PROM programmer* device is required for this purpose: these can either be purchased or fairly easily built since the manufacturer specifies all the appropriate details for programming. The process is irreversible, so the user must be certain that the bit pattern is correct first time.

Erasable PROMs (EPROMs) are PROMs which can not only be user-programmed but erased as well. Mistakes either in the bit pattern or in programming the device can thereby be rectifed (but note that the entire memory array is erased). Typically EPROMs can be erased and re-programmed up to 100 times. Erasing is possible by means of a perspex window in the top of the IC package, through which the memory chip itself is visible: the chip is exposed to ultraviolet (UV) light of a specified frequency for a recommended length of time. Note that when EPROMs are programmed and being used in a memory system the perspex window should be covered by an opaque material (such as black adhesive tape) to prevent any possible loss of information due to the UV in natural light.

Static RAMs are memory chips in which the cells do not lose information as long as electric power is supplied to them.

Dynamic RAMs, in contrast, need to be *refreshed* periodically otherwise the information would be lost. The distinction between the two types really applies only to MOS RAMs, since the bipolar memory chips are essentially static. The advantages of dynamic RAMs consist of the smallness of their memory cells compared with those in static memories, thus making possible the production of larger-capacity chips. Also they consume less power since when not selected (that is, with chip enable inputs disabled) they automatically go into a low-power-consumption *standby* mode. On the other hand dynamic RAMs do require external refresh circuitry which adds to the total memory cost. Generally, static RAMs are more cost-effective in small-memory systems (up to about 4K words). Otherwise dynamic RAMs are better.

Logic ICs include all digital chips other than memories and interfaces.

The name is rather general and is intended to cover all logic devices which may be used to implement the CPU of a computer system, including gates and flip-flops at the SSI level, MSI devices such as registers and adders, and also microprocessor (LSI) units, themselves complete CPUs. Though logic devices form the largest category, little need be said about them in this section: they are available in IC packages, as already described. Chapters 3, 4, 5 and 6, however, are primarily concerned with the design and implementation of logic within CPUs, where this category of IC will receive further attention.

Positive and negative logic
One last topic requires to be discussed in the present section. It brings the two streams, abstract and physical, back together. Basically, the point is that there are two forms of logic which may be used, depending on the way 1s and 0s are assigned to the physical realisations of HI and LO voltages. Either assignment is equally valid but the choice must be applied consistently. As we shall now see, the two forms of logic may be used to link together circuit design, expressed in terms of AND, OR and NOT operations, and implementation using the readily available NAND gates. The following also makes additional points about logic symbols and their use.

When we buy a logic gate, the function which it performs must be specified by the manufacturer, but since the gate physically operates by voltage levels this function is specified in terms of voltages — for example a NOR gate has the following truth table:

A	B	$\overline{A+B}=F$
LO	LO	HI
LO	HI	LO
HI	LO	LO
HI	HI	LO

where the two states or signals are represented by a HI and LO voltage level (which will be +3.5V and 0V for TTL gates). Normally the manufacturer also specifies that the gate is a *positive-NOR* which means that by convention we assign 0 to LO voltage and 1 to HI. Then the truth tables will have the same functional appearance:

	A	B	F
	0	0	1
	0	1	0
(again, a NOR gate)	1	0	0
	1	1	0

This is called the *positive logic* convention.

If, however, we choose to assign 0 to HI and 1 to LO the truth table becomes:

A	B	F
1	1	0
1	0	1
0	1	1
0	0	1

which looks like a NAND gate in this *negative logic* convention.

With the same physical gate, then, two different functions can be realised depending on the logic convention chosen.

How do we indicate on a drawing the logic convention chosen? We do this by means of a small circle on the inputs or outputs of a gate. Since there are distinctive shapes for only AND and OR (not NAND, NOR) we therefore have to indicate the positive and negative versions of nominal gate functions as shown in Fig. 2.29.

Nominal Gate Function	Positive Logic		Negative Logic	
	Function	Symbol	Function	Symbol
AND	AND	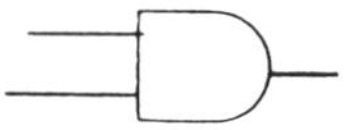	OR	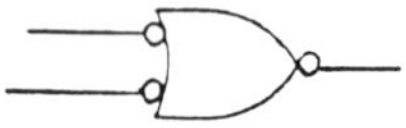
OR	OR	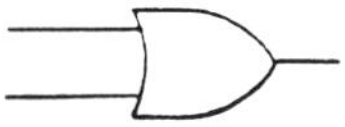	AND	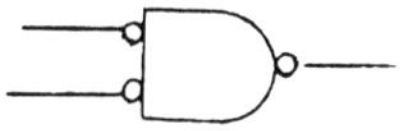
NAND	NAND	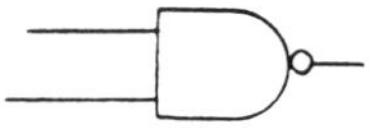	NOR	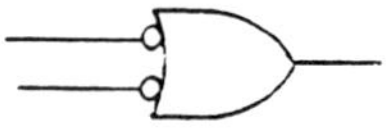
NOR	NOR	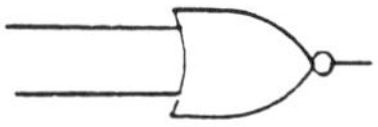	NAND	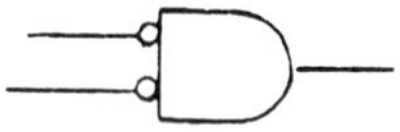
NOT	NOT	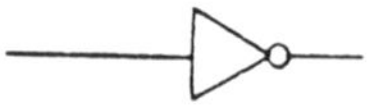	NOT	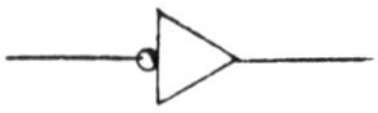

Fig. 2.29 — Positive and negative logic symbols.

To explain the table, let us look at the nominal AND function (in terms of HI and LO). If we apply negative logic, the truth table becomes that of an OR function (in terms of 1s and 0s). To indicate that negative logic is being used, the inputs and outputs are circled. Another way of looking at this change of logic convention is that is is equivalent to *inverting* the signal value. So we could say that if the inputs of an AND gate are inverted before the function and the output inverted after the function then the function looks like OR.

The reason why the NAND gate is shown as the AND symbol followed by a circle is that changing the logic convention at the output of an AND gate gives a NAND function, which is equivalent to inverting the output. The small circle can be interpreted as either a change of logic convention or as an inversion of the signal value.

Returning to the NAND gate with negative logic applied at inputs and output, this looks like the NOR function, which is normally written as

that is OR with an inversion at the output. The symbol, therefore, for a *negative* logic NOR is written as

and since two inversions cancel each other out the symbol is actually written as

as indicated in the diagram. This symbol can be interpreted as a NOR working in negative logic, or as an OR gate with the inputs inverted or having undergone a logic change.

This can be used to maintain, in a logic diagram, the functions of AND and OR which arise naturally from truth tables and Boolean expressions, while enabling us to interpret circuit symbols as physical NAND (or NOR) gates.

For example, consider the exclusive-OR function $\overline{A}B+A\overline{B}$. The circuit diagram can be drawn as in Fig. 2.30(a).

It would be helpful to keep the symbols for AND, OR so that we easily recognise the function which the circuit performs. By changing the logic convention between gates we can do this, as Fig. 2.30(b) shows. The gates keep their original functions but physically each can be realised by a 2-input NAND gate.

Notice that the NOT gate has a positive and negative logic version — it can be considered as an amplifier —▷— with *either* a logic convention change or inversion at input (negative logic) *or* output (positive logic).

The circuit in Fig. 2.30(b) can be realised entirely by 2-input NAND gates, since it is very easy to implement NOT using NAND. This can be done in two ways, either

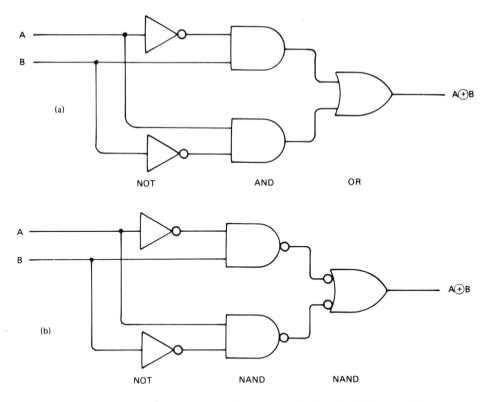

Fig. 2.30 — Exclusive-OR logic circuit: (a) in terms of AND, OR, NOT gates. (b) in terms of NAND, NOT gates.

by connecting both inputs together, or

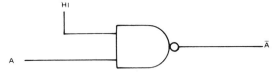

by connecting one of the inputs to HI. These can both be verified by inspecting the truth table for the NAND gate (in positive logic form). Similarly, NOT can be realised by NAND gates with more than 2 inputs — either by connecting all the inputs together or by connecting all but one to HI (via 1KΩ resistors).

Note that de Morgan's laws are consistent with the above interpretations of positive and negative logic, for example

$$\overline{A}+\overline{B}=\overline{AB}$$

shows that NAND is equivalent to a negated-input OR gate.

3

Combinational and sequential logic

3.1 REPRESENTATION OF LOGIC CIRCUITS

The terms *combinational* and *sequential* have already been defined for logic elements in Section 2.1: the outputs of a sequential element depend on previous as well as present inputs, whereas combinational elements are a special case in which only the present inputs affect their output values. From now on the word 'element' will be replaced by 'circuit' since any circuit can be represented as a black-box element.

As shown in Fig. 3.1 sequential circuits may be further sub-divided into the *asynchronous* and *synchronous* classes.

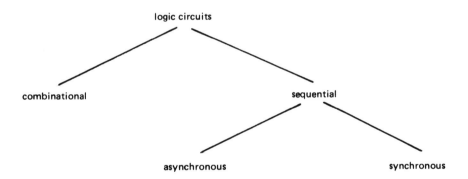

Fig. 3.1 — Classification of logic circuits.

In Sections 2 and 3 of this chapter combinational circuits will be studied first, followed by a discussion on sequential logic. Although asynchronous circuits are mentioned, and an example given, it is the synchronous type which is most frequently used in computers and consequently they will receive substantially more treatment. Design techniques and example circuits will be presented for both combinational and synchronous sequential logic.

In the present section we concentrate on the various different representations of logic circuits, some useful in the design techniques presented later while others are simply ways of presenting circuits to make their functions clearer. In general, logic circuits can be represented by the following means:

> written descriptions
> mathematical expressions
> tables/diagrams

and quite commonly by all three together. Tables or diagrams (for example *truth tables*) are usually very effective in communicating the meaning of (complex) ideas but often require annotation, particularly to explain symbols which may have been used from necessity. The compact, expressive power of mathematics (in the shape of Boolean algebra) may also be required to add precision to the (often generalised) table or diagram.

The combinational logic gates were expressed initially in this way — truth tables, written explanations and Boolean expressions. The ideas involved in these gates are so simple that we can replace the three modes of expression by a single distinctively-shaped symbol. There are also fortunately few different types of combinational gate and correspondingly few symbols to remember. The flip-flop varieties will also be introduced by means of tables, diagrams and a written explanation (in Section 3.3). They, too, are few and sufficiently simple to be represented by rectangular shapes bearing letters to label inputs and outputs. The input identities are adequate reminders of the function which the flip-flop performs.

MSI and LSI circuits of greater complexity than gates and flip-flops are represented also by simple rectangular shapes, in these cases showing the pin configuration of the IC packages as described in Section 2.4. All the pins are labelled, but the complexity of the circuits is such that a suitable explanation needs to be attached. In effect these circuits are represented by their respective data sheets.

Some pictorial representations

It is sometimes helpful to describe combinational logic circuits using pictorial forms related to the physical and abstract sides of digital logic.

Switching representations can be made as illustrated in Fig. 3.2. Each switch is equivalent to a Boolean variable, and their interconnections equivalent to the form of the Boolean expression.

The basic three Boolean operations, AND, OR and NOT are shown. The AND and OR operations are combinations of switches connected in series and parallel respectively. Inversion is achieved by a double switch arrangement: when one is closed, the other is open and vice versa. The value 0 is represented by an open, 1 by a closed switch. These switch forms may be employed in representing more complex combinational circuits or more useful still in demonstrating the postulates and theorems of Boolean algebra. For example Theorem T5:

$$A + AB = A \text{ (see Section 2.2)}$$

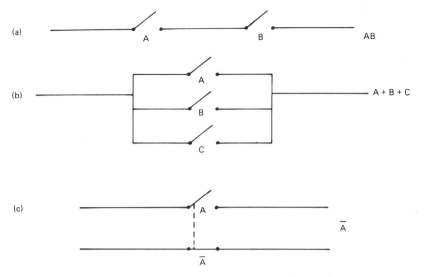

Fig. 3.2 — Switching representation of (a) AND, (b) OR, (c) NOT.

follows from Fig. 3.3 without further explanation.

Venn diagrams may also be used to give a pictorial representation of combinational circuits. These diagrams are used in mathematical theory to illustrate the relationships between sets in terms of the set operators: intersection, union and complementation. Fig. 3.4 illustrates that these operators are essentially equivalent to AND, OR and NOT. Just as for switching representations, Venn diagrams may be used to illustrate more complex combinational circuits and to verify the postulates and theorems of Boolean algebra. For example, theorem T5 follows from a little consideration of Fig. 3.4(a) and (b).

Karnaugh maps

Karnaugh maps, or *K-maps* as they will be called hereafter, are very useful in practice for representing combinational circuits. Their main purpose, as will be explained in Section 3.2, is to aid the process of *minimisation* whereby logic circuits are implemented as efficiently as possible (as we shall see there are various criteria by which minimisation may be measured).

The K-map is really an extension of the combined ideas of Venn diagrams and truth tables: it combines the idea of representing all possible combinations of *n* Boolean variables on a plane, with the idea of listing all the variable values and output results in a table.

The Venn diagram can be used to show, for example, all combinations of three variables A, B and C as in Fig. 3.5.

We can give each of the expressions a numerical value as shown in brackets. The value corresponds to the binary equivalent if we use 1 and 0 instead of A and $\overline{A}$ and so on. A particular logical expression can be plotted

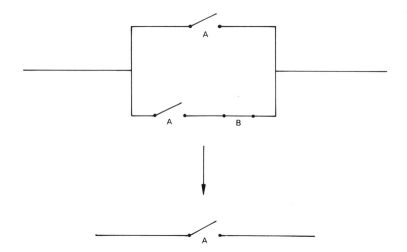

Fig. 3.3 — Demonstration of theorem T5: A + AB = A.

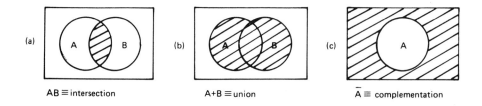

Fig. 3.4 — Venn diagram representation of (a) AND, (b) OR, (c) NOT.

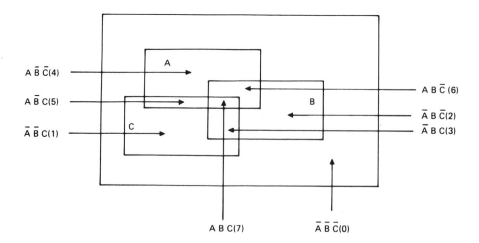

Fig. 3.5 — Venn diagram representation of 3 variables.

on the diagram by shading the area or areas desired, or by assigning an output value of 1 to the shaded areas and 0 to the unshaded. Thus, for example, the AND function for 3 variables is represented by shading area number 7, or by placing a 1 there (and 0s elsewhere).

Notice that in moving horizontally or vertically from one sub-region to another there is a change in only one variable (or a change in only one binary digit). Karnaugh maps are based on the same principle, except that the diagram takes the form of a map as in Fig. 3.6(a). The squares in the map have been given the same numerical values as in the Venn diagram.

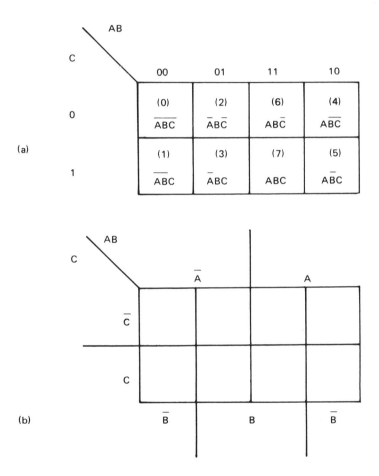

Fig. 3.6 — K-map representation of 3 variables: (a) significance of each square. (b) division into regions.

Notice that *reflected binary* (or *Gray code*) is used for listing the input variable values along the top and sides of the map — because Gray code involves a change in only one binary digit from one number to the next, as illustrated in Fig. 3.7. This figure shows the pure binary codes for the decimal digits 0–9 and their corresponding Gray code values. It is also called reflected binary because of the reflection symmetry which exists about a horizontal line drawn after two, four, eight rows and so on. For example this symmetry is evident for the least significant two bits from the line under the fourth row in the Gray code column.

Fig. 3.6(b) demonstrates the division of the K-map into regions according to the values of the individual variables. This can be useful for the minimisation procedure to be described in the next section.

K-maps may be used to represent 2-, 3- or 4-variable expressions on a single map. For 5 variables two adjacent maps are required; for 6, four maps. The K-map is impracticable for any greater number of variables. Outlines for 2-, 4-, 5- and 6-variable maps are given in Fig. 3.8, divided into regions as in Fig. 3.6(b). Care must be taken in noticing which variables are

Decimal	Pure binary	Gray code
0	0000	0000
1	0001	0001
2	0010	0011
3	0011	0010
4	0100	0110
5	0101	0111
6	0110	0101
7	0111	0100
8	1000	1100
9	1001	1101

Fig. 3.7 — Correspondence between decimal, pure binary and Gray code.

presented horizontally and which vertically. For example, Fig. 3.8(b) is differently organised from Fig. 3.6(b) in this respect.

State tables, state diagrams and finite-state machines

All the above representations apply to the special case of combinational circuits. Sequential logic systems, otherwise known as finite-state machines (FSMs) as explained in Section 2.1, have a more complex structure and necessarily require to be represented in a more suitable form.

The structure of FSMs may be elaborated as follows: an FSM consists of five sets (I, O, S, T_s, T_o) where

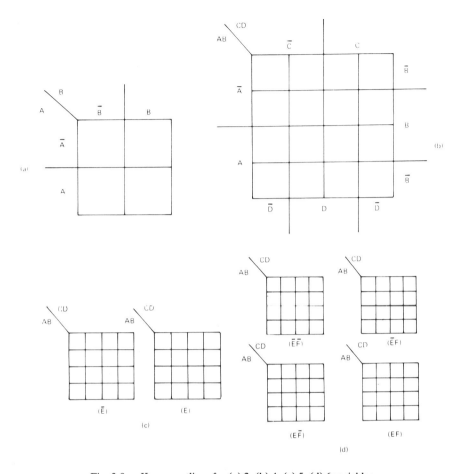

Fig. 3.8 — K-map outlines for (a) 2, (b) 4, (c) 5, (d) 6 variables.

I = input symbols
O = output symbols
S = internal states
T_s = inter-state transitions
T_o = output transitions

Less formally, any FSM has a finite number of states, in any one of which it can be at a given time. It changes from one state to another in discrete timesteps, depending on the input symbols and on the inter-state transitions. The FSM also outputs symbols as it progresses from state to state according to the output transitions. Thus, given any state and input symbol, the movement of the FSM is entirely predictable. This is the same as the generalised black box behaviour. The FSM can be represented in either of two ways, by a state table or a state diagram.

A *state table* is an extension of a truth table which includes extra columns for present and next internal states. The general form of a state table is shown in Fig. 3.9(a), and a very simple example table in (b).

For the simplest sequential circuits there may be no need to distinguish between next state S′ and output O — as in Fig. 3.9(b) — thus a reduced version of the state table may be used.

State diagrams contain exactly the same information as the tabular form. Internal states (or nodes) are represented by circles, and inter-state transitions by lines (called arcs) joining the circles. The lines are further labelled with the input symbol (or symbols) leading to this transition, and with the resulting output symbol. Fig. 3.10 gives the state diagram version of the example in Fig. 3.9(b).

The Moore/Mealy model
A very important representation of sequential circuits, as shown in Fig. 3.11, is due to E. F. Moore and G. H. Mealy. This gives a view of a sequential circuit in terms of the elements with which it will be constructed: a combinational logic network and a memory by which previous inputs are remembered. It also shows the element of *feedback* which is fundamental to the construction of sequential circuits.

Moore and Mealy independently reported on the structure and synthesis of sequential circuits but their models, although different in detail, are both essentially as shown in Fig. 3.11. Their work followed on from previous investigations into synthesis procedures by D. A. Huffman, who used a form of state table (called a flow table) to represent circuits. Huffman and Moore are credited with introducing the notion of an internal state into sequential design procedures (i.e. equating sequential circuits with FSMs). Moore, in addition, developed the idea of a state diagram for starting off the design process.

3.2   COMBINATIONAL LOGIC DESIGN

We begin the study of logic circuit design by considering combinational logic problems. This class of problem is characterised by the fact that output values are a function of only the present inputs. Furthermore, for the moment it can be assumed that a change of input values has immediate effect on the outputs.

In computer systems, there are many combinational circuits, such as

   adders
   ALUs
   carry look-ahead generators
   comparators
   code converters
   $n \times m$ decoders
   priority encoders
   multiplexers/demultiplexers
   parity generators/checkers

Present state/Inputs	Next state	Outputs
(a) all combinations of present state and input symbols	next state for each combination of present state and inputs	output symbol for each combination of present state and inputs

S	I	S′	O
0	0	0	0
0	1	1	1
1	0	0	0
1	1	1	1

(b)

Fig. 3.9 — Stable table: (a) general form, (b) example.

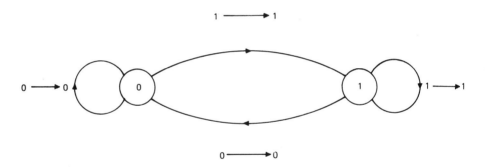

Fig. 3.10 — Example of a state diagram.

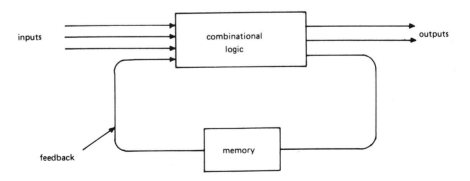

Fig. 3.11 — Moore/Mealy model of a sequential logic circuit.

These are all circuits available in MSI form. Within the CPU of a typical computer they would be amalgamated with registers to give a larger functional unit. Registers, being sequential circuits, will be studied in the following section. Our purpose in the present section, however, is twofold: to show how circuits such as the ones listed above are designed from SSI components, and to explain in the process of demonstrating examples the structure of some important parts of a computer. Further examples will be discussed in Chapter 4.

A simple design example

To illustrate the design process let us consider a simple problem not directly related to computer systems. It is a switching problem — how to construct a circuit to enable one light to be equipped with two switches. This arrangement is common in domestic lighting schemes. Expressing the problem in detail, there are two switches A and B, and one light L. When A and B are both down or both up L is off, otherwise L is on.

This statement is more concisely expressed in a truth table:

A	B	L
down	down	off
down	up	on
up	down	on
up	up	off

Let us substitute 0 for switch position down and light off, and 1 for up and on. We now have

A	B	L
0	0	0
0	1	1
1	0	1
1	1	0

As described in Section 2.2, the output L can be expressed in terms of A,B and the fundamental operators AND, OR and NOT. Consider the rows only where an output of 1 appears. It is those combinations of inputs which lead to the Boolean sum-of-products expression:

$$L = \overline{A}B + A\overline{B}$$

From this point we are in a position to draw a circuit diagram, depending on the availability of components with which to implement the circuit.

A suitable switching circuit can be drawn as follows:

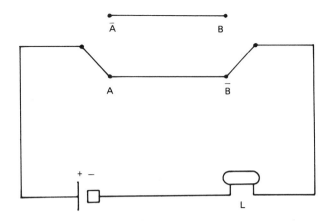

Notice that the function shown in the truth table is the exclusive-OR (EOR) as defined in Section 2.1. Although EOR is itself available as a (quad) MSI package it is instructive to show its implementation using SSI gates. Suitable circuits were presented in Fig. 2.24(a) and (b), the first using AND, OR, NOT and the second the corresponding NOT, NAND implementation. These circuits can be drawn from the Boolean expression for L.

    Fig. 2.24(b) can further be converted into a circuit using 2-input NAND operations only. This is shown in Fig. 3.12.

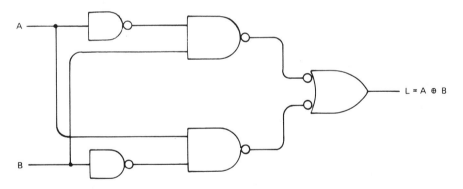

Fig. 3.12 — NAND gate version of the exclusive-OR (EOR) function.

    As described in Section 2.4, NOT may be implemented using NAND either by connecting all inputs together or by connecting all but one to HI. Either way, the NAND version of NOT may be indicated by a single-input NAND gate, as in the diagram.

    This simple problem illustrates the basic steps in designing a combinational logic circuit. These steps may be enumerated as follows:

(1) Think round the problem, particularly about the inputs and outputs which the circuit will have.

(2) Draw a truth table by listing all possible input variable combinations and filling in the required output values. Alternatively a K-map could be used (but see later).

(3) Extract from the truth table (or K-map) the Boolean expression for the output value and write it down as a sum-of-products form in terms of AND, OR and NOT.

(4) (Usually) convert the AND, OR, NOT form to one using only NAND or NOR gates. The circuit is now ready for implementation.

The simplicity of the lightswitch problem is such that little thought need be put into step (1). For more complex, multiple-input, multiple-output problems this step may be significantly more difficult. In the case of multiple outputs a truth table is required (step (2)) for each output. Alternatively all the truth tables can be merged as long as the outputs are all functions of the same set of inputs.

In general, the extracted Boolean expression will be much more complex than that for L above. It is often possible to reduce the circuit in terms of the number of gates (or IC packages) used, the number of interconnections between gates and the *levels of logic* in the circuit. Referring to Fig. 3.12, there are three levels in the circuit, corresponding to the maximum number of gates which an input signal passes through on its way to the output. All combinational circuits can be implemented, in theory, using only three levels of logic because they can all be expressed in a sum-of-products form with the three levels NOT, AND and OR. In practice the expression may have to be manipulated or factorised if the available gates do not have sufficient inputs for direct implementation of the three-level sum-of-products form. Such factorisation results in an increased number of levels of logic. The importance of minimising levels of logic is that each level corresponds to a gate delay in the circuit, in other words the smaller the number of levels, the faster the circuit will operate. The next example will illustrate how a circuit may be minimised in terms of the above criteria.

Wiring diagrams

As mentioned in Section 2.4 circuits are implemented using IC packages containing the appropriate logic elements. Implementation is the process of translating the circuit diagram into an interconnected array of ICs (or IC sockets) on a circuit board. For this purpose the wiring diagram is important.

The first step in implementing a logic circuit is therefore to add point-to-point wiring information to the designer's circuit. Alternatively a wiring list may be made up separately, listing the pins in each IC and the other pins/ICs they are to be connected to. In either case a layout of the circuit board must first be planned, to show the positions of ICs, as in Fig. 3.13.

Preferably the IC positions should be chosen to minimise the amount of wire used in making the interconnections. For all but the smallest of circuits this is a difficult task. Sometimes the criterion is to use the smallest board possible. This can be achieved by arranging the packages so that they occupy the minimum area, depending on their sizes. Fig. 3.13 shows an arrange-

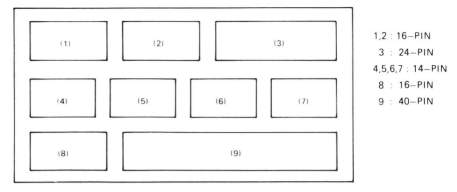

Fig. 3.13 — Example of an IC board layout.

ment chosen with this aim in mind. Generally it will not be possible to satisfy this criterion as well as minimising the amount of wire used.

If the wiring details are to be added to the circuit diagram the IC numbers on the board layout have to be used to label the appropriate symbols on the diagram as in Fig. 3.14, which illustrates one section of a circuit.

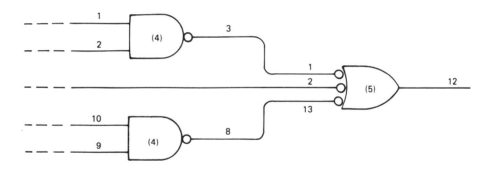

Fig. 3.14 — Section of a circuit diagram showing wiring connections.

Of the three logic gates two are to be implemented using a type 7400 IC, or quad 2-input NAND gate package, labelled as (4). The third, a 7410 or triple 3-input NAND, corresponds to IC number (5). Implementing the interconnections is a matter of reading the pin/package details directly from the drawing, and wire-wrapping each output pin to the appropriate input.

Design example — the binary adder
The basis of the arithmetic and logic unit (ALU) in computers is the *binary adder*. This takes two binary digit operands and produces their binary sum. The adder is also used to subtract numbers by the 2s complement (or the 1s complement) method and may be employed in multiplication and division units which are based on repetitive methods.

When we add two numbers manually, whether they be decimal or binary, we start at the least significant end and add the two corresponding digits together — we write down the result of the addition and take the carry digit, if any, to the next-to-least significant position where the procedure is repeated. This is a serial process; that is, we use the same 'circuit' (our mental faculties) to add each stage in turn.

Similarly, we can perform serial addition using electronic circuitry, providing one circuit for adding two digits and presenting the operands one pair at a time. We can represent this system as follows:

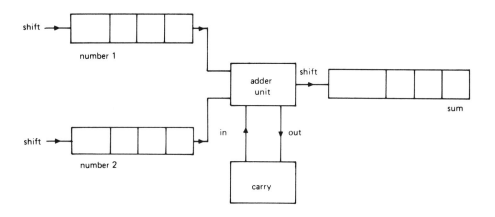

A more costly but effective method is to provide one adder circuit for each pair of digits in the numbers and to perform the addition in parallel, that is all the stages together.

Unfortunately the addition cannot truly be done in parallel because of the carry digit propagation delay — it takes a finite time for each successive carry digit to be passed to the next stage. This delay determines the speed with which two n-bit numbers are added. A method of improving the addition time will be presented later.

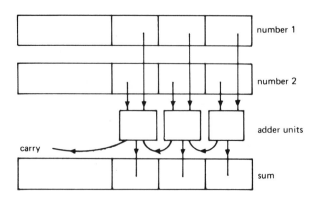

We now design a single-stage adder unit using combinational logic. It is usual to distinguish between the half-adder and the full-adder circuits, which are shown diagrammatically below.

In both cases, A and B are the binary operands, S is the resulting sum and C_O is the carry-out bit. The difference between the two is that the half-adder neglects the carry-in C_i from the previous stage while the full-adder takes it into account.

Truth-tables for these circuits can easily be constructed:

A	B	S_H	C_O
0	0	0	0
0	1	1	0
1	0	1	0
1	1	0	1

half-adder

C_i	A	B	S_F	C_O
0	0	0	0	0
0	0	1	1	0
0	1	0	1	0
0	1	1	0	1
1	0	0	1	0
1	0	1	0	1
1	1	0	0	1
1	1	1	1	1

full-adder

The Boolean equations for the outputs are:

HALF-ADDER $S_H = \overline{A}\,B + A\,\overline{B}$ (the exclusive-OR function)
$C_O = AB$
FULL-ADDER $S_F = \overline{C_i}\,\overline{A}\,B + \overline{C_i}\,A\,\overline{B} + C_i\,\overline{A}\,\overline{B} + C_i\,A\,B$
$C_O = \overline{C_i}\,A\,B + C_i\,\overline{A}\,B + C_i\,A\,\overline{B} + C_i\,A\,B$

Notice that amalgamated truth tables are used for both types of adder. Alternatively two separate tables could be drawn in each case, one for the sum and the other for the carry-out.

The half-adder is very simple and its corresponding circuit consists of an EOR part (for the sum) and the AND function of A and B for the carry-out.

On the other hand, the full-adder equations for S_F and C_O will both produce circuits consisting of four 3-input gates (for the product terms), one 4-input gate (for the sum) and three inverters (for C_i, A and B). Quite often it is possible to reduce the size of such circuits because of their inherent redundancy: variables can be eliminated from the expressions to make the product terms both smaller (i.e. fewer variables in each) and fewer in number. This can be done in one of two ways — using Boolean algebra to manipulate the expressions, or by plotting the expressions on K-maps.

The sum and carry expressions for the full-adder can be re-written using *algebraic manipulation* as follows:

$$S_F = C_i (AB + \overline{A}\,\overline{B}) + \overline{C}_i (\overline{A}\,B + A\,\overline{B})$$
$$= C_i \overline{S}_H + \overline{C}_i S_H$$

(since by applying de Morgan's laws $\overline{A\,B + \overline{A}\,\overline{B}} = \overline{A}B + A\overline{B}$).

Thus another way of implementing the full-adder sum is to use two half-adder circuits (i.e. two EOR gates): hence the names. The expression for S_F cannot otherwise (in terms of AND, OR, NOT) be reduced in size. However, the carry can be written as

$$C_O = \overline{C}_i\,A\,B + C_i\,A\,B + C_i\,\overline{A}\,B + C_i\,A\,B + C_i\,A\,\overline{B} + C_i\,A\,B$$

(adding two redundant C_iAB terms has no effect on the value of the expression)

$$= C_i\,A(B + \overline{B}) + C_i\,B(A + \overline{A}) + AB\,(C_i + \overline{C}_i)$$

$$= C_i\,A + C_i\,B + A\,B$$

(since $A + \overline{A} = 1$ and $A.1 = A$).

Thus we have a simplified form for C_O, with three 2-variable terms instead of four each of three variables. With the redundancy removed we can apparently now draw a minimal circuit. However, by manipulating the C_O expression in a different way:

$$C_O = A\,B\,(C_i + \overline{C}_i) + (C_i\,\overline{A}\,B + C_i\,A\,\overline{B})$$
$$= A\,B + C_i\,S_H$$

we can make use of the expression for S_H already available from the sum part of the adder. This will produce a smaller circuit than the previous manipulation would have. The circuit for a full-adder based on half-adders (EOR gates) is drawn in Fig. 3.15. The AND, OR circuit for the carry has been drawn directly in NAND gate form.

Reducing the size of expressions using Boolean algebra is basically simple: just look for the possibility of factorising the expression such that a term of the form $(A + \overline{A})$ emerges, which reduces to 1. In this way redundant variables are eliminated. If possible expressions should be closely inspected to see if they are amenable to manipulation to take advantage of common sub-expressions (such as S_H above), as this is likely to produce a smaller overall circuit.

A more convenient way to eliminate redundant variables is by use of *K-maps*. This method allows elimination to be effected with a quick visual scan

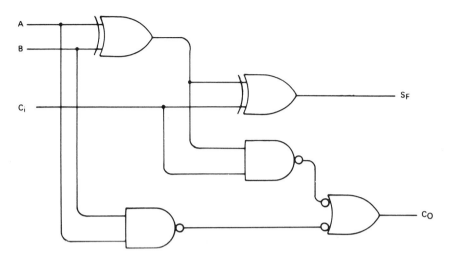

Fig. 3.15 — Binary full-adder circuit diagram.

because terms containing potentially redundant variables will be adjacent on the map. Consider the K-map for S_F:

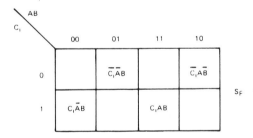

which is more usually drawn as:

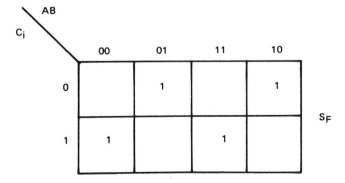

because the value of each expression is obvious from the position of the plotted 1s. Terms occupying adjacent squares horizontally or vertically differ only in the value of one variable: they may be combined to eliminate that variable according to the rule $A + \overline{A} = 1$. In the case of S_F there are no adjacent squares occupied by 1s therefore the expression cannot be reduced.

For C_O the K-map is:

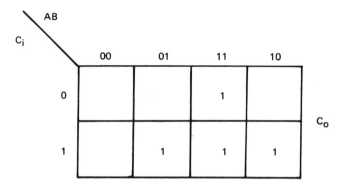

There are adjacent squares containing 1s — two pairs horizontally and one pair vertically. These are indicated by circles which group the adjacent 1s together:

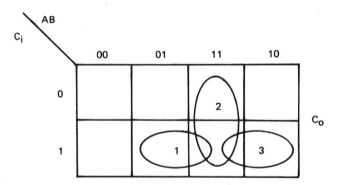

Group 1 consists of $C_i \overline{A}B$ and C_iAB which reduces to C_iB (eliminating A). Groups 2 and 3 similarly reduce to AB and C_iA, eliminating C_i and B respectively. Thus C_O may be written:

$$C_O = C_iA + C_iB + AB$$

the same expression which was obtained by the first of the two algebraic manipulations. The K-map inspection does allow a rapid elimination of any redundant variables and as such is very useful for reducing the size of circuits. It does not help the process of manipulating expressions to make use of already available sub-expressions. We shall be returning to the topic of minimisation criteria.

The use of K-maps

The adder example showed briefly how K-maps can be used to represent and reduce the size of combinational circuits. Let us more fully explore their use in logic design.

K-maps are really just a rearrangement of the information in a truth table. The 1s in the output column of the table are plotted on the squares of the K-map, and the 0s are represented by blank squares. The position of the squares is arranged so that if each one represents a combination (product term) of n variables, then $n-1$ variables have the same value in adjacent squares while one variable is complemented in one square but not in the other. Adjacent squares for a 3-variable map are shown in Fig. 3.16 by double-headed arrows. Note that adjacency includes wrapping round the map horizontally or vertically from each square at an edge to the square at the opposite edge.

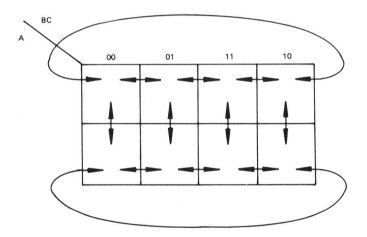

Fig. 3.16 — Adjacent squares on a 4-variable K-map.

Adjacency on a 4-variable map is similar, though for maps with 4 or more variables it is more difficult to spot adjacent 1s. For 5-variable maps (two 4-variable maps side by side) it helps to imagine one of the two maps in a plane above the other so that adjacent squares in the fifth variable are aligned along the third dimension.

In combinational logic design, K-maps may usefully be employed in a stage following the formation of the truth table. The expression is plotted on the map, reduced in size if possible and finally rewritten. Alternatively the

K-map may be used instead of the truth table as a direct means of plotting the desired logical function, and only the reduced form of Boolean expression written down. Expressions in a sum-of-products form derived from truth tables are suitable for direct translation onto a K-map: one product term maps onto one square.

Sometimes it may be wished to reduce the size of an expression, if possible, such as the following:

$$F = \overline{A}\,\overline{B}\,\overline{C} + \overline{A}B + \overline{A}\,\overline{B}C\overline{D} + AC\overline{D}$$

This is a 4-variable expression (variables A, B, C, D) but is not in *canonical* form, that is each product term does not contain all four variables. For direct mapping of each product onto a square of the K-map the expression should be converted to canonical form. This is done by expanding those terms not containing all four variables by ANDing them with the sum of each missing variable and its complement (since $A + \overline{A} = 1$ this has no effect on the value of the expression). Using the example:

$$\begin{aligned} F &= \overline{A}\,\overline{B}\,\overline{C}(D+\overline{D}) + \overline{A}B\,(C+\overline{C})\,(D+\overline{D}) + \overline{A}\,\overline{B}C\overline{D} + AC\overline{D}\,(B+\overline{B}) \\ &= \overline{A}\,\overline{B}\,\overline{C}D + \overline{A}\,\overline{B}\,\overline{C}\,\overline{D} + \overline{A}BCD + ------ \text{(expanded)} \end{aligned}$$

The function is now plotted on the K-map:

AB \ CD	00	01	11	10
00	1	1		1
01	1	1	1	1
11				1
10				1

F

Product terms in a canonical sum-of-products expression each occupy one square, the smallest area on a map, and are thus sometimes called *minterms*. K-maps are also sometimes referred to as minterm maps.

How do we group squares in general to give a reduced expression? The rules are that squares should be combined in groups of 2, 4, 8 and so on in powers of 2. In the 4-variable case the groupings can be 2, 4 or 8 squares (thus eliminating 1, 2 and 3 variables respectively). The largest possible groupings should be sought first. The squares being combined are circled and the aim is to cover all the squares containing 1s in the most effective way.

Squares can belong to more than one circled group — they can be covered more than once. Circled groups are known as *prime implicants* (PIs) of the plotted function, and groups containing at least one square which cannot belong to any other group are known as *essential prime implicants*.

The prime implicants in the example are shown circled:

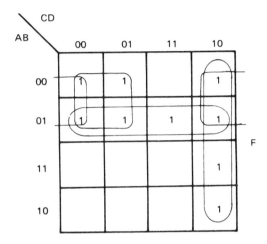

There are four circled groups, that is four PIs, each of four squares. However, the PI

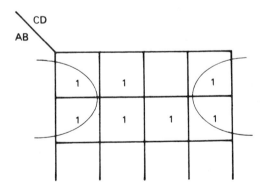

(corresponding to $\overline{A}\,\overline{D}$) is non-essential, containing only squares which belong to other circled groups. As such, this PI should not be included in the final expression. The other three PIs are all essential and between them cover all the 1s on the map. Thus the final reduced expression is

$$F = \overline{A}B + \overline{A}\,\overline{C} + C\overline{D}$$

To write down the reduced terms corresponding to each PI it is helpful to consider the K-map as a set of regions for each variable as in Fig. 3.6(b). The value of each PI is determined by the intersection it makes across the regions on the map.

In the above example the final reduced expression is unique since all 1s are covered by essential PIs. In some cases the essential PIs are not sufficient to cover all 1s, and there may be a choice of other PIs which cover the remaining 1s. The final expression, which will be non-unique, should consist of the essential PIs and sufficient other PIs to cover all the 1s on the map.

To summarise, squares containing a 1 should be included in the largest possible groupings and the minimum number of groupings selected to cover the function. Each square containing a 1 must be included at least once.

Design example — BCD to Gray code conversion
Some functions are *incompletely specified,* meaning that some combinations of input values cannot occur in practice. This should be taken into account in the design of a logic circuit to implement the function. An example is in the conversion of binary-coded-decimal (BCD) to Gray code values.

The truth table to represent the code conversion problem is essentially contained in Fig. 3.7. This does not, however, show the incompleteness of the function. BCD values require four bits to store the ten possible decimal values 0 to 9, leaving six unused combinations of the bits. These unused combinations cannot occur in practice. When the Boolean expressions corresponding to the code conversion are to be reduced (if possible) we can choose whether to include any of the outputs which would result from unused input combinations, if these will help the reduction process: these outputs are marked by Xs on the truth table and K-map to indicate *don't care conditions* (they can be 0 or 1 as we choose).

Fig. 3.17 shows the truth table for the BCD to Gray code conversion, including don't care conditions.

This is a multiple-output problem. Although all four inputs G_3, G_2, G_1, and G_0 are amalagamated into one truth table each requires a separate K-map for the reduction process. The K-map for the least significant output is as follows:

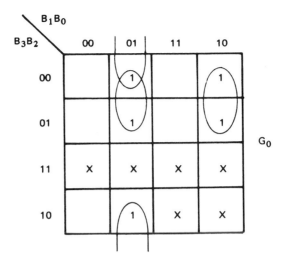

Without using the don't care conditions the grouped 1s give a final expression

$$G_0 = \overline{B}_3 B_1 \overline{B}_0 + \overline{B}_3 \overline{B}_1 B_0 + \overline{B}_2 \overline{B}_1 B_0$$

A quick visual scan tells us that by including appropriate don't care conditions (effectively as 1s) as shown:

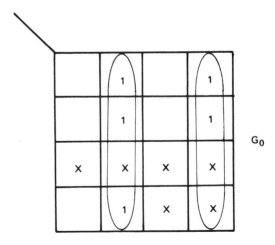

we obtain a very much reduced expression:

$$G_0 = B_1 \overline{B}_0 + \overline{B}_1 B_0 = B_1 \oplus B_0$$

BCD				Gray code			
B_3	B_2	B_1	B_0	G_3	G_2	G_1	G_0
0	0	0	0	0	0	0	0
0	0	0	1	0	0	0	1
0	0	1	0	0	0	1	1
0	0	1	1	0	0	1	0
0	1	0	0	0	1	1	0
0	1	0	1	0	1	1	1
0	1	1	0	0	1	0	1
0	1	1	1	0	1	0	0
1	0	0	0	1	1	0	0
1	0	0	1	1	1	0	1
1	0	1	0	X	X	X	X
1	0	1	1	X	X	X	X
1	1	0	0	X	X	X	X
1	1	0	1	X	X	X	X
1	1	1	0	X	X	X	X
1	1	1	1	X	X	X	X

DON'T CARE CONDITIONS

Fig. 3.17 — BCD to Gray code conversion showing don't care conditions.

eliminating B_3 and B_2, and reducing the number of terms to only two. The K-maps and reduced expressions for the other outputs are shown below:

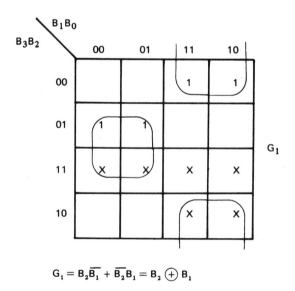

$$G_1 = B_2\overline{B_1} + \overline{B_2}B_1 = B_2 \oplus B_1$$

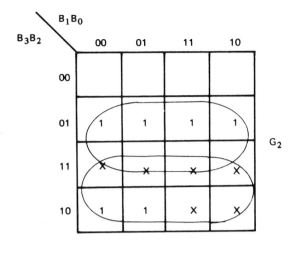

$$G_2 = B_3 + B_2$$

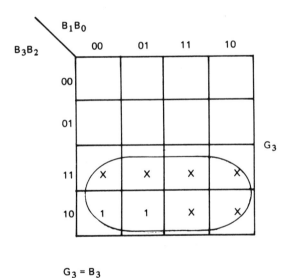

$$G_3 = B_3$$

In the cases of G_2 and G_3, groupings of eight squares are circled, thus eliminating three variables.

A circuit diagram for the BCD to Gray code conversion is illustrated in Fig. 3.18, using EOR gates. Although the expression above for G_2 has been reduced as much as possible it is better in this case not to use all the don't care conditions:

B_3B_2 \ B_1B_0	00	01	11	10
00				
01	1	1	1	1
11	X	X	X	X
10	1	1	X	X

but to circle only the groups shown to give

$$G_2 = B_3\overline{B}_2 + \overline{B}_3B_2 = B_3 \oplus B_2$$

Since EOR gates are available four in one IC package (with designation 7486) the converter may thus be implemented with one IC (leaving one spare EOR gate in it).

Some notes on circuit minimisation

Using K-maps, or indeed Boolean algebra, logic expressions can be reduced to a minimum size by eliminating redundant variables. This reduction process is usually called *minimisation*. Generally speaking, minimisation consists of reducing the number and size of the product terms in a Boolean expression to the minimum, although in practice the most effective solution depends on specific circumstances, for example the availability of certain types of gate, or the existence of common sub-expressions within a large circuit.

In the first generation of computers, AND and OR were implemented by inexpensive diode logic, but the NOT operations required a vacuum tube circuit which was relatively expensive. One of the principal aims, therefore, in building combinational circuits was to keep the number of inverters to a minimum. For sequential circuits amplification had to be provided to implement the feedback path (see Fig. 3.11). Again this was expensive to provide, so the aim in these circuits was to minimise the number of feedback loops. Second generation gates provided both inversion and amplification so the early criteria disappeared, to be replaced by a general requirement to reduce the total number of gates.

More recently, the cheapness of gates in IC packages has altered the balance of the criteria. The cost of wiring, including both materials and labour, has risen so much in comparison with IC costs that it is often cheapest to minimise the number of interconnections between gates. Small

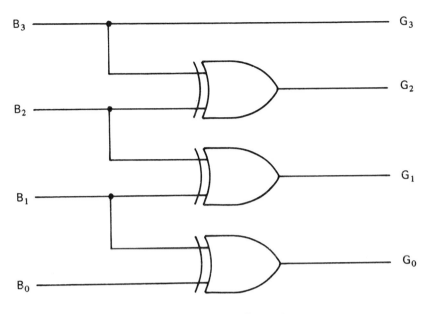

Fig. 3.18 — Circuit for BCD to Gray code converter.

circuit size is usually considered important: in these circumstances keeping down the IC package count and optimising their layout on the circuit board are key factors. Minimising the number of levels of logic in a circuit leads to faster circuit operation and may be the most important criterion in particular implementations.

Reducing the number of product terms in an expression using a K-map (or otherwise) corresponds to reducing the number of gates in the circuit, while reducing the size of each product is equivalent to minimising the interconnections. For example, consider the 4-variable expression introduced earlier:

$$\overline{A}\,\overline{B}\,\overline{C}+ \overline{A}B + \overline{A}\,B\,\overline{C}\overline{D} + AC\overline{D} \tag{3.1}$$

Using a K-map, we know that the expression reduces to

$$\overline{A}B + \overline{A}\,\overline{C} + C\overline{D} \tag{3.2}$$

which appears to be much cheaper to implement than (3.1).

The number of interconnections is important not only because of wiring costs but also because of the fan-in and fanout factors for the available gates. Fan-in is determined by the number of input pins for a gate — 2, 3, 4 or 8 for NAND gates. Depending on the number of inputs per gate a different number of gates can be accommodated in the IC package, as explained in Section 2.4. Fanout, the number of inputs which may be connected to a single gate output, is not physically limited by a pin count so care must be exercised by the designer in ensuring that gates are not overloaded by exceeding the permitted fanout. A fanout of 10 is usual for TTL gates, but such a figure must be carefully interpreted, since (usually) it is quoted for gates of the same type.

Continuing the example, the availability of only 2-input NAND gates means that (3.2) must be factorised to avoid the necessity of a 3-input gate. One of the ways this can be done is as follows

$$\overline{A}(B + \overline{C}) + C\overline{D} \tag{3.3}$$

Circuit diagrams for all three versions of the expressions are given in Fig. 3.19.

The gate count, number of interconnections (all gate inputs) and levels of logic (maximum number of gates through which any signal must pass) are compared below for all the circuits.

Circuit	No. of gates	No. of interconnections	Levels of logic
[1]	9	20	3
[2]	7	12	3
[3]	7	11	4

The best circuit would seem to be [2] or [3] depending on whether interconnections or gate delays would be the more important criterion. Let us also look at the number of IC packages required to implement each circuit, since in practice we must count these for board layout. The following information is useful:

Type of gate	IC package designator	Gates per IC package
Inverter	7404	6 (hex)
2-input NAND	7400	4 (quad)
3-input NAND	7410	3 (triple)
4-input NAND	7420	2 (dual)

Circuit [2] requires one 7404 (leaving 3 spare NOT gates), one 7400 (leaving

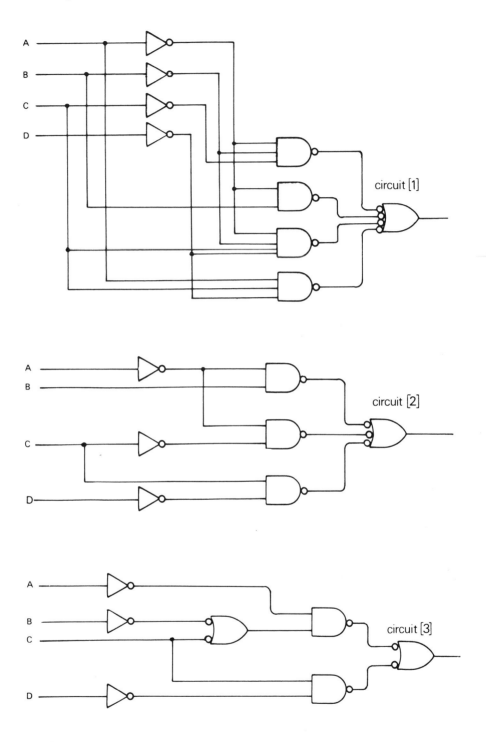

Fig. 3.19 — Three circuits to implement the same expression.

1 spare NAND gate) and one 7410 (2 spare gates) — a total of 3 IC packages. The third circuit requires one 7404 (3 spare gates) and one 7400 (none spare), giving only 2 packages in total. So in terms of package count, circuit [3] is preferable to [2].

However, note that [1] requires one 7404 (2 spare gates), one 7420 (none spare) and one 7410 (none spare, using one of these as a 2-input NAND by connecting the unused input to HI) — the same number of packages as circuit [2]. Although [1] has a larger gate count it needs only the same number of ICs to implement it.

Note also that spare, that is unused, gates in packages may be an important factor to consider if they can be incorporated into another circuit which will share the circuit board.

The Quine-McCluskey minimisation method

An alternative to reducing the size of expressions using K-maps is the *tabular* minimisation method due to W. V. Quine and E. McCluskey. This is useful for expressions containing large numbers of variables, for which K-maps are impracticable. The method is systematic and is suitable for programming on a computer to give an automatic minimisation tool.

The aim of the tabular method is the same as that for K-maps, namely to extract the prime implicants from the Boolean expression and then to select the essential PIs, and sufficient of the remaining PIs, to cover all the terms in the expression.

Let us demonstrate the method by means of an example. The four-variable expression in the notes on circuit minimisation will be used, for two reasons — first, the techniques can be illustrated more easily while using a fairly small set of tables and second, a comparison can easily be made with the K-map method.

Example: Tabular minimisation of the function:

$$F = \overline{A}\,\overline{B}\,\overline{C} + \overline{A}B + \overline{A}\,BC\overline{D} + AC\overline{D}$$

(1) The first step is to convert the expression into canonical form, by expanding as follows

$$F = \overline{A}\,\overline{B}\,\overline{C}(D+\overline{D}) + \overline{A}B(C+\overline{C})\,(D+\overline{D}) + \ldots\ldots\ldots$$
$$= \overline{A}\,\overline{B}\,CD + \overline{A}\,B\,\overline{C}\,D + \ldots\ldots\ldots\text{(expanded)}$$

(2) The next step is to list the minterms (canonical product terms) in a table using 1s to represent uncomplemented and 0s to represent complemented variables, grouping the terms according to the number of 1s they contain. Thus $\overline{A}\,\overline{B}\,\overline{C}D$ would be written 0001 and grouped with the other terms which contain only a single 1. Further, the terms are indexed by their decimal equivalent, so for example 0001 would be labelled '1' and 0101 ($\overline{A}B\overline{C}D$) labelled '5'.

The complete table is shown below:

	Decimal index	Binary equivalent of switching terms	
√	0	0000	group with no 1s
√	1	0001	
√	2	0010	group with one 1
√	4	0100	
√	5	0101	
√	6	0110	group with two 1s
√	10	1010	
√	7	0111	group with three 1s
√	14	1110	

(√ see explanation below).

(3) Now proceed to find, for each term in the table, those other terms which differ from that term in only one variable — this necessitates investigating the group below the current group in the table. So compare term 0 with all terms in the second group and compare, for example, term 5 with terms in the very last group.

The above process continues for each group from the first to the second last inclusive — since all terms in the last group will have been compared with all other terms during the process, this group need not be inspected again.

Whenever any pair of terms is found to differ in only one variable they are both ticked in the table. The pair is combined, replacing the variable which differs in the two terms by a dash (–), and inserting the combined pair into a new table. Thus, for example, term 1 and term 5 are combined to form 0–01, thus eliminating the variable B. The new table has the following entries (which should be checked by going through the first table systematically as described — note that all the terms in the first table have been ticked).

0,1	000–
0,2	00–0
0,4	0–00

1,5	0–01
2,6	0–10
2,10	–010
4,5	010–
4,6	01–0

5,7	01–1
6,7	011–
6,14	–110
10,14	1–10

(4) The second table is again organised into groups depending on the number of 1s in each term. The process carried out for table one is repeated for table two, where only terms with dashes in corresponding positions can be compared. Again, terms differing in only one variable are combined, the variable eliminated and an entry made in a new table. Terms which have been combined are ticked. In this example, all terms in table two will be ticked, and the new table is as follows.

0,1/4,5	0–0–
0,2/4,6	0––0
0,4/1,5	0–0–
0,4/2,6	0––0

2,6/10,14	––10
2,10/6,14	––10
4,5/6,7	01––
4,6/5,7	01––

(5) The same procedure is applied to this table, and so on until no more combinations can take place.

In the present example the third table yields no combinations so the process stops here. All remaining unticked entries in all the tables are the prime implicants of the expression.

Note that duplicate entries may arise, as in table three — in each case it is sufficient to include only one copy of each duplicated term. The third table therefore reduces to

0,1/4,5	or 0,4/1,5	0–0–	P
0,2/4,6	or 0,4/2,6	0––0	Q

2,6/10,14	or 2,10/6,14	––10	R
4,5/6,7	or 4,6/5,7	01––	S

The expression has four prime implicants, labelled P, Q, R and S. Compare this result with the Karnaugh map method for this example — in the tabular method all the prime implicants arise from the systematic procedure, whereas they are not always all obvious on K-maps.

(6) A prime implicant table is formed as shown below,

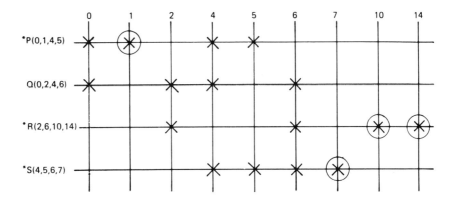

where each PI is given a name (in this example P, Q, R and S) and a cross placed on the intersection of each PI row with any column representing a variable contained in that prime implicant.

To mark the essential prime implicants, look for columns containing exactly one cross. A circle is placed round the cross and the PI containing that variable has an asterisk placed alongside it. The PIs not asterisked are the other prime implicants. The essential prime implicants must be included in the answer, with a selection of the other PIs sufficient to cover all the terms in the expression.

In this example, since P, R and S are the essential prime implicants they are essential to the answer, but since they also cover all the terms in the original expression the fourth PI is not necessary, and can be excluded.

(7) The minimised expression is obtained by looking at the labelled entries for the finally selected PIs in the combination tables and writing down the logical sum of the minimised terms, so in this example

$$F = \overline{A}B + \overline{A}\,\overline{C} + C\overline{D}$$

using the prime implicants, P, R and S.

3.3 SEQUENTIAL LOGIC DESIGN

The Moore/Mealy model of sequential logic circuits in Fig. 3.11 shows that the essential difference between combinational and sequential circuits is the ability of the latter to remember previous outputs. Sequential circuits have a memory. As we shall see shortly, an important use of sequential circuits in computers is to implement registers; the simplest sequential circuits are basic memory elements.

The S–R flip-flop

The main components of a sequential circuit are a combinational logic part and a feedback path from output to input (via a memory element or delay path). The simplest sequential circuit is constructed with two NAND gates:

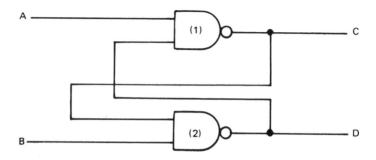

where the outputs are fed back and used as inputs. Let us analyse the operation of this simple circuit. We shall use the positive logic convention for all circuit analyses, in other words LO (low voltage) input is the same as 0, and a HI (high voltage) input is equivalent to 1. In analysing circuits it is important either to have a mental picture of the appropriate gate truth table (in this case for a 2-input NAND) or if this is found to be too difficult (at first) the truth table should be consulted (see Fig. 2.4). When A is 0, C must be 1. If B is 1, then both inputs to gate (2) are 1 and its output D is 0. If the input values are reversed, that as if A is 1 and B is 0, the outputs are similarly reversed: C and D are 0 and 1 respectively. If from either of these input cases (A = 1, B = 0 or A = 0, B = 1) B or A is changed so that both A and B are 1, then the values of C and D remain in their present states. Thus the circuit is capable of remembering which output, A or B, was last set to 0. The case A = B = 0 ensures that both C and D become 1.

The circuit is the basis of the *set-reset* (S–R) flip-flop which is used as a basic memory element. It is also called, in common with some other circuits which we shall be studying, a *bistable*: an element with two stable states. The S–R flip-flop circuit diagram is detailed in Fig. 3.20. It differs from the previous diagram in that the inputs are inverted (using single-input NAND gates).

The normal state of the inputs is S = R = 0: in this state the outputs do

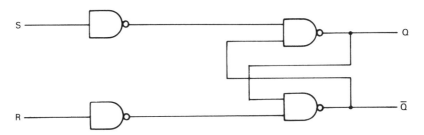

Fig. 3.20 — S–R flip-flop circuit diagram.

not change but depend on which input, S or R, was previously applied. Applying an input means that it is changed to 1, then back to 0 again. In other words the input is *pulsed*: we shall look at the notion of pulses shortly. If S = 1 (and R = 0) then the output Q becomes 1. When S is returned to 0 the output Q remains at 1. If R = 1 (and S = 0) then Q changes to 0 and will remain so when R is returned to 0 (until the next time S is changed). In both cases (Q = 1 or Q = 0) the other output is the inverse of Q and is labelled $\overline{Q}$ for this reason. The operation of the S–R does not allow for the case when S = R = 1: this input combination must be avoided in practice. The behaviour of the S–R flip-flop is best summarised by using a state table or state diagram. Both are presented in Fig. 3.21. Note that Q_o labels the present internal state.

	Present state Q_o	Inputs S	R	Outputs Q	$\overline{Q}$
(a)					
	0	0	0	0	1
	0	0	1	0	1
	0	1	0	1	0
	0	1	1	X	X
*	1	0	0	1	0
	1	0	1	0	1
	1	1	0	1	0
*	1	1	1	X	X

(b)

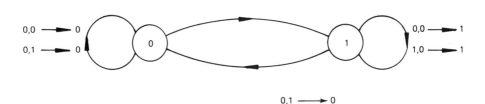

Fig. 3.21 — (a) State table and (b) state diagram for the S–R flip-flop.

In (a) the rows marked with an asterisk (*) label the disallowed input conditions (and the corresponding undefined outputs). Notice that the state table lacks the 'next state' column of the general table in Fig. 3.9(a). In common with the other bistables the next state is exactly the same as the output Q so this column would merely contain redundant information. More complex sequential circuits, with more than two internal states, would not in general have the same correspondence between their observable outputs and internal states. In (b) the order of inputs causing inter-state transitions is exemplified by $S = 1$, $R = 0 \rightarrow Q = 1$. The output $\overline{Q}$ is not specifically mentioned in this diagram, but is taken for granted. All flip-flops have complemented outputs available: they are often required in circuit implementations.

Pulses and clocks
The notions of pulses and clocks are very important in digital logic. Events in logic circuits take place over periods of time which we represent by means of *timing diagrams*. The basis of these diagrams is shown below:

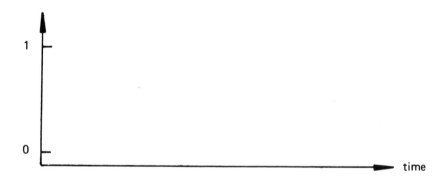

Time is represented along a horizontal axis, which is calibrated into suitably sized intervals, if necessary. Typically for logic circuits we would show time in a range between nanoseconds (10^{-9}s) and microseconds (10^{-6}s). The timing diagram is used to record the behaviour of voltage levels at a sampling point (an input or output) in a circuit. Usually it suffices to represent only the two logic levels, HI and LO (0 and 1 using positive logic) since, apart from very short intervals, the sampled output will be at either one level or at the other. As a first approximation, the *transition* between logic levels (0 to 1, or vice versa) may be assumed to be instantaneous. As we shall see, there are circumstances in which it is important to know the transition times in detail. For TTL logic, the levels 0 and 1 correspond approximately to 0 volts and 3.5 volts respectively (although the voltage supply level V_{cc} is at 5 volts the output stage of TTL gates is such that there is a voltage drop from V_{cc} through a resistor in the transistor ON state — see Fig. 2.14).

Two consecutive logic level transitions constitute a *pulse,* either a *positive* pulse as shown in Fig. 3.22(a), or a *negative* pulse (Fig. 3.22(b)). We shall deal exclusively with positive pulses in our examples.

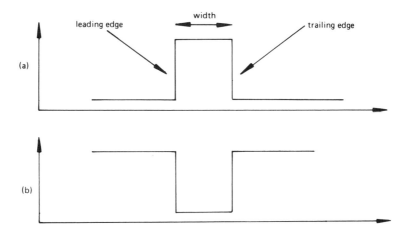

Fig. 3.22 — Pulses, (a) positive, (b) negative.

A $0 \rightarrow 1$ (LO $\rightarrow$ HI) transition is referred to as a *leading edge* (or *rising edge* for positive pulses) and the $1 \rightarrow 0$ (HI $\rightarrow$ LO) transition as a *trailing edge* (or *falling edge*). An important characteristic of a pulse is its *width* (or *duration*).

Some circuits are sensitive to a leading or trailing edge — these *edge-triggered* devices will be described in the section on other flip-flops. Some flip-flops are *pulse-triggered* which means that a whole pulse — two transitions — must be applied to effect output changes. The S–R flip-flop, however, is perhaps best described as *level-sensitive*: a HI logic level at S or R causes changes in Q. As explained above, the mode of use of the S–R is to return the S or R level to LO after the appropriate input has been asserted. One of the main operating problems with logic circuits is *noise*. This manifests itself in the form of pulses, often called *spikes* (or *glitches*), which have very small width. Such narrow pulses may not be fast enough to cause changes and subsequent problems in pulse-triggered or level-sensitive circuits but they can produce unwanted output changes in edge-triggered devices. Elimination of noise is usually achieved by sound circuit construction techniques which include shielding from sources of external noise, good earthing contacts and the use of decoupling capacitors. Noise is a topic which will not be further discussed in this book.

In computer systems most sequential circuits are synchronised together by a common source of timing signals called a _clock_. The clock emits a stream of pulses at regular _intervals_ as illustrated in Fig. 3.23.

The pulses initiate changes in the various circuits to which the clock is connected, and in between pulses the circuits are allowed to operate or settle down. The settling down time can be the sum of many gate propagation delays, as for example in a basic parallel binary adder where carry bits are generated for each stage of the addition in turn. The _clock frequency_, which is the number of pulses emitted per unit of time, is chosen to suit the operating speed of all the circuits for which it provides timing signals: the speed of the slowest of these circuits ultimately determines the upper frequency limit of the clock source. Typical computer clock frequencies are of the order of 1 MHz (1 Megahertz = 10^6 pulses per second), in other words the clock pulse interval is about a microsecond or hundreds of nanoseconds. Pulse widths are typically about half the pulse interval, but may sometimes be much smaller than half. Frequency is measured only in terms of pulse intervals and says nothing about the width of clock pulses. Data sheets will, however, refer to the _duty cycle_ which means the ratio of pulse width to interval. So a 50% duty cycle means that the width is half the pulse interval. The other flip-flops, which will be described next, are all provided with a _clock input_ CK which is intended to be connected to a clock source. Such _clocked_ flip-flops are the basis of the sequential circuits in computers.

Other types of flip-flop

There are two other types of flip-flop: the D and the J–K. Both are developments of the circuit described earlier for the S–R flip-flop. Their names, as for the S–R, are the labels used to denote the inputs. In the case of the D-type the name stands for _delay_ (but is sometimes called _data_). However, the name J–K does not represent any words describing the J–K's mode of operation: the origin of J and K is unclear but they appear to have been chosen simply because they differ from S and R.

The circuit symbol for a flip-flop is a rectangular shape as explained in Section 2.1. Each type is distinguished by the input labels as illustrated in Fig. 3.24. This shows the approved circuit symbols for all three types, with some variations which are found in available IC packages.

In the diagram the S–R is unclocked, but the D and J–K both have clock inputs CK (the shape > is used to indicate the clock input). The D is provided with preset (PR) and clear (CLR) inputs which are active-LO (normal, inactive state HI) and asynchronous with the clock input; in other words if PR is set LO at any time the value of Q changes to 1, if CLR becomes LO the flip-flop state Q becomes 0. The CK input of the J–K is shown as active-LO: this will be explained shortly. Flip-flops are available in IC packages, usually in a dual configuration. The TTL IC version of the J–K in Fig. 3.24 is illustrated in Fig. 3.25. Its package designator is 7473. Notice the unconventional pin positions for V_{cc} and GND — usually they are assigned pins 14 and 7.

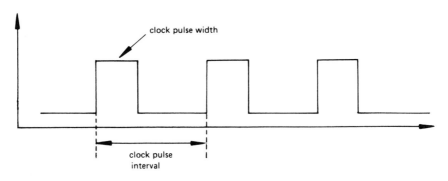

Fig. 3.23 — Pulses emitted by a clock source.

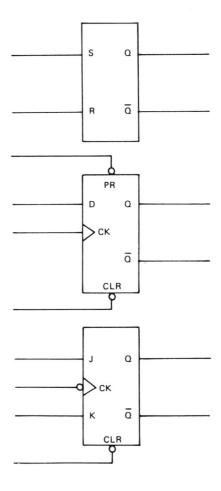

Fig. 3.24 — Circuit symbols for the main types of flip-flop.

D-type input is a single input which replaces the S and R inputs of Fig. 3.20, as illustrated below:

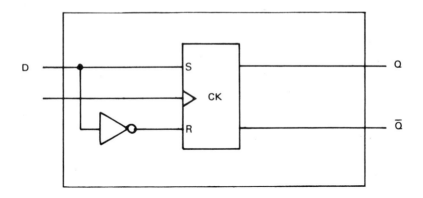

This arrangement is more accurately called a *gated latch* (or just a latch) because of its operation. Whenever the clock input is HI the output Q changes to the value currently at input D: Q follows D during a clock pulse. If the clock input is LO, Q cannot change. Effectively the clock is an *enable* input to the circuit. The latch operation is shown by the following timing diagrams:

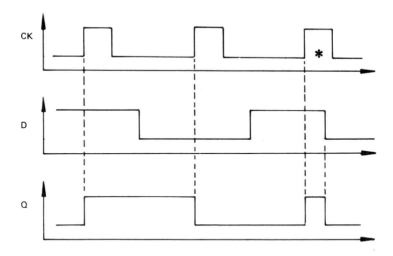

The important point to note is that if D changes while CK is HI, as during the clock pulse marked *, Q will change to follow it.

There are applications in which it is required to sample a data input at a particular time and to allow no further changes at the input to affect the output. A suitable way of achieving this is to sample on the edge of a pulse, during the very small time interval (typically a few nanoseconds) it takes the level to change from LO to HI or vice versa. The true D-type flip-flop is an edge-triggered device rather than a latch, most commonly *positive-edge-*

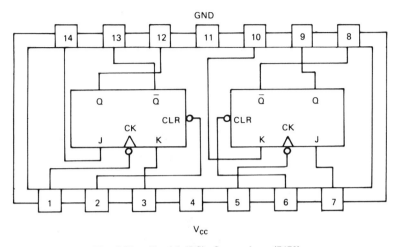

Fig. 3.25 — Dual J–K flip-flop package (7473).

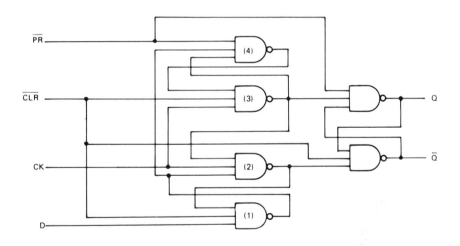

Fig. 3.26 — Circuit diagram of positive-edge triggered D-type flip-flop.

triggered meaning that it is the LO–HI transition of the clock input which causes changes. The circuit diagram of such a flip-flop is presented in Fig. 3.26. Clear and preset inputs, consistent with the D-type shown in Fig. 3.24, are included.

The circuit has the basic two NAND gates with crossed feedback paths as for the S–R flip-flop, but extra input gating is necessary to produce edge-triggered operation. Two cases must be considered in order to understand the operation of the device. First, when D is LO, the output of gate (2) becomes LO at the top of the leading edge of the clock pulse, and this effectively disables gate (1) throughout the clock pulse duration. Thus no subsequent changes in D can affect the circuit until the output from gate (2) is reset to HI by CK returning to LO. Second, if D is HI at the top of the leading clock edge, gates (2) and (4) are disabled by a LO output from gate (3), again preventing changes in D from affecting the circuit until the next leading edge.

This type of flip-flop is available in a dual form in an IC package designated 7474. Along with the pin configurations, data sheets describe the operation of flip-flops using a *function table* which is more like a truth table than the state table form introduced earlier. Such a description is exemplified for the 7474 in Fig. 3.27.

	Inputs			Outputs	
Preset	Clear	Clock	D	Q	$\overline{Q}$
LO	HI	X	X	HI	LO
HI	LO	X	X	LO	HI
LO	LO	X	X	HI*	HI*
HI	HI	↑	HI	HI	LO
HI	HI	↑	LO	LO	HI
HI	HI	LO	X	Q_o	$\overline{Q}_o$

*nonstable configuration.

Fig. 3.27 — Function table for 7474 positive-edge-triggered D-type flip-flop.

As usual for manufacturers' data sheets, the information is presented in terms of LO and HI rather than 0 and 1. Don't care Xs are used to keep the table to a compact size, for example the first row in the table where preset is LO (and clear is HI) could be expanded to show each of the combinations of clock and D, but the essential information is that it doesn't matter what the values of clock and D are, so they are better shown as Xs. The basis of the circuit operation is denoted by the upward arrows, which mean that on the leading edge of the clock input, Q follows D. The state table form can be avoided by using Q_o and $\overline{Q}_o$ to denote previous states of Q and $\overline{Q}$.

The J–K flip-flop is a *master–slave* device. Each J–K contains effectively two S–R flip-flops, as shown in Fig. 3.28. The idea of the master-slave operation is that either the master or the slave inputs are enabled at any time, but not both: the inverted clock input to the slave ensures this. Thus the J–K may be used as a one-bit storage element in a CPU register where certain operations require the register to supply a value while, within the same clock pulse interval, receiving a result from another source. Examples of such operations occur in a shift register, where on each clock pulse data is shifted one place right or left, and in an ALU where a register may be used to provide operands and receive results (a so-called *accumulator* register). The operation of the J–K of Fig. 3.25 (the 7473) is summarised by the function table in Fig. 3.29.

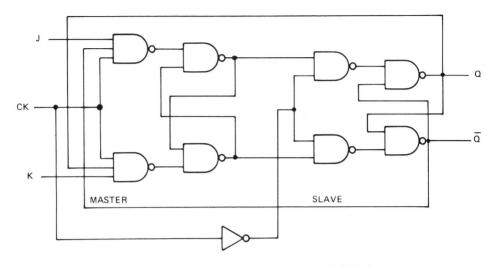

Fig. 3.28 — Circuit diagram of a master–slave J–K flip-flop.

	Inputs			Outputs	
Clear	Clock	J	K	Q	$\overline{Q}$
LO	X	X	X	LO	HI
HI	⊓	LO	LO	Q_o	$\overline{Q}_o$
HI	⊓	HI	LO	HI	LO
HI	⊓	LO	HI	LO	HI
HI	⊓	HI	HI	TOGGLE	

Fig. 3.29 — Function table for 7473 J–K flip-flop.

Apart from the asynchronous clear input, there are four input cases to consider. When J = K = LO the flip-flop stays in its former state (that is Q_o and $\overline{Q}_o$) after a clock pulse has been applied (signified by ⎍ in the table). J = HI, K = LO sets the state of Q to HI; J = LO, K = HI resets Q to LO. Thus if J and K are both LO, or are different, they behave like S and R inputs, with the distinction that any changes in J and K while the clock input is HI do not become evident at Q until the trailing edge of the pulse: this is why the CK inputs in Fig. 3.25 have an active-LO appearance. The final input combination, J = K = HI, causes the flip-flop to TOGGLE, meaning that Q_o (and $\overline{Q}_o$) are complemented when a clock pulse is applied. Toggling is achieved by the extra feedback loops from Q and $\overline{Q}$ to the master input stage as in Fig. 3.28. The master–slave operation is perhaps best considered from the point of view of the clock pulse: while the clock is HI the master inputs are enabled but the slave inputs disabled. Thus changes can be clocked into the master during this time. When the clock returns to LO changes may no longer be recorded into the master since its inputs are disabled, but the state of the master flip-flop at the trailing edge of the clock pulse is now passed to the output Q.

Of the different types of flip-flop the J–K is the most versatile, and the most frequently used. It may be employed in constructing general-purpose registers in computers — one flip-flop for each bit — and as a memory element in any sequential logic circuit.

Designing sequential logic circuits

Sequential logic circuits are characterised by having a number of internal states by which previous outputs are remembered. As well as memory, they also contain logic which guides the circuit through a sequence of states depending on the input values applied over a period of time, as illustrated by the Moore/Mealy model in Fig. 3.11. Examples of sequential circuits are counters, shift registers, accumulators and (not directly related to computers) pattern detectors and traffic light sequencers.

The internal state of a sequential circuit is physically represented by as many flip-flops (one-bit memory elements) as are necessary. Each flip-flop corresponds at the abstract level to a *state variable*. To explain the distinction between internal states and state variables we use an example. Say a sequential circuit has 16 possible internal states. Each of these is represented on a state diagram by a single node (or circle). To implement the circuit, however, only 4 state variables (that is, flip-flops) are required since 16 different combinations of stored 1s and 0s can thus be represented. It is equally possible, without redundancy, to use as many as 16 flip-flops, each one corresponding to a state variable. Thus the n internal states of a sequential circuit can be realised by at least m flip-flops where m is the smallest integer greater than or equal to $\log_2 n$. If the minimum number (m) of flip-flops is used, the combinational logic required to *decode* the states may be substantially more complex to design than the logic necessary if n are used instead. Design complexity, however, is less important than implementation cost, so in practice the circuit using fewest IC packages — gates and flip-flops together — would probably be preferred.

There are two classes of sequential logic circuits, synchronous and asynchronous. The latter are composed of unclocked or free-running elements and are not our prime concern here. They are also more difficult to design than synchronous circuits and require the use of *flow·tables* and *excitation matrices* to represent their internal states and output transitions. An example of this class of circuit, and discussion of some of the associated problems, is given later. Synchronous circuits are our main concern — they predominate in computers. We shall see how they can be designed and some examples will be described.

Synchronous circuits consist of a number of flip-flops, all connected to the same clock source, and appropriate combinational logic interconnecting the flip-flops.

In general terms, the steps in sequential logic design are:

(1) Consider the given problem carefully and determine the number of internal states, inputs and outputs. A state diagram may be very useful for representing the desired operation of the circuit.
(2) Decide how many state variables, and therefore flip-flops, will be used in the implementation. Represent the circuit operation by means of a state table and for each state variable derive the associated combinational logic.
(3) Combine the separate flip-flops and their associated logic into the final circuit diagram, converting as appropriate for the available circuit components.

Typically the circuit implementation would be in terms of J–K flip-flops and NAND gates. To enable part (2) of the design process to be applied we begin by looking again at the state table for the S–R flip-flop in Fig. 3.21(a). It is possible to plot the information in the state table on a K-map, using the present state Q_o as an input:

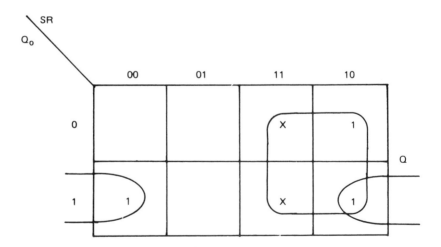

We obtain a minimised expression for the next state

$$Q = S + Q_o \overline{R} \qquad\qquad (3.4)$$

called the *characteristic equation* for the S–R flip-flop.

A similar K-map can be drawn for the J–K flip-flop:

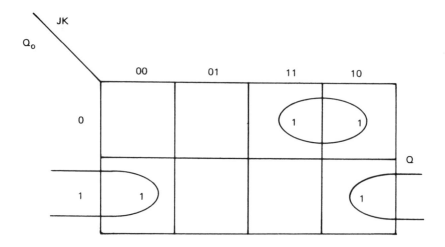

The characteristic equation for the J–K is

$$Q = \overline{Q_o}J + Q_o\overline{K} \tag{3.5}$$

Equations (3.4) and (3.5) may be used to help implement sequential circuits in terms of (clocked) S–R or J–K flip-flops respectively by enabling the appropriate combinational logic to be extracted from the state table produced in the design process. They allow us to identify the logic which acts as S–R or J–K inputs for each state variable. An example will illustrate the design of synchronous sequential circuits and show how the characteristic equation is used.

Design example — modulo-8 counter

Counters have a wide range of applications in digital systems for counting or sequencing events. An event is represented by a pulse, for example a radiation counter records the number of particles of radiation which have been incident on a collecting chamber: each particle causes an avalanche effect which is converted into a pulse of electrical energy. Counters are employed in digital watches and clocks, where the triggering pulse is derived from quartz crystal oscillations, and in computers they may be used to sequence the actions of the control unit or control the steps in a serial shift operation according to timing pulses from the common clock.

They are useful examples for illustrating the design and operation of sequential circuits because they are simple to explain. Counters also demonstrate well the sequencing action of sequential circuits. There are various types — binary up and down counters and ring counters being particularly important — but they may be devised to count in any code we like (for example, Gray code). Our design example is a (synchronous) re-cycling modulo-8 binary up counter, meaning that it counts in an increasing sequence through 8 states then repeats the sequence. It is usual to count from 0, so the 8 states correspond (in binary) to the decimal values 0 through 7. As our first step in the design process we must consider how many internal states, inputs and outputs the circuit will have. There is only one input — the source of pulses which are being counted. The outputs must show the current count value, which is the same as the internal state. In the next section we shall design a (combinational) decoder circuit which can translate the internal state for representation on a seven-segment light-emitting diode (LED) display. There will be eight internal states, usefully represented on the state diagram of Fig. 3.30.

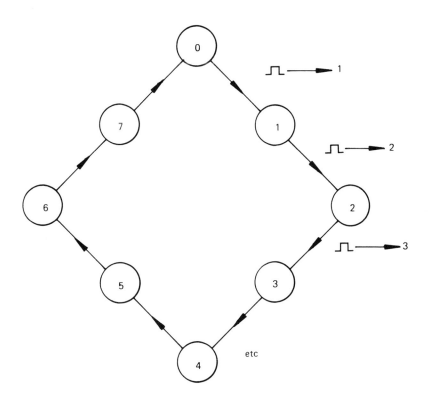

Fig. 3.30 — State diagram of re-cycling modulo-8 up counter.

This shows the eight states as eight nodes, and the cyclic nature of this counter. An input pulse causes the counter to sequence to its next state and to output the new states.

How many state variables, that is flip-flops, do we require to implement this counter? A minimum of three is required since there are eight states to represent. With three state variables we can use a pure binary representation of the eight states. Let us proceed with the design using three state variables, which we shall call A, B and C. The logic circuit will consist of three flip-flops and appropriate combinational logic. To find out what logic is required could be done intuitively, given a good understanding of the operation of the flip-flops to be used in the design. However, a methodical approach is possible making use of the characteristic equation of the flip-flops we intend to use. We begin by writing down a state table in terms of the state variables A, B and C. This is shown in Fig. 3.31. The input pulse is not represented; it is assumed for all synchronous circuits that changes can occur only when triggered by a pulse at the clock input of the flip-flops, so it is not necessary to show this input in the table. A_o, B_o and C_o represent the previous states of A, B and C before a pulse is applied.

A_o	B_o	C_o	A	B	C
0	0	0	0	0	1
0	0	1	0	1	0
0	1	0	0	1	1
0	1	1	1	0	0
1	0	0	1	0	1
1	0	1	1	1	0
1	1	0	1	1	1
1	1	1	0	0	0

Fig. 3.31 — State table for re-cycling modulo-8 binary up counter.

Let us design the circuit with J–K flip-flops. We consider each state variable separately and write down the relationship between its new state and the previous state of the counter. In the same way as for combinational logic design we look for 1s in the output column and write a Boolean sum-of-products expression of the input combinations giving rise to the 1s. Thus:

$$A = \overline{A}_o B_o C_o + A_o \overline{B}_o \overline{C} + A_o \overline{B}_o C_o + A_o B_o \overline{C}_o \tag{3.6}$$

(the four product terms corresponding to the 1s in the 'next state' column for A).

The characteristic equation of the J–K flip-flop is (substituting A for Q in equation (3.5)):

$$A = \overline{A}_o J_A + A_o \overline{K}_A$$

Re-writing (3.6),

$$A = \overline{A}_o (B_o C_o) + A_o (\overline{B}_o \overline{C}_o + \overline{B}_o C_o + B_o \overline{C}_o) \tag{3.7}$$

Equation (3.7) tells us that the required logic at the J input of the flip-flop representing A is B_oC_o, and the logic at the K input is the inverse of $(\overline{B}_o\overline{C}_o + \overline{B}_oC_o + B_o\overline{C}_o)$. Evaluating the inverse using Boolean algebra, or more easily by means of a K-map (the inverse of a plotted function consists of the blank squares), we obtain B_oC_o as the K input logic. That is,

$$J_A = K_A = B_oC_o$$

A more direct way of extracting the J and K input logic is to inspect the state table for $0 \rightarrow 1$ and $1 \rightarrow 0$ transitions of the state variables. Input combinations giving rise to $0 \rightarrow 1$ transitions correspond to $\overline{Q}_oJ$ whilst those producing $1 \rightarrow 0$ changes correspond to Q_oK (K, not $\overline{K}$: this will give the K logic directly). Using this technique for A in our example,

$$0 \rightarrow 1 \text{ transitions:} \quad \overline{A}_oJ_A = \overline{A}_oB_oC_o$$
$$J_A = B_oC_o$$
$$1 \rightarrow \text{ transitions:} \quad A_oK_A = A_oB_oC_o$$
$$K_A = B_oC_o$$

giving J_A and K_A as before.
    The logic for state variable A in the modulo-8 counter is:

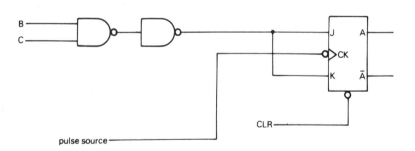

where B and C are derived directly from the Q outputs of flip-flops B and C.
    Repeating the procedure, this time for state variable B:

$$0 \rightarrow 1: \quad \overline{B}_oJ_B = \overline{A}_o\overline{B}_oC_o + A_o\overline{B}_oC_o$$
$$J_B = \overline{A}_oC_o + A_oC_o = C_o$$
$$1 \rightarrow 0: \quad B_oK_B = \overline{A}_oB_oC_o + A_oB_oC_o$$
$$K_B = \overline{A}_oC_o + A_oC_o = C_o$$

The circuit for B is:

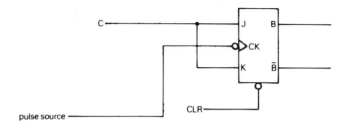

For state variable C:

$$0 \to 1: \quad \overline{C}_o J_c \quad = \overline{A}_o \overline{B}_o \overline{C}_o + \overline{A}_o B_o \overline{C}_o + A_o \overline{B}_o \overline{C}_o + A_o B_o \overline{C}_o$$
$$= \overline{C}_o$$
$$J_c \quad = 1 \text{ (or HI)}$$
$$1 \to 0: \quad C_o K_c \quad = \overline{A}_o \overline{B}_o C_o + \overline{A}_o B_o C_o + A_o \overline{B}_o C_o + A_o B_o C_o$$
$$= C_o$$
$$K_c \quad = 1 \text{ (or HI)}$$

The circuit for C is:

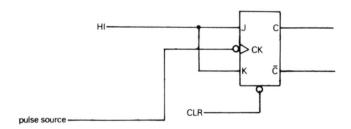

The complete counter circuit is obtained by combining the separate circuits, as in Fig. 3.32. Strictly speaking, our state diagram of Fig. 3.30 should indicate a starting state. The starting state of the implementation we have derived is ABC = 000, which is obtained by activating the asynchronous CLR input to the circuit.

The same design technique may be used for any synchronous sequential logic circuit. Variations on the counter such as different modulo number, down counting instead of up, or self-stopping instead of re-cycling can be taken account of in the state diagram and state table — and the design follows as before. Further design examples are given in the next chapter.

An asynchronous counter

As an example of an asynchronous sequential circuit, a modulo-8 binary counter is illustrated in Fig. 3.33. The circuit consists of three J–K flip-flops as for the synchronous version, but the pulse source is connected only to one

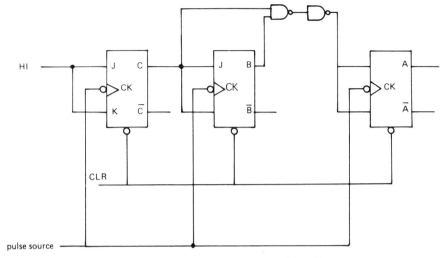

Fig. 3.32 — Circuit diagram of synchronous modulo-8 binary counter.

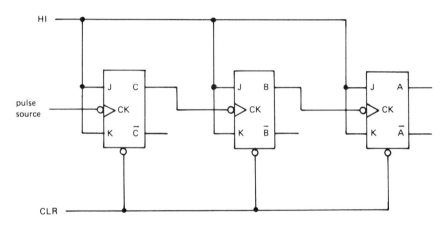

Fig. 3.33 — Circuit diagram of an asynchronous modulo-8 binary counter.

flip-flop: the flip-flops in the circuit are not synchronised by a common signal. This counter operates according to the state diagram of Fig. 3.30 — that is it counts 0 through 7 and re-cycles — but the state diagram does not indicate the internal changes in the circuit following an input pulse. Since there is no synchronisation, changes are propagated through the circuit rather than affecting all the flip-flops simultaneously. For this reason, the asynchronous counter is often referred to as a *ripple-through* counter.

Each J–K operates in toggle mode, that is whenever a pulse is received at CK the output is complemented. The effect is summarised by the timing diagrams in Fig. 3.34.

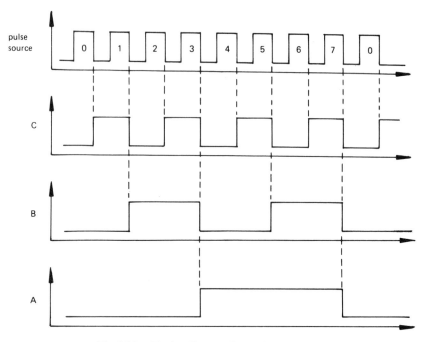

Fig. 3.34 — Timing diagrams for modulo-8 counter.

Note that changes take place effectively on the trailing edge of the clock pulse for J–K flip-flops. Each flip-flop divides the number of input pulses successively by two (extra stages could be added to make modulo-16, modulo-32 counters and so on), so this counter is sometimes alternatively called a *divide-by-two* counter. It has no combinational logic external to the flip-flops and is thus minimal in terms of IC packages. However, it has a disadvantage: it takes longer to settle down into a new state than the synchronous counter when a new pulse arrives. This is because flip-flops, like gates, have a *propagation delay* time. Typically, a TTL flip-flop takes 30 nanoseconds before its output has changed in response to the trailing edge of a pulse at its CK input. This is illustrated below:

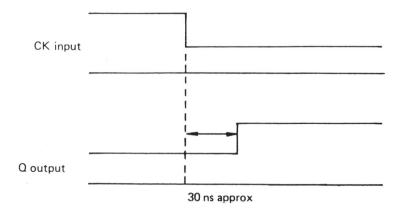

Such a delay is of course present in synchronous counters, but the total delay is exactly the same: 30 nanoseconds. For the asynchronous counter, however, consider the pulse labelled 7 in Fig. 3.34. There will be three consecutive 30 ns delays before the counter changes from 111 to the 000 state, a total of 90 ns. For larger asynchronous counters even longer delays occur. When using an asynchronous counter, these longer settling times must be accounted for when sampling the state of the counter, otherwise erroneous readings could be taken. A problem with logic circuits in general is the possibility of erroneous operation because of circuit *hazards* — faults which arise because of the interaction of changing internal signals in circuits. These are particularly likely to occur in asynchronous circuits and can be difficult to eliminate. Hazards in combinational circuits will be discussed briefly in the next chapter.

Further remarks on sequential design
Synchronous sequential circuits, for which a design method was described, are in practice more commonly used. While the design method outlined is sufficient for the majority of requirements, two refinement techniques should be mentioned.

Just as combinational circuits can be minimised, so techniques can be applied to reduce both the number of flip-flops and the amount of combinational logic in sequential circuits. In more complex design problems two or more internal states may be equivalent, that is given the same input sequences they produce exactly the same outputs (even though their next internal states are not the same). *Internal state reduction* (or *state minimisation*) can produce a design solution with fewer flip-flops, though this may have the effect of increasing the associated combinational logic.

The technique of *state assignment* is used to assign binary codes optimally to the internal states identified in the design process. This can have the effect of reducing the combinational logic in the final circuit. For simple examples, however, it is possible to rely on intuitive methods.

4

Logic circuits in practice

4.1 DESIGN EXAMPLES

We begin this chapter by presenting further design examples of both combinational and sequential logic circuits, three of each type. They will consolidate the design techniques introduced in Chapter 3 as well as providing examples of logic circuits which may be put to practical use. The present chapter continues with a discussion of some problems which are encountered in using logic components, followed by some remarks on analysing (rather than synthesising) logic circuits.

Priority encoder
A priority encoder has several input lines which are normally at 0. When any of the inputs goes to 1 the encoder outputs a value identifying that input line. Furthermore, the inputs have each a different priority, and if two of them are at 1 the encoder outputs the identity of the higher priority line. The encoder has another output line which indicates whether any input line is at 1. Such an encoder could be used in a priority interrupt scheme whereby peripheral devices are connected to a CPU and require to interrupt its operation on completion of a data transfer. The highest priority device must be given attention if more than one device signals completion at the same time.

   The circuit for a 4-input priority encoder is to be designed. In order to identify uniquely one of 4 lines, 2 outputs are required at least. These we shall call the address lines for the inputs. A black-box diagram of the encoder is shown below:

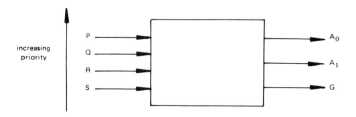

P, Q, R and S are the input lines and have relative priorities as indicated in the diagram, A_0 and A_1 the address lines, and G the output which tells if any input line is set to 1. To design the required combinational logic the following truth table is constructed:

P	Q	R	S	G	A_1	A_0
0	0	0	0	0	X	X
0	0	0	1	1	0	0
0	0	1	X	1	0	1
0	1	X	X	1	1	0
1	X	X	X	1	1	1

The use of don't care conditions in both input and output columns makes the table much more compact and readable than if they are expanded to show all combinations explicitly.

Treating each output separately we draw the following K-maps:

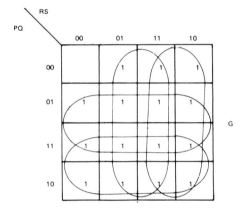

which gives simply

$$G = P + Q + R + S$$

so $A_1 = P + Q$

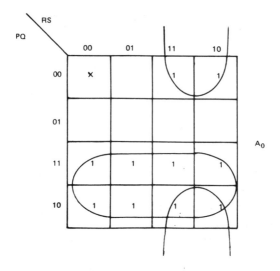

and $A_0 = P + \overline{Q}R$.

Thus the circuit diagram for the priority encoder is as shown in Fig. 4.1. It is drawn in terms of NAND gates and inverters. Note that above it is possible to plot directly from truth table to K-map without canonical expansion (with a little practice) and this is recommended.

(An 8-line to 3-line priority encoder, for example, is available as a TTL MSI package, designated 74148.)

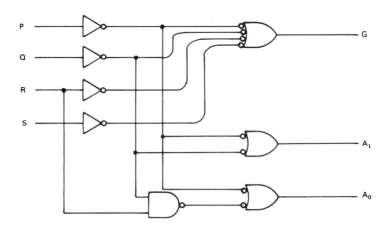

Fig. 4.1 — Circuit diagram of 4-line to 2-line priority encoder.

Parity generator/checker

Parity generators and checkers are used in the input/output part of a computer system. It is usual for information to be transmitted in groups of bits representing a character or symbol. Errors may occur in transmission; therefore it is important to be able to detect their occurrence at the receiving end, and better still to correct the error as well. Single-bit errors may be detected by a parity bit sent with the data. There are two basic schemes: if the number of 1s in the data is even, a parity bit of 0 is included, otherwise parity sent is 1 (this is called *even parity*); or the other way round, namely parity is generated to ensure the total number of 1s sent is odd (*odd parity*). At the receiving end, parity is checked by looking for either an even or an odd number of 1s.

To illustrate the generation of even parity, consider a 4-bit data word, ABCD. A single parity bit P is to be produced as shown by the black-box diagram:

The truth table for the generator is as follows:

A	B	C	D	P
0	0	0	0	0
0	0	0	1	1
0	0	1	0	1
0	0	1	1	0
0	1	0	0	1
0	1	0	1	0
0	1	1	0	0
0	1	1	1	1
1	0	0	0	1
1	0	0	1	0
1	0	1	0	0
1	0	1	1	1
1	1	0	0	0
1	1	0	1	1
1	1	1	0	1
1	1	1	1	0

Using a K-map directly:

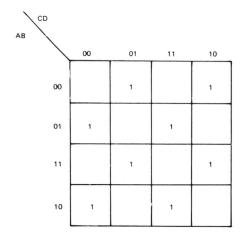

No reduction can be effected. However, this table has a form similar to the one on page 80 for the binary full-adder sum. Writing out the Boolean expression for P:

$$P = \overline{A}\,\overline{B}\,\overline{C}D + \overline{A}\,\overline{B}\,C\overline{D} + \overline{A}\,B\,\overline{C}\,\overline{D} + \ldots.$$

which can be regrouped as

$$P = (\overline{A}\,\overline{B}+A\,B)(\overline{C}D+C\overline{D})+(\overline{A}\,B+A\,\overline{B})(\overline{C}\,\overline{D}+C\,D)$$
$$= (\overline{A\oplus B})(C\oplus D)+(A\oplus B)(\overline{C\oplus D})$$
$$= X\oplus Y$$

where

$$X = A\oplus B \qquad \text{and} \qquad Y = C\oplus D$$

Another way of writing this is simply

$$P = A\oplus B\oplus C\oplus D$$

(brackets may be placed anywhere within this expression).

The circuit is a cascade of EOR gates as in Fig. 4.2. Note that the generator circuit can easily be extended for any number of data bits. A realistic word length over which to generate parity is 7 bits (as for the ASCII international code to represent characters) plus 1 bit for parity. In this case P would be given by

$$A\oplus B\oplus C\oplus D\oplus E\oplus F\oplus G$$

where A–G are the seven data bits.

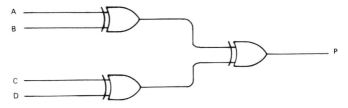

Fig. 4.2 — Circuit diagram of 4-bit parity generator.

Parity checking uses the same form of circuit, except that at the receiving end the parity bit is itself an input. A general-purpose 9-bit parity generator/ checker is available in TTl MSI form, designated 74180, with 8 data bits and a ninth input (actually 2 bits) used for selecting odd or even parity if the circuit is used for generation and for the parity bit itself when the circuit is used as a checking circuit.

Modulo-n counters

In Section 3.3 a modulo-8 binary counter was designed. The eight states could be represented by three flip-flops leaving no spare states. In general, modulo-n counters require a minimum of $\log_2 n$ flip-flops rounded up to the nearest integer but unless n is a power of two there will be spare states left over. An example is a modulo-10 counter which needs 4 flip-flops. The state table is shown below:

A_o	B_o	C_o	D_o	A	B	C	D
0	0	0	0	0	0	0	1
0	0	0	1	0	0	1	0
0	0	1	0	0	0	1	1
0	0	1	1	0	1	0	0
0	1	0	0	0	1	0	1
0	1	0	1	0	1	1	0
0	1	1	0	0	1	1	1
0	1	1	1	1	0	0	0
1	0	0	0	1	0	0	1
1	0	0	1	0	0	0	0
1	0	1	0	X	X	X	X
1	0	1	1	X	X	X	X
1	1	0	0	X	X	X	X
1	1	0	1	X	X	X	X
1	1	1	0	X	X	X	X
1	1	1	1	X	X	X	X

Only ten states are required — the remaining 6 are spare and can be used as don't care conditions.

This is a cyclic counter as before — returning to state 0000 after 1001. This counter can be used in digital clocks or watches along with modulo-6 and modulo-3 counters (for a 24-hour clock) as illustrated below:

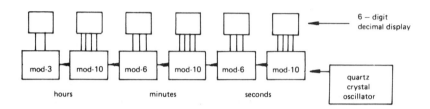

The oscillator provides a 1-second interval clock pulse to the least significant counter. Typically the crystal will oscillate at a frequency of 32768 Hz so the pulse rate will be divided down by a counter arrangement to provide the 1-second timing. Each counter triggers the next more significant one by a pulse when it recycles from its maximum count to zero. This simple arrangement gives a ripple-through effect for the digital clock. Extra logic must be included (though it is not shown) to cause the modulo-10 hours counter to recycle from 3 to zero (instead of from 3 to 4) when the most significant modulo-3 counter is already at 2. This can be taken account of in the design of the modulo-10 hours counter, by including an input derived from the mod-3 counter in the state table. A 6-digit decimal display would normally be provided. Suitable logic to drive the displays will be designed in the next example.

Meantime the design of the synchronous modulo-10 counter may proceed from the state table above. The don't care conditions are included to improve the solution where appropriate. For state variable A, we look for $0 \rightarrow 1$ and $1 \rightarrow 0$ transitions as before. We shall design the circuit using J–K flip-flops:

$$0 \rightarrow 1: \quad \overline{A}_o J_A = \overline{A}_o B_o C_o D_o$$

$$1 \rightarrow 0: \quad A_o K_A = A_o \overline{B}_o \overline{C}_o D_o (+ A_o \overline{B}_o C_o \overline{D}_o + A_o \overline{B}_o C_o D_o +$$
$$A_o B_o \overline{C}_o \overline{D}_o + A_o B_o \overline{C}_o D_o + A_o B_o C_o \overline{D}_o + A_o B_o C_o D_o)$$

(don't care conditions are in brackets).

In the case of the first equation there are no don't care conditions. Thus we may write

$$J_A = B_o C_o D_o$$

Eliminating A_o from the second equation, the solution for K_A is best found by plotting the right-hand side on a 3-variable K-map:

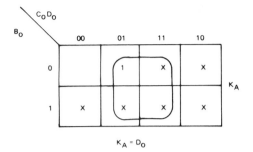

Similarly for state variables B, C and D we derive:

$$0 \to 1: \quad \overline{B}_o J_B = \overline{A}_o \overline{B}_o C_o D_o (+A_o \overline{B}_o C_o \overline{D}_o + A_o \overline{B}_o C_o D_o)$$

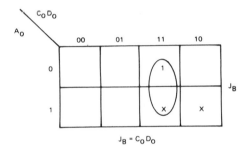

$$1 \to 0: \quad B_o K_B = \overline{A}_o B_o C_o D_o (+A_o B_o \overline{C}_o \overline{D}_o + A_o B_o \overline{C}_o D_o$$
$$+ A_o B_o C_o \overline{D}_o + A_o B_o C_o D_o)$$

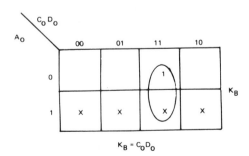

$$0 \to 1: \quad \overline{C}_o J_c = \overline{A}_o \overline{B}_o \overline{C}_o D_o + \overline{A}_o B_o \overline{C}_o D_o (+A_o B_o \overline{C}_o \overline{D}_o + $$
$$A_o B_o \overline{C}_o D_o)$$

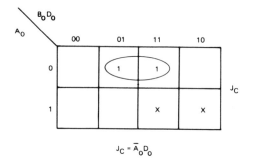

$$J_C = \overline{A}_o D_o$$

$$1 \rightarrow 0: \quad C_o K_c = \overline{A}_o \overline{B}_o C_o D_o + \overline{A}_o B_o C_o D_o (+ A_o \overline{B}_o C_o \overline{D}_o +$$
$$A_o \overline{B}_o C_o D_o + A_o B_o C_o \overline{D}_o + A_o B_o C_o D_o)$$

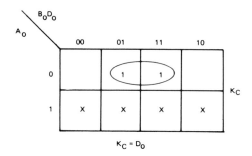

$$K_C = D_o$$

Lastly, the K-maps for D are both:

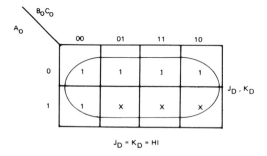

$$J_D = K_D = HI$$

The circuit diagram for the modulo-10 counter is shown in Fig. 4.3.

A simple method of providing the clock pulses for the next more significant counter in the 24-hour clock would be to NAND the $\overline{Q}$ outputs of the flip-flops together as shown below for the modulo-10 counter:

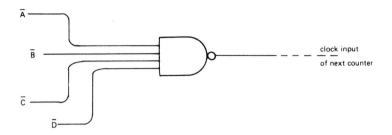

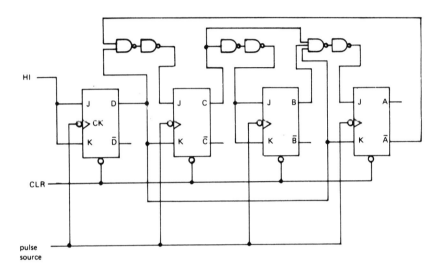

Fig. 4.3 — Circuit diagram of modulo-10 binary counter.

Whenever the counter is in the zero state the output of the NAND gate is LO; otherwise it is HI. When the counter changes from zero to one the leading edge of a pulse is produced. At the change from the maximum count to zero the trailing edge of the pulse triggers the next counter.

A TTL MSI modulo-10 counter is available in a positive-edge-triggered variety, designated 74160.

BCD to seven-segment LED decoder
Binary-coded-decimal (BCD) employs four bits to represent the decimal digits 0–9. An example of its use is in the digital clock described in the previous section. Each modulo-10 counter is capable of storing a BCD value (the other counters a subset of the possible values). For display purposes a seven-segment light-emitting-diode (LED) device is often used, particularly

in digital clocks and watches. This is available as a chip with the LEDs arranged on the top as follows:

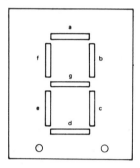

The seven segments a–g (the labels are for identification and do not appear on the chip) may be lit or unlit in combinations to form all the decimal digits, as:

Two small round LEDs are also provided, one on each side of the seven segments as shown above. These are for use as decimal points — in practice only one can be used at a time. We shall not consider the decimal points for this example. A black-box diagram of a BCD to seven-segment LED decoder has the following inputs and outputs:

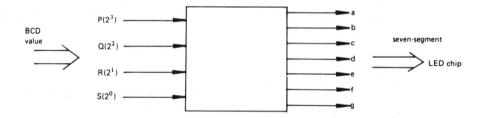

P, Q, R and S are the four bits of the BCD value, a–g the output lines which will cause the appropriate segments to be lit (considered active-HI in our example). The truth table for our decoder design follows:

decimal	P	Q	R	S	a	b	c	d	e	f	g
0	0	0	0	0	1	1	1	1	1	1	0
1	0	0	0	1	0	1	1	0	0	0	0
2	0	0	1	0	1	1	0	1	1	0	1
3	0	0	1	1	1	1	1	1	0	0	1
4	0	1	0	0	0	1	1	0	0	1	1
5	0	1	0	1	1	0	1	1	0	1	1
6	0	1	1	0	0	0	1	1	1	1	1
7	0	1	1	1	1	1	1	0	0	0	0
8	1	0	0	0	1	1	1	1	1	1	1
9	1	0	0	1	1	1	1	0	0	1	1
	1	0	1	0	X	X	X	X	X	X	X
	1	0	1	1	X	X	X	X	X	X	X
	1	1	0	0	X	X	X	X	X	X	X
	1	1	0	1	X	X	X	X	X	X	X
	1	1	1	0	X	X	X	X	X	X	X
	1	1	1	1	X	X	X	X	X	X	X

including don't care conditions for the six unused input combinations. The K-map and reduced expression for each output are listed below:

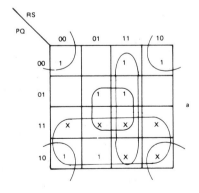

$$a = P + RS + \overline{Q}\,\overline{S} + QS$$

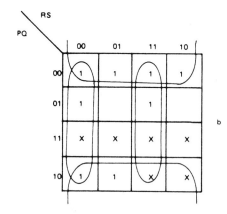

$$b = \overline{Q} + \overline{R}\,\overline{S} + R\,S$$

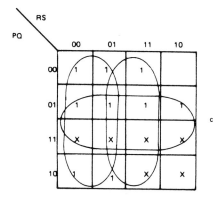

$$c = \overline{Q} + \overline{R} + S$$

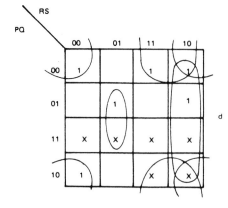

$$d = \overline{Q}\,\overline{S} + \overline{Q}R + R\overline{S} + Q\overline{R}S$$

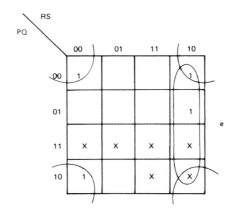

$$e = \overline{Q}\,\overline{S} + R\,\overline{S}$$

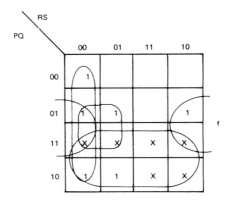

$$f = P + Q\overline{R} + \overline{R}\,\overline{S} + Q\,\overline{S}$$

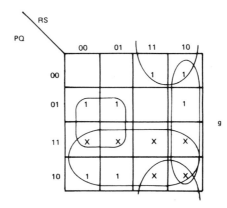

$$g = P + Q\overline{R} + R\,\overline{S} + \overline{Q}\,R$$

Note that the different shapes for 6 and 9, namely,

could be used in the design, producing slightly different expressions for a and d.

The logic circuit for the decoder is shown in Fig. 4.4. A similar TTL MSI component, the 7448, is available.

Pattern detector

A pattern detector is a finite-state machine (FSM) which inputs an indefinitely long string of symbols and outputs a special symbol whenever it recognises a particular pattern. Let us consider a simple version of the problem: we wish to be able to detect the binary pattern 0101 on an input line X, outputting a 1 on line R if the pattern is recognised (otherwise 0s will be output). The input bits are to be clocked into the pattern recogniser as illustrated below:

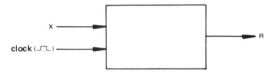

Since we shall design a synchronous sequential circuit to implement the recogniser, we can assume that the clock line is fed to the CK input of each flip-flop in the circuit.

Let us begin by drawing a state diagram to show how many internal states are required, and how the recogniser sequences between them: Four states

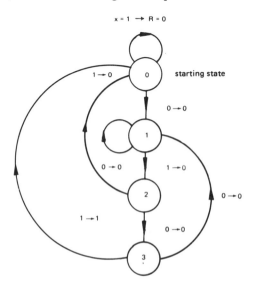

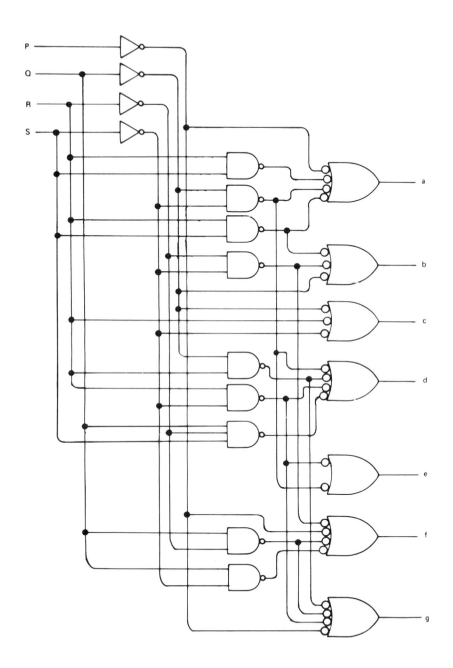

Fig. 4.4 — Circuit diagram of BCD to seven-segment LED decoder.

are required. The sequence 0–1–2–3–0 means that the required pattern of 0101 has been recognised and a 1 will then be output. Each interstate transition is actioned by an input clock pulse. Thus we require 2 state variables (A and B, say) and 2 corresponding flip-flops in the circuit. As usual we write down a state table and look for $0 \rightarrow 1$ and $1 \rightarrow 0$ transitions for each variable:

X	A_o	B_o	A	B	R
0	0	0	0	1	0
1	0	0	0	0	0
0	0	1	0	1	0
1	0	1	1	0	0
0	1	0	1	1	0
1	1	0	0	0	0
0	1	1	0	1	0
1	1	1	0	0	1

Note that the assignment of binary codes to internal states has been made as follows:

State	Code A	B
0	0	0
1	0	1
2	1	0
3	1	1

but could equally well be re-allocated in a different order.

Designing in terms of J–K flip-flops, we have for state variable A:

$$0 \rightarrow 1: \quad \overline{A}_o J_A = X \overline{A}_o B_o$$
$$J_A = X B_o$$

$$1 \rightarrow 0: \quad A_o K_A = X A_o \overline{B}_o + \overline{X} A_o B_o + X A_o B_o$$
$$K_A = B_o + X \overline{B}_o = B_o + X$$

For B:

$$0 \rightarrow 1: \quad \overline{B}_o J_B = \overline{X} \overline{A}_o \overline{B}_o + \overline{X} A_o \overline{B}_o$$
$$J_B = \overline{X}$$

$$1 \rightarrow 0: \quad B_o K_B = X \overline{A}_o B_o + X A_o B_o$$
$$K_B = X$$

(without the need for K-maps)

Extra combinational logic is required for output R. From the state table

$$R = XA_oB_o$$

Thus the complete circuit can be drawn, as in Fig. 4.5 (CLR inputs are not shown).

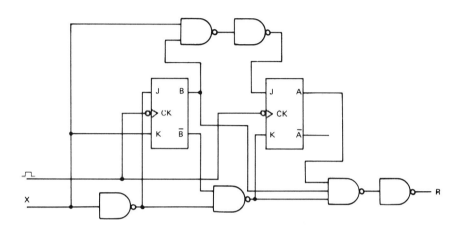

Fig. 4.5 — Circuit diagram of 0101 pattern recogniser.

The problem can be tackled in quite a different way, using an ad hoc technique. Notice that what we are really doing is interposing a logic circuit on the stream of input bits and looking at a window, four bits wide.

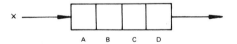

This is just a *right-shift register* arrangement, a group of flip-flops connected together such that at each clock pulse the bits move one flip-flop to the right (left-shift registers can be built similarly). The J and K inputs of each flip-flop are derived from the Q and $\overline{Q}$ outputs respectively of the flip-flop on the left. To recognise 0101 we simply add NAND gating as shown in Fig. 4.6.

Using the shift register arrangement a programmable recogniser could be constructed. The pattern to be recognised could be set up in a 4-bit register and comparison logic designed so that R would output 1 only when that register and ABCD (as in Fig. 4.6) contained the same pattern.

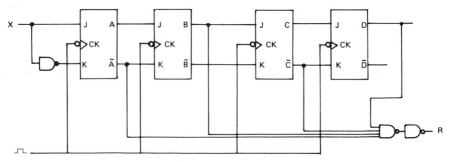

Fig. 4.6 — Alternative circuit diagram of 0101 pattern recogniser.

Traffic lights controller

The last example in this section is slightly more complex than the previous ones, and requires more explanation, although it concerns a realistic problem from everyday life. The problem is one of designing a controller to sequence the lights at a two-way traffic junction.

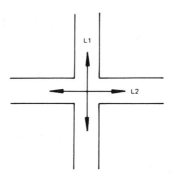

There are two distinct sets of lights, L1 and L2, each with a green, amber and red lamp. The lights work in a sequence which may be illustrated as follows:

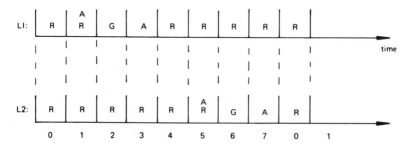

There are eight different combinations of lit lamps, labelled 0–7. A sequential logic circuit to implement the sequences will thus have eight internal states. In each state the appropriate combination of lamps must be lit, for example in state 0 both L1(R) and L2(R) are lit but none other. The lamps are the outputs of the circuit and are lit by *decoding* the states of the sequencer appropriately. Let us say that a 1 (or HI) lights a lamp, and a 0 (LO) extinguishes it. The input to the circuit is a pulse source to drive the sequencer from state to state, but it has this distinction: it must have irregular pulse intervals because the eight states will not all have equal durations. In particular state 0 will be short whereas state 2 will be much longer. The problem of this timing pulse will be dealt with shortly.

Meantime, assuming a suitable pulse source we now proceed to design the sequencer and its lamp decoding logic. Eight internal states can be suitably provided by the synchronous modulo-8 counter which was described in Section 3.3. We shall not reproduce the state table nor the design here. An amalgamated truth table for the lamp logic is, however, necessary:

State	A	B	C	L1 R	L1 A	L1 G	L2 R	L2 A	L2 G
0	0	0	0	1	0	0	1	0	0
1	0	0	1	1	1	0	1	0	0
2	0	1	0	0	0	1	1	0	0
3	0	1	1	0	1	0	1	0	0
4	1	0	0	1	0	0	1	0	0
5	1	0	1	1	0	0	1	1	0
6	1	1	0	1	0	0	0	0	1
7	1	1	1	1	0	0	0	1	0

Using K-maps the Boolean expressions for the lamp logic are derived:

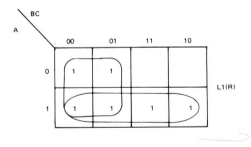

$$L1(R) = A+\overline{B}$$

Similarly (without drawing the K-maps):

$$L1(A) = \overline{A}C$$
$$L1(G) = \overline{A}B\overline{C}$$
$$L2(R) = \overline{A}+\overline{B}$$
$$L2(A) = AC$$
$$L2(G) = AB\overline{C}$$

The traffic light sequencer circuit therefore consists of the modulo-8 counter of Fig. 3.32 plus the combinational logic shown in Fig. 4.7.

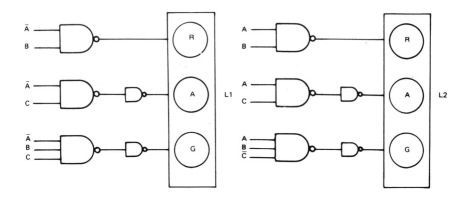

Fig. 4.7 — Lamp driving logic for the traffic lights controller.

Lastly, let us look at the problem of generating a suitable stream of timing pulses, or timing *waveform*. Assume that we have a source of clock pulses with a 1-second interval (say the pulse width is 100 ns). A suitable waveform might have the following time intervals:

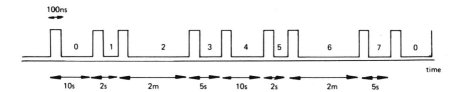

allowing 10 seconds for red-red, 2 minutes for green-red and so on. We have chosen the same timing sequence for both traffic directions, so this gives the basic operating pattern or cycle of:

We have to generate such a pulse interval pattern from the regular 1-second clock source. One solution is to use a 7-bit counter (modulo-128) and divide the cycle up into

where 111 seconds is near enough to 2 minutes for our purposes. Effectively we provide a filter circuit which allows the input clock pulse (of 1-second frequency) through the traffic light controller only at the arrowed points in the above diagram, that is after a count of 10, 12, 123 and 0 in the 7-bit counter. A suitable circuit diagram is outlined in Fig. 4.8.

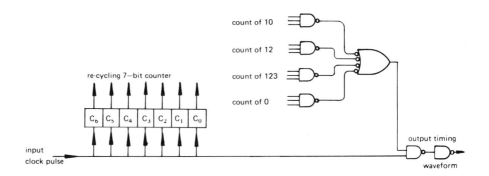

Fig. 4.8 — Circuit diagram of timing waveform generator for traffic lights controller.

4.2   CIRCUIT PROBLEMS IN PRACTICE

In previous sections the point was made that although logic circuits can be designed entirely in terms of abstract operators (AND, OR, NOT) their physical realisation has an important influence on the design process. The wide availability of NAND gates in particular — and the fact that any circuit can be built using only this type of gate — means that circuit designs are usually altered from an AND, OR, NOT form to a NAND (often a NAND, NOT) form. As we have shown, using positive and negative logic conventions, this is a particularly easy conversion to make. It may on occasion be desirable to factorise a Boolean expression to be able to make use of, say, 2-input NAND gates instead of the 3-input type — either because there is a short supply of 3-input gates at the time or more likely to minimise the number of IC packages in a circuit which has some spare 2-input gates from other parts of the circuit. Likewise the use of spare 4-input gates to implement 2- or 3-input functions may be beneficial in terms of gate costs: in the case of NAND gates the unused inputs are simply connected to HI. As we have also seen, NAND gates may be used as inverters in a similar way.

Quite apart from the handling of the circuit design to available components, there are operational problems associated with logic circuits which may not be apparent at the design stage. These problems arise because of the non-ideal performance of circuit components: once again, therefore, they have an impact on the design. The purpose of the present section is to illustrate some of the problems which arise, and how they are solved.

Hazards

Logic gates, flip-flops and circuits of all kinds have inherent *propagation delays*: they take a finite, if small, time to operate. The delay time of a component is characteristic of the speed at which its associated logic family operates. For normal TTL gates and flip-flops propagation delays are about 10 ns and 30 ns respectively.

Consider the operation of an inverter:

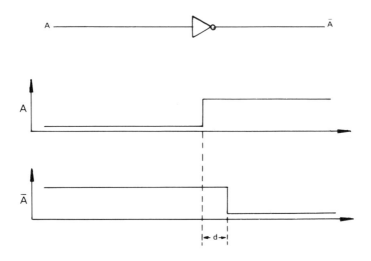

A change at input A causes an inversion at the output $\overline{A}$ a short time later. The propagation delay is shown for d. For time d the law $A\overline{A} = 0$ does not hold true. Likewise the law $A+\overline{A} = 1$ does not hold during the propagation time of the input signal. The violation of these laws of Boolean algebra, even for a very short time, can have serious consequences on the operation of a circuit. The following example demonstrates this.

The Boolean function $F = A\overline{B}+BC$ is implemented by the circuit:

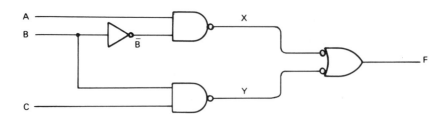

Suppose the initial conditions are $A = B = C = HI$ and that B undergoes a transition from HI to LO. The circuit operation can be represented by the following timing diagrams, where X sample $A\overline{B}$ and Y samples BC (strictly speaking these expressions should be inverted but it is convenient here to use the functional appearance of AND-OR instead of the actual NAND-NAND implementation):

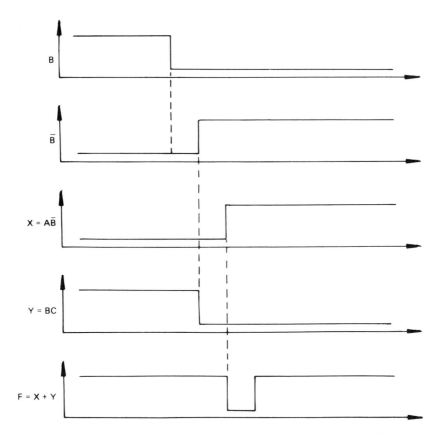

Assuming all the gates have approximately the same propagation delay d, the output F — which theoretically should remain at HI throughout — experiences a negative pulse of duration d. This output *spike* is due to the unequal path lengths for input B in the circuit and to the consequent *race* between the two paths to the output: along one path, B experiences two gate delays, along the other a total of three. The resulting output spike is one example of a circuit *hazard*. This particular example illustrates a *single-variable, static* hazard because it involves changes to only one variable and the output remains static (at HI) having undergone a pair of logic transitions.

On its own this circuit malfunction poses no problems, but if F happens to be the input to a sequential circuit it is possible for an incorrect data value to be input to a flip-flop, particularly if F feeds the clock input of an edge-triggered circuit. In practice we want to avoid hazardous operations, but how can this be predicted at the design stage? In the case of a static hazard this can be done by inspecting the K-map for the Boolean expression:

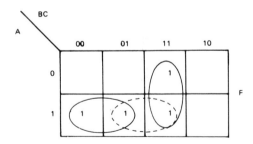

The hazard arises because there are two adjacent 1s not included in the same PI. These are shown by dotted lines round the offending pair. If this (redundant) PI, AC, is included in the final expression, as

$$F = \overline{A}\,B + B\,C + A\,C$$

then hazard-free operation results. This is clearly true if we consider the input conditions A = B = C = HI as before. Since A and C are both HI throughout, while B changes from HI to LO, then AC always remains HI, so F cannot experience an output spike.

Other techniques used in general to eliminate hazards include equalising path lengths by introducing appropriate delays, and avoiding complemented terms (NOT gates) if possible by suitably manipulating the Boolean expression at the design stage.

As well as static hazards, there are two other types of single-variable hazard, called *dynamic* and *essential*. Dynamic types, like the static example above, occur in combinational circuits but there are three different path lengths for the one variable, with inversion in at least one path but not in all three. This type usually arises out of factorisation of the Boolean expression (for example to use 2-input instead of 3-input gates) and can be eliminated by careful re-factorising of the expression. The essential hazard occurs in asynchronous sequential circuits, as a result of a race between an input signal and an internal circuit signal (called a *secondary* signal). Elimination of the hazard can be achieved by inserting delays (non-inverting) in the paths of appropriate signals to equalise the competing path lengths. Lastly there are *multi-variable* hazards which arise when more than one input signal changes at the same time. This type of hazard is generally difficult to eliminate by circuit modification particularly in the case of asynchronous sequential circuits.

Fanout

The data sheets for available logic gates supply a variety of information specifying the physical tolerances of the component, including the supply voltage requirements for successful operation, the power consumed by the gate and the range of ambient temperatures within which it will work. Some of the most important specifications, however, are the low-level and high-level input and output currents which the gate will tolerate. These indicate the *fanout* for the gate, that is the number of other gates (of a similar kind) which may be connected to its output, and also the *load* which this gate imposes on other gate inputs. These facts are extremely important in practice and must be taken into account by the circuit designer.

Let us explain the low- and high-level currents in terms of TTL logic, which is a very popular logic family for gates and other SSI components. The output stage of the standard TTL gate consists, as described in Section 2.4, of two transistors in a totem-pole arrangement. At any time one is ON and the other OFF, or vice-versa, giving the two output voltages LO and HI. The two output cases are illustrated in Fig. 4.9, where (a) shows a HI at the

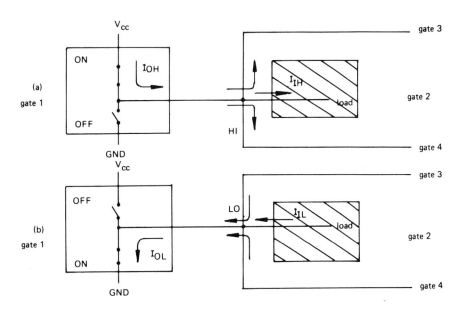

Fig. 4.9 — Schematic diagram of (a) current sourcing and (b) current sinking.

output of gate 1, and (b) a LO voltage.

In each case gate 1 is connected to a load (gate 2). Other loads (gates 3, 4, etc.) may be connected as indicated, up to the fanout for gate 1. The two cases, (a) and (b), are referred to as *current-sourcing* and *current-sinking* modes respectively: when the output is at HI, current flows out of gate 1, and when LO it flows into the current gate. In current-sourcing mode if too many loads (represented by I_{IH}) are driven from one gate, the output current of that gate becomes higher than I_{OH} and the output voltage will fall below HI. In current-sinking mode the gate output must be able to sink current I_{IL} from each attached load: if the total current exceeds I_{OL} the output voltage will no longer be at LO. The current values I_{OH} and I_{OL} are *worst-case* values and determine the fanout of the gate. Values I_{IH} and I_{IL} represent the load which a gate imposes on the output of another. To allow comparisons between different types of TTL gates the manufacturers quote a *standard load* which is:

$$I_{IH} = 40 \, \mu A \text{ (microamps) maximum}$$
$$I_{IL} = 1.6 \, mA \text{ (milliamps) maximum.}$$

A standard TTL gate has a fanout of 10: it can drive 10 standard loads in either a HI or LO state. It must be realised that not all gates represent one standard load nor have the same output characteristics, so when using other than standard gates (for example the increasingly popular low-power Schottky (LS) version — see Fig. 2.24) care must be taken to ensure the fanout is never exceeded otherwise the circuit may malfunction.

The H and S versions of TTL represent larger than standard loads and have a higher fanout, while L and LS varieties impose smaller loads but also have smaller fanouts. In fact the L, S and LS types each have different fanouts for HI and LO cases, but it is safer to quote a *normalised* fanout which is the smaller of the two. Normalised fanouts and input loads are presented in Fig. 4.10 for the five types of TTL component. All figures are

TTL Series	Input load	Fanout
Standard	1	10
H	1.25	12.5
L	0.5	2.5
S	1:25	12.5
LS	0.5	5

Fig. 4.10 — Input load and fanout for the five types of TTL component.

quoted in terms of a standard TTL load.

Manufacturers' specifications vary, so it is recommended that data sheets be always consulted — the appropriate data is quoted in terms of the currents, I_{OH}, I_{OL}, I_{IH} and I_{IL}. There are, of course, other logic families but we shall not discuss their fanouts here: this information can be found again from the appropriate data sheets. Note, however, that sometimes it is important to consider the *interfacing* of one logic family with another. The popularity of the TTL family has led to logic interfaces being described as *TTL-compatible* or otherwise. This implies compatibility with TTL voltages (V_{cc} = +5 volts, GND = 0 volts) as well as with current loadings which would enable a fanout of at least one. The most important of these logic interfaces are MOS-TTL and CMOS-TTL.

Note that although it is convenient to think in terms of only HI and LO voltages there is a specified range of values over which voltages at gate inputs and outputs will be effectively HI or LO. In the data sheets the following values are defined:

V_{IL} is the voltage level required for LO at an input: it is 0.8 volts maximum for TTL;
V_{IH} is the voltage required for a HI at an input: it is 2.0 volts minimum;
V_{OL} is the voltage at a gate output in the LO state: it is guaranteed to be 0.4 volts maximum;
V_{OH} is the voltage at a gate output in the HI state: it is guaranteed to be a minimum of 2.4 volts.

Typical, rather than maximum or minimum values, are 3.5 volts for HI and 0.2 volts for LO. The minimum acceptable voltage for a HI output (2.4V) is 0.4 volts greater than the minimum (2.0V) required to constitute a HI input. Similarly the maximum LO output voltage (0.4V) is 0.4 volts less than the maximum LO input (0.8V). These differences of 0.4 volts are referred to as the high- and low-state *noise margins* of the gate: it is guaranteed to operate successfully when subjected to noise spikes of not more than 0.4 volts amplitude.

Interfacing logic families
While many SSI (and many MSI) components are manufactured in TTL, the majority of LSI components are being made in MOS logic. In particular, microprocessors and associated ICs are mainly MOS devices, and it is often required to interface these to TTL components. Some MOS devices do not have sufficient drive capability for interfacing with TTL: the standard TTL load is too great. However, the L or LS versions present a smaller load and can be so driven. The ease of interfacing depends on the supply voltage of the MOS device in question. If this is a negative value (for example −5V and −12V are common) then interface devices (available in IC form) must be used to translate voltages suitably. If the supply voltage is +5V, which it increasingly is for microprocessors and associated components, the connection is straightforward in terms of voltages. Current loadings are no longer a problem for the newer NMOS devices, and usually one standard TTL load can be interfaced: most NMOS microprocessors and interface devices are designed to be TTL-compatible in this way. Once again, the data sheets should be consulted in specific cases. Older PMOS devices may require the use of an external pull-up resistor (of 1K or less) between the TTL output and +5V when driving MOS from TTL, and an external resistor from the

MOS output to GND when driving TTL from MOS. PMOS devices are quite likely to drive only low-power TTL loads.

Increasing use is made of CMOS devices. These may be mixed in a circuit along with TTL components, the CMOS being used where low power consumption is a requirement (but not high speed), and the TTL being used for higher-speed operation. Most CMOS devices have a wide range of supply voltages over which they will operate. For compatibility with TTL a voltage of +5V would be chosen. Some CMOS components will drive a TTL load while others will not. However, special CMOS *buffers* are available which have a fanout of three or four, and which can be used in the interface beween CMOS and TTL to improve drive capability. When TTL is used to drive CMOS gates an external pull-up resistor between the TTL output and +5V is recommended. This measure is intended to increase the noise margin at the input to the CMOS gate to an acceptable level.

Schmitt trigger circuits
We have seen how an inverter (or any other gate) has a propagation delay between input and output. When the output of a gate changes state, from LO to HI or vice versa, we have idealised the logic transition as an instantaneous change, giving a perfectly vertical slope on a timing diagram. Logic transitions are in practice not instantaneous, but take a finite time, as illustrated below:

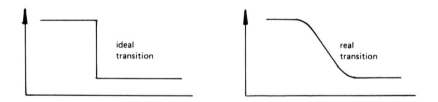

ideal transition   real transition

The outputs of TTL gates produce *transition times* of only several nanoseconds and this causes no problems. However, the inputs to TTL gates must change rapidly (transition times of 1 microsecond are unacceptable) otherwise unreliable operation will result: usually oscillations would be produced at the output of the gate, causing problems if this input is connected to a sequential circuit. If the input to a gate is very slow-changing it can be speeded up — the transition time made shorter — by passing it through a Schmitt trigger circuit, which typically gives transition times of a few nanoseconds. Some TTL gates are available with Schmitt trigger circuits built into their inputs. An example is the 7414, a hex inverter package. This type of gate is distinguished by a special shape (indicating a pair of superimposed idealised logic transitions) inside the normal logic symbol as for example:

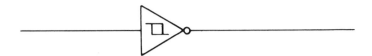

for the 7414 gate.

Monostables

Using the Schmitt trigger circuit a pulse shape can be improved so that its leading and trailing edges have rapid transition times. This can be important for the successful operation of a circuit which requires rapidly-changing inputs. Another important parameter of a pulse is its width or duration. Sometimes the width requires to be altered — lengthened or perhaps shortened. An example where a pulse has to be lengthened is in driving a stepping motor from a logic circuit: the stepping pulse may be required to be as long as 20 or 30 microseconds. A shorter pulse produced by the logic circuit can be lengthened by the use of a *monostable multivibrator*, usually called simply a monostable or a one-shot. This is a device with one stable and one unstable state: it is triggered by pushing it into the unstable state and it reverts after a time to its stable state, the time being dependent on external resistor and capacitor values. An example of a monstable available in IC form is the 74123, which contains two of the devices. A monostable circuit is illustrated below:

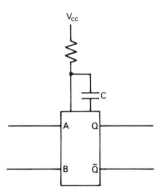

The device has A and B inputs as shown, and can be triggered either by a HI or LO transition at A or a LO to HI transition at B. In the data sheet a graph is given showing the variation of the output pulse width against the values of R and C, thus enabling R, C to be selected for a particular application.

A pair of monostables, such as the pair in the dual 74123 package, can be used to provide a clock pulse without the need for a crystal oscillator circuit. For this purpose they may be connected as follows:

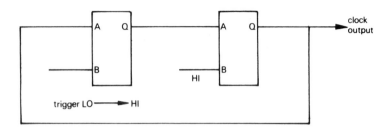

The operation is triggered by a LO to HI transition at one of the B inputs, and thereafter the circuit outputs clock pulses whose width and interval are determined by the R, C values for the two monostables.

4.3 ANALYSIS OF LOGIC CIRCUITS

At least as important as the ability to design logic circuits is the capability of analysing and comprehending circuit diagrams. In the case of the well-practised logic designer this can be taken for granted: synthesising logic circuits is difficult and the practice will lead to the ability to understand other designers' work.

However, for the majority of computer practitioners the opportunity or even the desire to design logic circuits will never arise. It is much more likely that they will be confronted at some time with logic diagrams which have to be understood to enable a hardware fault to be traced or even to clear up a point to allow a program to be written or amended. This type of activity is most likely to occur for those involved with microprocessor work, where often the microprocessor is monitoring or controlling some physical process through a special-purpose hardware interface. Possibly some logic may have to be added to a circuit which is unsuitable for its intended purpose in this specific application: thus in such a case a modest amount of design work may have to be undertaken. The addition of logic to an existing circuit will not in general be possible using a particular design technique, but more usually will be achieved using ad hoc methods: the ability to read and comprehend the original logic diagram is therefore of prime importance.

The choice of material in Chapters 2 to 4 inclusive was motivated partly by the aim of helping the reader to acquire a basic reading knowledge of circuit diagrams. The essentials are the understanding of the various logic symbols and the technology and labelling used on diagrams and in any accompanying literature. Also important is a readiness to consult manufacturers' data sheets when, inevitably, an unfamiliar IC package designator is encountered.

This is not to say that given an understanding of the material in this book all circuit diagrams will become transparently easy to comprehend. More complex diagrams require time and effort to follow through the signal paths, in order to determine the part which each component plays in the overall circuit operation. The sheer number and density of logic symbols on the diagrams of larger circuits make for confusion and consequent difficulties in understanding. It ia advisable to try to identify major sub-functions of the circuit and to concentrate on each in turn. Quite often these functions will be separated geographically on the diagram; in such cases boundary lines may usefully be added to help visual discrimination.

A somewhat historical example of a circuit diagram of modest complexity is given in Fig. 4. 11. This is a diagram of the interface logic for connecting a simple paper tape reader to an 8-bit microprocessor (the Motorola M6800). It is nevertheless offered as an exercise in attempting to follow the structure and operation of a realistic logic circuit. Some remarks should be made as follows, however, to set the circuit in its context.

The M6800 to reader connection is illustrated by the diagram below:

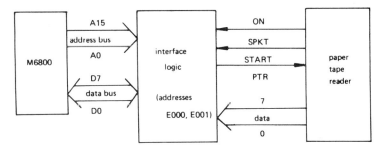

The M6800 has a 16-bit-wide address bus and a bidirectional 8-bit-wide data bus. It employs memory-mapped input/output, which means that any peripheral device is assigned its own address values. Suitable address decoding logic must be provided in the logic interface to recognise these address values when they are generated by the processor. It is common to quote addresses (and data values) in *hexadecimal* (hex for short), that is the base-16 number system with digits 0–9 and A–F (to stand for 10 to 15 inclusive). Each hex digit is represented by four bits. In this case the paper tape reader has two addresses, E000 for exercising *control* and reading *status*, and E001 for inputting *data* from the reader. *Partial address decoding* is used in the interface: only address bits A15–A12, and A0, are decoded. This is possible since no other addresses starting with E are assigned in this particular system.

The paper tape reader has a built-in stepping motor which moves the paper tape on by one frame each time the motor is pulsed. A 30 microsecond pulse is required for this purpose. Each frame or section across the tape has eight data positions — a 1 is represented by a hole, 0 by the absence of a hole — and a *sprocket* hole used for driving the tape by means of a toothed wheel. One step pulse to the motor causes the tape to move so that the next sprocket hole comes to rest over a row of photocells. A light source at the opposite side of the tape allows the binary pattern of the new character to be read — these are available as data bits 0–7. The fact that a new character is ready is conveyed by the SPKT signal which becomes set when a frame is over the photocells. Thus the processor can determine when new data is available by inspecting the CHARACTER READY bit derived from the SPKT signal.

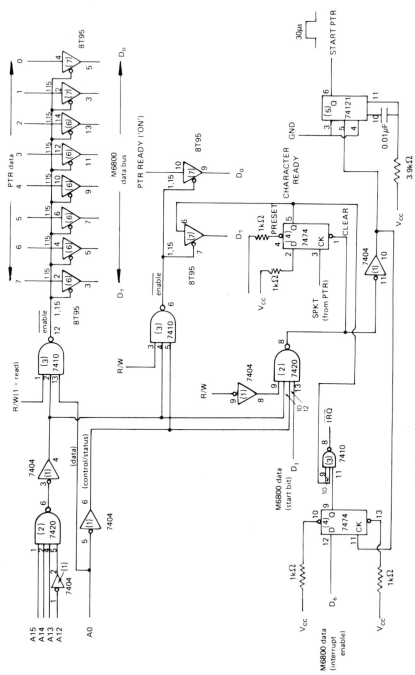

Fig. 4.11 — Microprocessor to paper tape reader interface logic.

This ready bit is passed by the interface logic to the data line D7 of the M6800, but only when the control/status address E000 is generated. Another status bit, PTR READY, is derived from the ON signal which indicates whether the reader is switched on. The processor reads data by reading lines D0–D7 from the data address (E001) of the reader. When a character has been read, the processor can cause the tape to move on by one frame by writing 1 then 0, on data line D1, to the control/status address. The control/status and data addresses may conveniently be regarded as registers with the following layout:

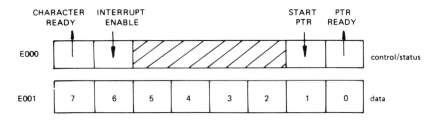

Note that a second control signal, INTERRUPT ENABLE, optionally allows the processor to be interrupted (by means of the $\overline{\text{IRQ}}$ line) when a character is ready, instead of the *polling* arrangement whereby the CHARACTER READY line is repeatedly read by the processor.

In Fig. 4.11 the following types of gates are used:

> 7404 — hex inverter package
> 7410 — triple 3-input NAND gates
> 7420 — dual 4-input NAND gates
> 7474 — dual edge-triggered D-type flip-flop
> 74121 — monostable
> 8T95 — hex tri-state buffers

The buffers are used for driving onto a common bus and are tri-state devices. This type of component is represented

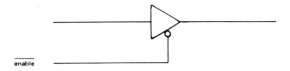

by a (non-inverting) amplifier with the tri-state enable shown entering the side of the symbol. The wiring information — package and pin numbers — is included in the diagram.

5

Very large-scale integrated circuits

5.1 INTRODUCTION

Modern technology makes possible the production of integrated circuits containing many hundreds or even many thousands of individual components on a single silicon chip a few millimetres square — the so-called large-scale integrated circuits, LSI, and very large-scale integrated circuits, VLSI. The million component chip is envisaged in the not-too-distant future and research is being conducted into WSI — wafer scale integration — in which an integrated system will be constructed on silicon wafers some 75–125 mm in diameter and potentially containing many millions of components. There are many different ways of exploiting this technology, and this chapter is aimed at highlighting them and describing the design tools needed to make the most of them. In the late 1970s and early 1980s, the heyday of medium-scale integration, MSI, system designers were able to treat their basic building blocks as 'black boxes': counters, registers, adders, etc. It was not necessary for a system designer to know in detail about the internal workings of a black box in order to design with it, providing certain interconnection and loading rules were obeyed. Certainly little knowledge of device physics was needed. To some extent this is still true but, at present, it is an advantage for a designer to have a wider knowledge of these matters in order to exploit fully all the available technologies. The design task is somewhat eased, however, by the fact that the very complexity of the circuits has made it essential that high-powered computer aids be developed to facilitate the tasks of designing, checking, laying out, manufacturing and testing the circuits produced. As these aids become more sophisticated, the system design task will again become largely that of black box interconnection, the device physics and circuit knowledge being built into the computer package. In general the more 'customised' the design is to be, the more fundamental knowledge the designer will require.

Fully customised circuits are designed down to the level of individual components, the designer having full control over the size, geometry and hence switching properties of each device in the system, and complete freedom to choose the interconnection paths between devices. He therefore needs a detailed knowledge of the electronic circuit properties of devices of different sizes and shapes and sufficient knowledge of device physics to appreciate such problems as the production of parasitic components (capacitors or even transistors) by the unwise choice of interconnection patterns.

Semi-custom design is available at a number of levels and, whilst imposing more constraints in terms of the range of devices available to the designer, frees him from the need to have such a deep understanding of the underlying principles of circuit operation. The two lowest levels of semi-custom design are generally referred to as gate array design and standard cell design. Both involve a system designer in choosing interconnection paths to be laid onto silicon to link devices which have otherwise been fully designed in terms of component size and geometry up to that stage. The role of the designer is therefore to provide a specification for the final stage of the fabrication process — the metallisation layer or layers (some processes have two). To a certain extent the design task is analogous to that of designing a printed circuit board (p.c.b.) holding a number of SSI (small-scale integration) or MSI components. The finished product will not, however, be a p.c.b. but a silicon chip — a device which has far fewer available test points. The testing problem is analogous to having access only to the edge connector — a very important point which will be elaborated later.

A gate array comprises a regular matrix of cells which contain logic gates or standard components which can easily be configured into gates. Interconnection of the gates can then be specified to realise any required logic function. Just as when designing with SSI components on a p.c.b., a designer will aim for a system of gates to realise the function he requires whilst seeking to minimise the number of individual components and interconnections. The standard cell approach 'moves up a level' in terms of the kinds of predefined circuit available. The designer may select the circuits he requires from a library of predesigned functional cells. This task is usually performed at a computer terminal via access to a powerful computer-aided design (CAD) package. The cells may then be laid out in an optimum way to facilitate interconnection. Systems now available provide libraries containing designs ranging from single gates through counters, registers and adders to complete microprocessors. The 'customising' specification for a gate array affects only the final step in the chip manufacturing process — determination of the metallisation pattern. A chip design using the standard cell approach requires the specification of a complete integrated circuit mask set. The boundary between the two levels is, in some cases, a bit hazy. Most gate array design systems now offer the designer a library of standard cells, the interconnection patterns for which have already been optimised. The cells will, however, consist of gates selected from those in the array.

The next family of devices which may be regarded as offering the facility of semi-custom logic design include Programmable Logic Arrays (PLAs), Programmable Array Logic (PAL) and Programmable Read Only Memories (PROMs). All of these devices are marketed as fully processed components, usually in dual-in-line packages. The 'customising' process involves applying for a brief time specified electrical signals to designated programming pins on the package. Some kinds of these devices are given a permanent identity by the programming process and, from that point on, perform specific logic functions. Some may be erased and re-programmed many times.

Of the various kinds of switching circuit which have been developed over the past few decades those currently finding most favour in VLSI applications are ECL or current mode logic from amongst the bipolar technologies, and NMOS and CMOS from amongst the unipolar or insulated-gate technologies. Developments in these technologies are aimed at reducing device sizes and thus increasing packing density and increasing the switching speed of circuits without increasing power dissipation too much.

5.2   THE ROLE OF CAD IN VLSI

The essential problem of VLSI design consists of specifying the logical function of a system which may contain many thousands of components and ultimately realising that system as a single silicon chip. To achieve this end — a task involving many hundreds of man-hours of work — would be impossible without extensive use of the computer as a design aid. To see where a computer can help in the design process the overall task may be broken down into a series of sub-tasks which are hierarchical in nature — subsequent tasks depending on parameters that have been defined in previous ones. Ideally each of these sub-tasks should be capable of being tackled using a software package and all such packages should be integrated into a design suite so that changes which may be necessary at any stage can conveniently be passed through the hierarchy and their effects evaluated.

At the highest level of the hierarchy must be a description of the logical function of the system. This may be in the form of a logic diagram (a device often favoured by engineers) or written in a hardware description language or HDL (a method often preferred by computer scientists or those more used to expressing functional ideas in algorithmic form). Some CAD packages include a graphical input facility or schematic capture package with which a logic diagram may be constructed on-screen using logic symbls selected from a menu occupying a peripheral area of the screen. Positioning of the symbols on the screen is achieved either by manipulating the cursor control keys on a keyboard or, more conveniently, by use of a mouse, a hand-held device whose movement over a flat horizontal surface causes a graphics cursor to move in sympathy across the screen. The most flexible systems provide a 'window' facility — an interactive graphics technique whereby a small section of the screen may be defined and then enlarged to fill a larger part of the screen — in some systems simultaneously being superimposed on the rest of the logic diagram of which it forms a part. Similar window facilities are often provided at many levels of design and, in some systems, windows may be defined which enable an operator to 'zoom' up and down between levels of the design hierarchy.

The schematic capture package or HDL leads to a 'netlist' — a description of all the interconnections between gates and all the connections to inputs and outputs. This netlist constitutes the database on which all the other software packages in the design suite will operate. Both schematic capture packages and HDLs usually allow designers to create user-defined macros: groupings of the logic symbols interconnected to perform a higher

level function such as a counter or an adder. These macros may then be held
in a library and called up when required again. Larger macros may then be
made up of smaller macros, and additional gates if necessary. The initial
design stage itself is thus a hierarchical process.

Once the functional description is complete the logic system it represents
must be checked for correctness. This function is performed by another
software package — the simulator. Simulators may work at behavioural
level, at gate level, at circuit level or in mixed mode. At behavioural level the
overall function of the system is checked in terms of the functional blocks it
contains. At gate level the operation of all gates is checked and the detailed
logical function of all its elements examined including postulated gate
delays. At circuit level all circuit elements are modelled in terms of voltage
and current processing devices, resistors and capacitors, so precise details of
waveform rise and fall times, etc., may be obtained.

To exercise a simulator a further software package must be run to
provide a set of input test waveforms to stimulate the simulated device. A
waveform description language is used to define these. Some simulators also
require the designer to specify the expected output responses to the test
waveforms. The output of the simulator may be viewed as a listing of
sequential logic values on input and output pins or, if a graphic display
package is available, as a simulated multi-channel oscilloscope waveform
display.

Once the logic design has been verified, layout design may proceed. In
some gate array and standard cell chip design suites further software
packages may be used to provide autoplacement of gates and autorouting of
interconnections. The regular arrangement of cells on the chip illustrated in
Fig. 5.2(b), which is typical of standard cell and some gate array systems,
makes this possible. Full custom designs, however, require layout design to
be done from the bottom up. Each cell or device must be positioned on the
chip and the appropriate connections made. Software packages are again
used to facilitate this, particularly for checking the layout design against the
functional design already completed.

When layout design is complete another simulation run should be made
to evaluate the effect on circuit timing of added capacitance due to the actual
interconnection leads used in the layout.

Assuming the design passes all checks, the layout design information can
then be used to produce a set of masks for the device to be made or to
provide the information required by an electron beam (E-beam) machine.
When the chips have been processed, the test waveform file can be used to
specify test routines for a probe test machine or other automatic tester which
may be used on the encapsulated devices.

5.2.1 The silicon compiler
The most recent research in software aids to VLSI design is towards
automating every stage in the design and layout of a silicon chip, thus
providing the ultimate CAD tool — the silicon compiler. This software
package will allow a complete system to be described in terms of a functional

high level language. This system description then forms a database from which all the subsequent hierarchical processes down to complete information for chip layout will be produced automatically. The high-level language description will lead to the compilation, not of source code for a computer, but of an actual piece of hardware realised on a silicon chip. The design of systems on silicon will thus be opened up to a much wider range of people. Those who possess high-level computing skills but are not necessarily well-versed in engineering matters will be able to realise working hardware designs on a relatively short timescale.

Pilot systems have already been produced and there is no doubt that more powerful ones will appear in the next few years.

5.3   INTEGRATED CIRCUIT MANUFACTURING PROCESSES

References 1 to 5 (see the Reading List for Chapter 5) give full details of the many ways in which integrated circuits can be made. A brief description is given here to allow the reader to appreciate the main problems involved and to understand the demands made on a chip designer.

As described in Chapter 2, integrated circuits are produced by selectively doping different areas in a wafer of silicon, selectively coating parts of the surface with oxide and laying down interconnections. The process involves a series of steps each of which requires a pattern of discrete polygons — rectangles, L-shapes, T-shapes and more complicated figures — to be produced on or close to the surface of the silicon. The appropriate process — diffusion, ion implantation, oxidation or metallisation — is then carried out with reference to these polygons. Each diffusion or ion implantation process will be preceded by coating the surface with an oxide through which 'windows' are etched. The remaining oxide acts as a barrier to the dopant. After doping, this oxide too is etched away. The windows are produced by coating the surface of the wafer with a thin layer of a substance called photoresist which changes its properties by polymerisation when exposed to ultraviolet light or a beam of electrons. The required pattern is produced on the photoresist by placing a suitable photographically produced mask against it which is transparent where areas are to be exposed or alternatively by 'writing' directly onto the surface with an accurately controlled electron beam machine. Unexposed areas can be removed by washing with an organic solvent. The result is that the wafer surface is then covered with a layer of photoresist except for a pattern of windows. The photoresist acts as a barrier to the etchant which, when applied, produces corresponding windows in the underlying oxide. The exposed photoresist is then removed with another solvent and the doping can proceed.

With masking techniques employing photographic lithography, minimum line widths of 1.5 μm to 2.0 μm may be achieved. Electron beam lithography allows line widths down to 0.5 μm to be achieved. It is this dimension which limits the size of devices which can be produced on a chip and thus the number of devices which can be included in a given area. Processes are often characterised and spoken of by the minimum line width in microns (micrometres) which they allow. Of the CMOS gate array processes in common use, one allows a minimum line width of 5 μm, another a width of 3 μm. These are spoken of simply as 5 micron and 3 micron processes.

To produce a complete integrated circuit involves many steps such as the one described above, and many masks or sets of instructions for an E-beam machine must be produced. It is the production of this information which is the task of the chip layout designer or the software package he uses. When doing a hand layout a designer may start from a 'stick diagram' — essentially a skeleton representation of the final component layout. This can later be 'fleshed out' to define completely the different mask patterns required. Some software packages allow this process to be carried out at a VDU terminal. The designer specifies end points for a component and the software completes it.

5.4   VLSI CHIP DESIGN METHODOLOGIES

5.4.1   Full-custom VLSI design

The design of a complex IC chip containing many hundreds of thousands of components is a task which, even with powerful CAD packages, cannot be performed in a reasonable time by one person working alone — it is essentially a team effort. The overall design must be from a top-down approach — the basic function of the chip must be decided first and this function then broken down into sub-functions until unit sizes are reached, the detailed design of which can be assigned to individuals. When a full-custom design is being initiated the layout of these sub-function units will constitute a 'floor-plan' for the chip. Agreed areas of the chip will be assigned to given functions and individual designers will work on these functions whilst keeping their layout designs within the agreed areas. A typical chip floor-plan is illustrated in Fig. 5.1. Interconnections between the areas must be agreed by the designers and any modifications to these agreements monitored as an ongoing process. The CAD tools used in the design must be able to accommodate this approach.

The logical functions of the various units will first be designed, simulated and checked. The layout then becomes a bottom-up task. Each individual component must be laid onto the chip and the circuit built up as required. Two points need to be taken account of: as each logical component of the design is realised as a circuit its function in the overall system must be checked against the database created by the logic simulator; at all stages of the layout each component must be checked to ensure that it conforms to the design rules of the IC process being used. This latter point is particularly important across the boundaries of different areas in a floor-plan. Layout at this level requires a detailed knowledge of device physics and, in the past, it has been essential for designers of full custom circuits to possess this knowledge. Intelligent knowledge-based design packages are now becoming available which largely remove much of this load. Information about the physical properties of the devices being used, and their design rules, are built into the package so that a designer can tell, when a set of components has

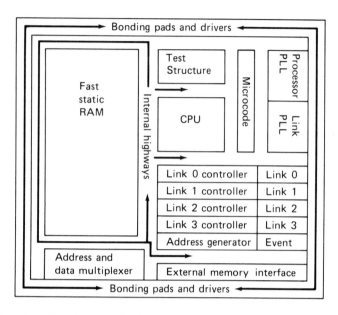

Fig. 5.1 — Floor-plan of the IMST 414 transputer (Reproduced courtesy of INMOS Ltd).

been laid down, whether they will fulfil the function for which they are intended. When this kind of checking is done off-line several iterations may be needed before a correct design is achieved but packages with on line design rule checking are now becoming available which ensure that chips, as laid out at the VDU terminal, are correct by design.

When layout design is completed a database will have been created which contains the information needed for each step of the manufacturing process. This database is used by a software package which can produce a complete mask set for a given chip (there may be a dozen or more masks depending on the process) or a set of data for feeding the same information to an E-beam machine.

The main advantages of full custom design are that designs which are economical of chip area may be realised and that full advantage of the available technology may be taken to optimise device performance. Novel system architectures may more easily be explored using this technique. Chapter 8 discusses advances in computer architecture.

5.4.2 Gate arrays

A gate array, otherwise known as an Uncommitted Logic Array or ULA, consists of a regular matrix of 'cells' of semiconductor components contained on a silicon chip. The layout pattern of the components is predefined and so therefore are all the production processes except that of providing the interconnections between the devices. These interconnections are provided by one or two layers of metal or, alternatively in some two-layer systems, a layer of polysilicon and a layer of metal. 'Customising' or 'committing' these arrays consists of defining the interconnection patterns required to realise a specific logic function. In essence the design process is analogous to designing with SSI devices. In fact it is, to some extent, even more restrictive in that the basic cell on a ULA frequently consists of no more than a single 2-input NOR or NAND gate.

Three basic patterns of cell layout may be identified as shown in Fig. 5.2:

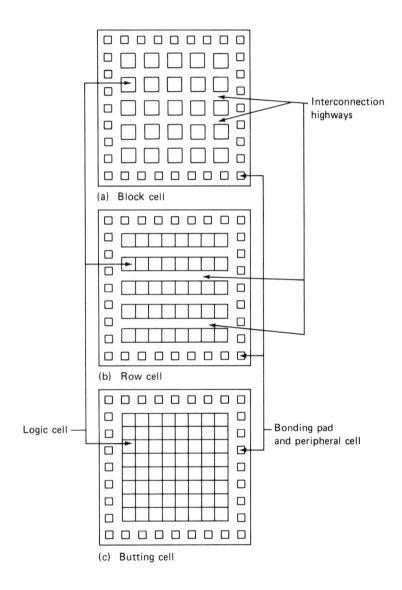

Fig. 5.2 — Cell layout patterns for gate arrays.

(a) The Block Cell pattern — cells are spaced apart at regular intervals on a two dimensional matrix. The vertical and horizonal channels created by the gaps between the cells are available for routing the interconnections between cells.

(b) The Row Cell pattern — cells are set out in rows with gaps between the rows, providing space for one level of interconnections. A second level, if needed in the process, may be laid down at right angles to the first and, generally, may cross both cells and first level interconnections.

(c) The Butting Cell pattern — the cells abut one another and no gaps are left for routing. Instead, the cells are so designed that inter-cell connections may be made within the cells themselves.

In all three patterns peripheral cells are available around the edge of the chip to provide input-output buffering between the logic on the chip and the outside world. These peripheral cells are located adjacent to bonding pads and may provide, for example, level conversion between on-chip logic and the industry standard TTL.

Two examples are given here to illustrate the kinds of layout which can occur. Fig. 5.3(a) shows a bipolar CDI (Collector Diffusion Isolation) technology cell, containing a group of uncommitted transistors and resistors which can be interconnected to form typically a pair of 2-input CML (Current Mode Logic) NOR gates as shown in Figs 5.3(b and c). Cells in this kind of ULA abut one another, and interconnections between cells are facilitated by prediffused polysilicon cross-unders. Power supplies are distributed through the bulk silicon and only a single metallisation layer is required.

Fig. 5.4(a) shows a CMOS cell from part of a row-cell pattern array. The typical gate element made in this array is a 2-input NAND gate as shown in Figs 5.4 (b and c). The cell contains two p-channel and two n-channel MOSFETs with extended polysilicon gates which also act as cross-unders through the cell. A number of contact holes are provided at preset locations to enable contact to be made between the metal layer and the diffusion (source and drain) and polysilicon levels. Two predefined metal power lines pass through the cell and further 'intracell' connections may be made at the metal level. Interconnections between cells are carried in routing channels between rows of cells and may include predefined polysilicon cross-unders and orthogonal metal tracks.

Design advantages

The greatest advantage of the gate array design principle is in the fast turn round time it gives to a designer. Since a manufacturer can hold a stock of preprocessed slices lacking only a metallisation pattern he can, under favourable circumstances, provide packaged devices within a few days of receiving the information needed to produce the metal layer or layers. This information may come in the form of metallisation masks or, for a process using E-beam technology, as software to drive an E-beam machine. This

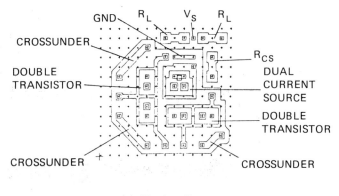

(a) Matrix cell

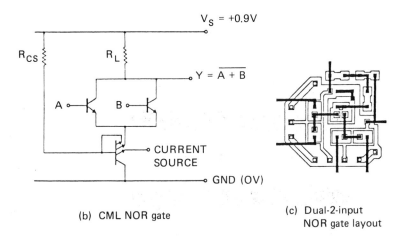

(b) CML NOR gate

(c) Dual-2-input
NOR gate layout

Fig. 5.3 — A single matrix cell from a 440–cell ULA is shown in (a). The circuit schematic of a 2-input CML NOR gate appears in (b), and the metal interconnections required to produce a pair of such gates from one of the matrix cells can be seen in (c). (Courtesy of Ferranti Electronics Ltd.)

latter process makes the multi-project wafer a viable concern and sample circuits of many different designs may thus be provided very economically.

Fig. 5.5 illustrates the 'route to silicon' using the gate array design method. Initial logic design is likely to be done on paper and then transferred to computer via a schematic capture package or hardware description language. Logic simulation should come next, followed by layout which may be manual (using an interactive graphics package) or automatic. Layout design rule checks will be carried out by a further software package and, once an acceptable layout has been achieved, a further simulation run should be carried out. Test data files will be created to drive pattern

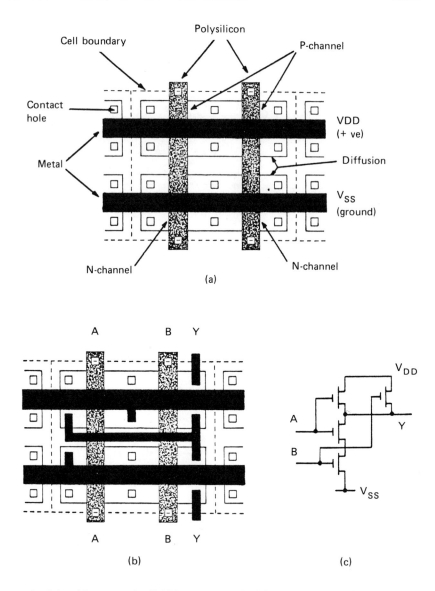

Fig. 5.4 — (a) Layout of a CMOS gate array cell of the row-cell type. (b) Internal connections required to produce a 2-input NAND gate (c).

generators which can then be used to exercise the simulators. Once a design has passed all the logical connectivity checks, design rule checks and test pattern checks for a complete layout the metallisation processes may be specified. When packaged chips are received the test data files can, if suitable equipment is available, be used to drive the hardware test machines.

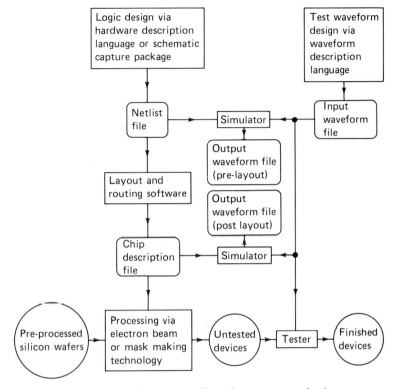

Fig. 5.5 — The 'route to silicon' for gate array technology.

5.4.3 Standard cell design

This technique falls somewhere between full custom design and design using gate arrays. As may be seen from Fig. 5.6 the placement of devices on the chip has much in common with the row-cell approach to gate arrays. Each cell is custom designed to fulfil a given function and to fit on a row. All cells have the same height but the width is determined by the function. Power rails are in standard positions within the cells. Since cells are placed wherever they are needed on a row to realise a given system function, each chip design is unique and therefore requires a full mask set for production. Cell designs covering a wide range of functions are held in a cell library and called up as required. Each cell library is unique to the process for which it is designed since the individual cells are laid out according to the design rules of a given process. Inputs and outputs are provided at the top and bottom of the cells so that they will be on the edges of rows when the cells are placed in position. Interconnections are made in routing channels between the rows, two layers of interconnection usually being provided. The system thus lends itself to the use of the same kind of placement and interconnection routing algorithms as have become established for the layout of printed circuit boards. Standard cell design is, in fact, directly comparable to p.c.b. design

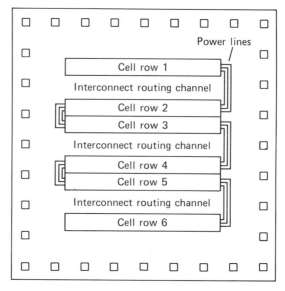

Fig. 5.6 — Organisation of a standard cell IC.

using off-the-shelf SSI and MSI circuits. Automatic placement and routing software packages available for standard cell design are capable of laying out chips containing several hundred cells without any operator intervention. The complete process can be achieved in a few minutes of CPU time. The price to be paid, compared with full custom design, is a far less efficient use of silicon area although, for a given system, this would be better than a gate array design. As system size increases the disparity becomes more apparent between the relatively inefficient use of space in the routing channels and the densely wired custom designed cells themselves. At present, therefore, standard cell design is only really useful at the low end of the VLSI chip complexity spectrum. Here, however, because of its similarity to p.c.b. design, it offers a design system which provides a rapid, cheap realisation of a system using design and layout tools which are already well understood and widely used.

5.5   PROGRAMMABLE LOGIC DEVICES

This name covers a range of devices which are supplied to the customer fully processed and packaged but whose function can be defined by the application of electrical signals to specially provided programming pins. Mask programmable versions are also available and are useful where prototype production using an electrically programmable device leads to a foreseen quantity requirement. Some devices, once programmed, have their function fixed forever. Others may be erased and reprogrammed many times. The devices are programmed to realise a particular function by making or breaking a physical connection (such as a fusible link) between two cross points on a matrix.

All devices in the range depend on the fact that a combinational function of a number of variables can be realised as a 2-level AND–OR expression — the sum-of-products form. Fig. 5.7 shows the general arrangement of

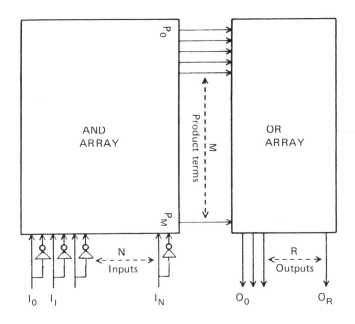

Fig. 5.7 — A comparison of programable logic devices.

(a) PROM: AND array preprogrammed. Fully decodes N inputs to yield all $M=2^N$ possible product terms.

OR array user-programmable. Any combination of the M products can be ORed onto any of the R outputs.

(b) PLA: AND array user-programmable. Generates a chosen subset of M ($<2^N$) product terms from N inputs.

OR array user-programmable. Any combination of the M products can be ORed onto any of the R outputs.

(c) PAL: AND array user-programmable. Generates a chosen subset of M ($<2^N$) product terms from N inputs.

OR array preprogrammed. Groups of product terms are ORed onto the R outputs according to a pre-arranged pattern.

programmable logic devices. The difference between the various devices in the range lies mainly in the degree of programmability afforded at the AND and OR levels. Sequential logic can be realised in the form of finite state machines by making feedback paths around the devices, in some cases with the addition of external registers. Some manufacturers provide devices within the family with built-in registers.

5.5.1 Programmable read only memory (PROM)

The ROM was introduced in Chapter 2, and its variations the PROM and EPROM described. ROMs are widely used in computers to store fixed programs or data. They may equally well, however, be used to realise combinational or sequential circuits. The ROM structure, with reference to Fig. 5.7, corresponds to the case where the AND array is preprogrammed giving all $M=2^N$ possible product terms of N inputs, and the OR array is user programmable, any combination of the M products being ORed onto any of the R outputs by suitable selection of 1s in the ROM matrix.

ROMs are available in a variety of configurations. Most, since they were originally intended for use in computers, have one, four or eight outputs and can thus define a corresponding number of different functions. One example, the 32×8 ROM, is illustrated in Fig. 5.8. There are five address inputs

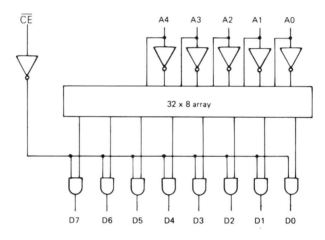

Fig. 5.8 — A 32×8 ROM.

A0–A4, and a chip enable input $\overline{\text{CE}}$ which allows data to be read out on the eight data lines D0–D7. Address decoding logic is included on the chip to select one of the 32 stored words of data for output. The contents of the ROM may be viewed as follows:

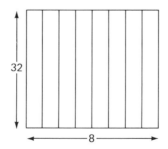

This view shows eight columns each of 32 bits. The columns may each be used to implement directly the output column of a five-variable truth table. The input variable combinations correspond to the 32 different addresses which may be generated by A0–A4. Thus the 32×8 ROM can be used to implement any 5-input combinational circuit with (up to) 8 outputs, simply by setting appropriate 1s and 0s into the ROM. If only single output functions are to be realised, however, much of the area in this ROM configuration would be wasted and thus the ROM would be an expensive implementation tool. For large combinational networks the ROM approach may well be cost-effective, particularly because it avoids the wiring interconnections required in a conventional SSI implementation. Note that no minimisation is possible since there is a bit in the ROM for every canonical product term. This is wasteful of space, particularly in the case of functions with few product terms (thus leading to a ROM sparsely populated with 1s), but on the other hand no circuit hazards can occur since these are a result of the minimisation process.

Asynchronous sequential circuits can be readily implemented using ROMs: feedback connections are made simply by linking appropriate ROM outputs to input address lines. Synchronous sequential circuits are not so easily realised, and external flip-flops (J-K or D-type) may have to be added to store the values to be fed back to the inputs. The flip-flops are all connected to a common clock; in this way circuit changes can be properly synchronised. This arrangement has the appearance of the Moore/Mealy model of Fig. 3.11.

5.5.2 Programmable logic array (PLA)

The PLA is a structure corresponding to the general form of Fig. 5.7 in which both AND and OR levels are user-programmable. Only a chosen subset M ($<2^N$) of the product terms of N inputs may be selected, any combination of these M products being ORed onto the R outputs.

Fig. 5.9 shows a logic circuit defining three possible functions of three product terms. Fig. 5.10 shows how this function can be implemented using an NMOS PLA structure. Note that the AND–OR function is realised by a NOR–NOR structure, a technique similar to that mentioned in the latter part of Section 2.4, inverters being used as necessary on inputs and outputs. The function F_1, as written directly from the PLA, is

$$F_1 = \overline{\overline{(\overline{A} + \overline{B} + C)} + \overline{(A + \overline{C})}} \tag{5.1}$$

Application of de Morgan's laws shows that it can also be represented in the sum-of-products form as

$$F_1 = AB\overline{C} + \overline{A}C \tag{5.2}$$

This kind of manipulation is typical of PLA design.

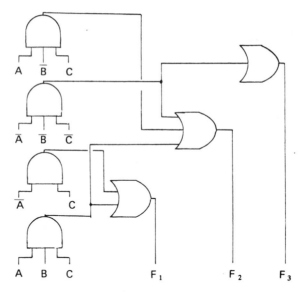

Fig. 5.9 — An AND–OR representation of three functions of three variables.

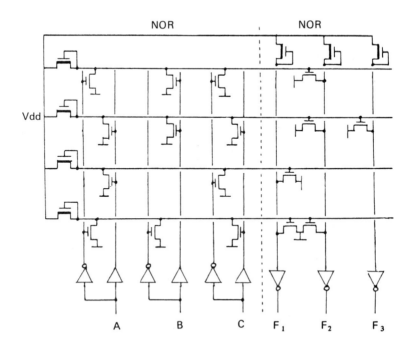

Fig. 5.10 — A NOR–NOR NMOS PLA realisation of the above functions.

5.5.3 Programmable array logic (PAL)

PAL structures are basically similar to PLAs but feature OR arrays which are preprogrammed. The AND array is user programmable so a chosen subset $M(<2^N)$ of the product terms of N inputs may be selected. Groups of product terms are ORed onto the R outputs according to a pre-arranged pattern.

Many varieties of PLAs and PALs are available commercially. A typical size would have 16 input variables, 48 possible product terms and 8 function outputs.

Some typical PAL design sheets are given in Appendix 2.

5.6 'SOFT' PROGRAMMABLE LOGIC DEVICES

The programmable logic devices just described all retain their programming information once programmed. Even if power is disconnected from them they are immediately ready for use again, as programmed, once power is reconnected. Two devices in widespread use depend on dynamically alterable programming for their operation. In terms of complexity they are at opposite ends of the spectrum. One is the multiplexer (MUX), the other the microprocessor.

5.6.1 Multiplexers

The multiplexer (MUX) is a combinational circuit which has several input data lines and a single output data line. Any one of the inputs can be connected to the output at any time, the selection being made by appropriate settings of control inputs. A circuit diagram of a 1-of-4 MUX is shown in Fig. 5.11. The Boolean equation for the 1-of-4 MUX is:

$$X = A\overline{S}\overline{R} + B\overline{S}R + CS\overline{R} + DSR \qquad (5.3)$$

which is to say that if S and R are both 0 the input line A is selected, and thus effectively connected to X. Similarly if S is 0 and R is 1, B is selected and so on for the other control input combinations. Other MUX configurations deal with larger numbers of input lines (in powers of 2), for example a 1-of-8 MUX has eight data inputs and three control lines.

Multiplexers may be used as universal logic modules for implementing combinational logic functions. Notice that in equation (5.3) all the combinations of S and R are represented. If combinations of 0s and 1s are applied appropriately at the inputs A, B, C and D any of the Boolean functions of two variables can be generated at the output X. In fact the circuit is capable of producing all the Boolean functions of three variables — consider how to apply combinations of 0s and 1s to two of the data inputs together with combinations of three variables applied to the two control inputs and the other data inputs. In general a 1-of-2^n MUX can generate all the Boolean functions of $n+1$ variables. To implement functions of larger numbers of variables a hierarchy of MUXs may be used. Thus any combinational logic function produced at the design stage may be implemented using MUXs by

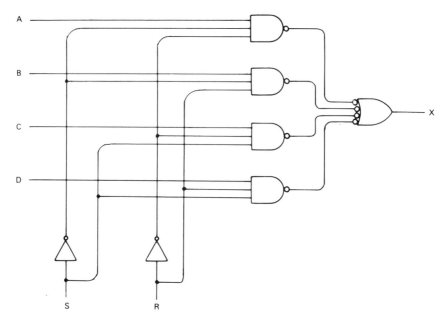

Fig. 5.11 — 1-of-4 multiplexer circuit. A, B, C and D are the data inputs, S and R the control inputs.

making the appropriate input connections. Multi-output functions require the use of MUXs arranged in parallel.

Despite the apparent usefulness of MUXs as universal logic modules their cost hardly justifies using them for low-complexity circuits, while for circuits with large numbers of variables there are better alternatives than either MUXs or random logic. MUX structures may, however, be useful as parts of larger VLSI systems. Since MOSTs can be used as controllable low-valued resistors they lend themselves very well to MUX construction. In full custom design some functions can be realised very conveniently with MUXs.

5.6.2   Microprocessors

In contrast to the *hard-wired* logic units described above, the microprocessor is a general-purpose device which can be programmed to suit the needs of a customer. Programs, unlike custom logic, can easily be changed so, where flexibility is required, the microprocessor is preferable. The unit cost of microprocessors is very small but, as for custom LSI, high design and development costs may have to be borne (for software instead of hardware): the greater the complexity of the task, the higher the costs. In terms of operating speeds a custom LSI chip will probably be better, although faster versions of microprocessors are likely to narrow the gap. Microprocessors are now being used very widely in digital applications previously dominated by hard-wired logic. Even in very low-volume applications the microprocessor may be preferred because of its attractive property of flexibility.

Microprocessors themselves do not constitute a complete logic module. They are basically CPUs which require the addition of a system clock, memory for programs and data — usually a mixture of ROM and RAM — and input/output interfaces which allow communication with the system being monitored or controlled. Thus a complete microcomputer typically consists of not one but several ICs: a computer on a circuit board, in effect. The latest trend in general-purpose devices is that of single-chip microcomputers with all the components contained in one IC. Usually this type of microcomputer has an 8-bit CPU, with integral clock, a few hundred bytes (8-bit words) of RAM, a few thousand bytes of ROM (or EPROM) and twenty to thirty single-bit lines for input-output. All that requires to be added is a (5-volt) power supply. These single-chip devices can be used for low-to-medium complexity tasks. Typical application areas include control functions in motor cars, domestic appliances and gaming machines. Higher complexity problems require more storage for programs, and possibly for data, so external memory must be added. As IC technology improves, the capabilities of single-chip computers will be extended by faster processors, 16–bit CPUs, larger memories and more input/output lines: the trend continues.

5.7 DESIGN FOR TESTABILITY

VLSI systems are very complex! Testing them to see if they work correctly is a formidable task and may even be impossible if not considered at the design stage. The number of components in a VLSI chip and the number of internal states such a chip may assume can equal those of a complete p.c. board made of MSI components. Whereas p.c. boards can be tested by 'bed of nails' testers where test probes can be applied at many points on the board, VLSI chips can be tested only by making connections to the pins of the package (or at the probe test stage to the bonding pads). In p.c. board terms this is equivalent to doing all tests via the edge connector.

Various techniques have evolved to facilitate chip testing and, for large chips, inevitably involve an 'overhead' in the loss of a certain amount of 'useful' chip area or a reduction in the number of 'useful' pins available. Certain bonding pads can be connected to special outputs which are used only at the probe test stage, special outputs can be brought out to test pins and special circuits may be incorporated into the design simply to make it testable.

References 8 and 9 give much information on design for testability. One popular method of enhancing chip testability is given here by way of example. Many synchronous systems can be subdivided into sections of combinational logic interspersed between stages of register storage. By adding gates, a control input, test data input and output lines and a test clock input, a 'scan path' can be set up within the chip so that it can be completely tested by a sequence of 'test vectors'. All register stages, as well as performing their desired purposes, can be configured into a long shift register or 'scan path' by a suitable setting of the control input. A HI on the control input could denote normal operation, a LO could set the chip into scan path mode. When in scan path mode, all register stages in the chip can be set to known values by serially inputting an appropriate 'test vector' into the shift register under the control of the test clock. The chip can then be set into normal mode and one pulse of the normal system clock applied. On returning to scan path mode, a new test vector can be input whilst the first test result vector is output. Logic values contained in this vector can then be checked to see if they correspond with predicted values. Repeating this process with a suitably chosen sequence of test vectors allows comprehensive testing of the chip to be carried out. This approach typically leads to an overhead of 12% lost useful chip area as well as the four pins required for test purposes.

System designers are traditionally antagonistic to 'wasteful' test requirements, but the necessity of including testability as part of the design process cannot be overemphasised. Without it many designs may be produced in which errors prove very difficult to locate.

5.8   WHAT OF THE FUTURE?

Silicon compilers have already been mentioned, and it is not in doubt that VLSI design and construction processes will become more and more automated over the next few decades. As wafer-scale integration becomes a reality, software aids to cope with its complexity will need to be developed and it is likely that intelligent knowledge-based systems (IKBS) will be employed to do this.

The technology itself, meanwhile, will not stand still, and new substances will be used which will allow faster and smaller devices providing for more and more logical power in smaller and smaller spaces. Gallium arsenide devices look promising for the late 1980s and beyond. Research is even being done into the use of biological materials as controllable switching and storage devices so these may become available before the turn of the century.

6

von Neumann computer architecture

6.1 COMPUTER LOGIC CIRCUITS

In Chapter 1 (Fig. 1.6) the structural layers of computer logic were outlined. The subsequent three chapters dealt successively with the following layers: the parallel streams of Boolean algebra and physical realisations; the nature of gates and flip-flops; and their use in designing and implementing logic circuits. We have now reached the stage of describing the uppermost level — how logic circuits are used in constructing computers.

The basic structure of a computer is illustrated by the von Neumann machine of Fig. 1.4. This will be used as a model for the present chapter. The von Neumann machine has three main parts: the CPU, memory and input/output unit. We shall concentrate mainly on the CPU and regard the memory and input/output unit as peripheral devices connected to the processor by means of the address and data buses.

Memory (RAM and ROM) is available in an IC form, as described in Chapter 2, and contains no logic of interest other than the address decoding circuits necessary to locate specific words in the memory matrix.

Choice of memory for a computer system depends on the word length of the computer and on the read/write timing cycles generated by the CPU. The maximum amount of memory depends on the width of the address bus — but also on the requirements of a particular application: in some cases the entire memory address space is not filled because a subset of the total memory is sufficient. A mixture of RAM and ROM is commonly used, especially in microcomputer systems, so that programs (in ROM) need not be reloaded whenever the computer is powered on. Indeed the bootstrap program which is responsible for initiating the loading of other programs from magnetic disc or tape is almost universally stored in ROM and is automatically entered when power is applied to the CPU.

Input/output units are connected to the CPU by means of I/O interfaces, either special ICs or printed circuit boards with the appropriate interfacing logic. Interfaces are either serial or parallel in nature, serial being used for slower peripheral devices like visual display units (VDUs), and slow matrix printers, while parallel are employed for fast devices like magnetic discs and tapes, and line printers. Standard interface ICs are very popularly used with microprocessors: the serial types are called ACIAs (asynchronous communications interface adapters) and the parallel ones PIAs (parallel,

or peripheral interface adapters). These are generally available as part of the
family of components for a particular microprocessor and tend to have
associated IC designators. For example the Motorola M6800 microprocessor has as relatives the M6820 PIA and the M6850 ACIA. A very simple
example of interface logic was given in Chapter 4 (Fig. 4.11) for a paper tape
reader to microprocessor connection. This interface logic can in fact be
rather easily implemented using an M6820 PIA.

The broad structure of a CPU

Computer architectures are many and various, but are often classified
roughly under three headings:

> mainframes
>
> minicomputers
>
> microcomputers.

The differences between these classes are becoming difficult to distinguish as
microcomputers and minicomputers both become more powerful, but the
distinctions are mainly connected with the richness of hardware and software features which they offer. Mainframes have long word lengths, as
mentioned in Chapter 1, with the consequent ability to address more
memory and to have a larger repertoire of machine-code instructions.
Standard mainframe hardware features tend to include virtual and cache
memory to improve the CPU performance. Minicomputers, with a typical
word length of 16 or 32 bits, offer a more modest set of instructions and have
smaller address spaces, but are more often than not equipped with some
form of virtual memory, and increasingly with cache as well. Microcomputers are characterised partly by short (8-bit or 16-bit) word lengths but
mainly by the fact that the CPU (the microprocessor itself) is entirely
contained on one chip. The problems of circuit packing density limit the
amount of hardware which can be packaged into a single IC, hence the
earlier microprocessors had a very restricted instruction repertoire, few
registers and slow performance. Advances in technology now permit 32-bit
microprocessors to be fabricated which are at least as powerful as the CPUs
of many minicomputers. Thus the distinction between mini and micro is
tending to disappear.

   Whether a computer is classified as a mainframe, mini or micro it has an
architecture which in detail depends on a variety of factors — word length,
instruction repertoire, number and type of registers amongst others. Some
computers, for example, have multiply and divide instructions — others do
not – while many have a register called a stack pointer used for implementing
interrupt handler software calls and subroutines. Nevertheless the majority
of computers share a broadly similar CPU structure, as illustrated by our
generalised von Neumann machine. In order to discuss the use of logic
circuits in computers we look more closely at the black-box units in the CPU.
Fig 6.1 reproduces the CPU part of our von Neumann machine.

The CPU bus is simply a parallel group of wires along which data can be transferred, in either direction, between registers. The number of parallel wires is the same as the word length of the CPU (for example 8 or 16 bits). The important part of the bus is its connection with each register. This is achieved by means of a *bus buffer* (not shown in Fig. 6.1) placed between the bus and the register. The buffer is a bi-directional device with *tri-state outputs* for allowing several devices to be driven on to a common bus.

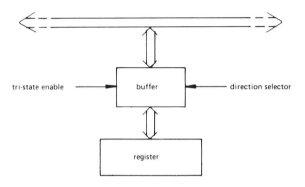

A similar uni-directional device, the 8T95 driver, was described in Section 4.3. Bus buffers, otherwise called *transceivers*, are available as octal IC packages. An example is the 74245 (or its low-power Schottky equivalent, the 74LS245) illustrated below:

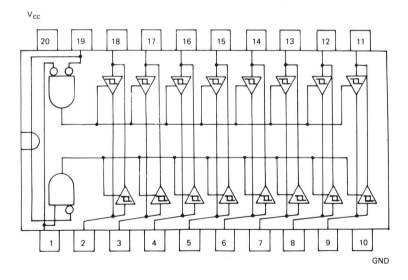

The eight non-inverting buffers for each direction have a common tri-state enable line (active-LO). A direction selector line chooses the direction of data transfer. Note that the tri-state property is used only in the direction of

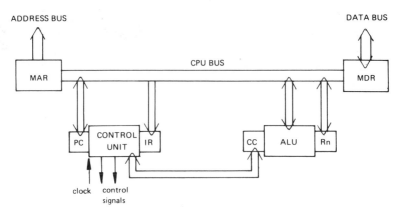

Fig. 6.1 — Outline CPU structure.

transfer to the bus. It is not required for connection between the buffer and the (single) register. This chip would be used also for the external data bus to the memory and input/output units. An octal bus driver, the 74244, is available for use in driving the external address bus from the MAR register.

The control unit is responsible for sequencing all the actions within the CPU, deriving its basic timing from a system clock which is usually a crystal oscillator circuit external to the CPU. As described in Chapter 1, a computer fetches machine-code instructions stored in memory, decodes and obeys them one by one. These actions correspond to micro-instructions which are mostly *register transfers* — the transfer of data from one register to another across the CPU bus. The order in which machine-code instructions are obeyed is determined by the program itself. Unless the present instruction is a JUMP or conditional BRANCH the next instruction to be obeyed is the one stored immediately after the present one in memory. Each micro-instruction is initiated by control signals issued by the control unit. In particular, register transfers are controlled by the opening of a path between a source register and a destination; this is achieved by enabling the (tri-state) output of the source register and then pulsing the clock inputs of the flip-flops in the destination register to cause data to be transferred across the bus.

In the next section the detailed operation of the control unit will be demonstrated by a simple example. The design of the control unit is one of the most important activities in computer design. Two approaches are used — the hard-wired and the microprogramming methods — and these merit further description in the last section of the chapter. The remainder of the present section deals with the other two main units in the CPU — the ALU and the registers.

Register structure
Basically a register consists of a number of flip-flops each capable of storing a single bit of information. The number of flip-flops depends on the size of register required, but typically would be 8 or 16. Edge-triggered D-type or

master–slave J–K flip-flops may be used — the former triggering on the leading edge of the clock pulse, the J–K effectively on the trailing edge. Registers are available in IC form, a package typically containing 4 to 8 flip-flops. Some of these registers are already provided with tri-state outputs and can therefore be connected directly onto a bus without the need for a bus buffer.

The transfer of data between registers can be either *serial* (one bit at a time) or *parallel* (all bits together) as illustrated below:

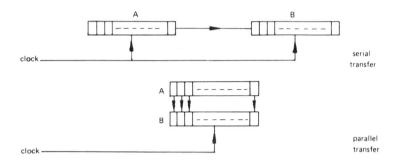

In serial transmission, data is shifted one bit at a time in one direction in both the source (A) and destination (B) register. Thus each register must be internally organised as a *shift register* in which the output of each flip-flop is connected to the input of its neighbour. Computers usually provide machine-code instructions to shift data in general-purpose registers right or left, either transferring the data into another register or shifting it simply within a single register, in which case data bits are lost from one end. *Rotate* instructions move data round from one end of a register to the other and require an end-to-end connection as illustrated:

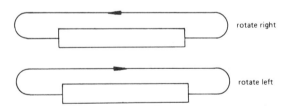

In a shift transfer, each source and destination flip-flop is connected to a common clock source. An n-bit shift operation requires n pulses of the clock. However, only one wire need link the two registers in the transfer.

In contrast a parallel data transfer requires one wire for each register bit. Only the flip-flops in the source register need to be connected to the clock source since the flip-flops in the source register are not themselves receiving new data. The transfer can be accomplished with one pulse of the clock.

A section of a general-purpose register based on J–K flip-flops is shown in Fig. 6.2.

This shows the logic required for bit i of the register, an effective

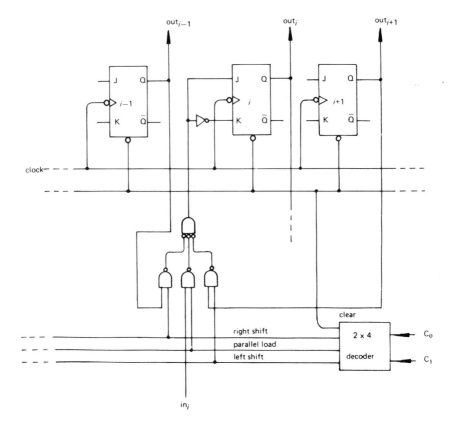

Fig. 6.2 — Section of general-purpose register.

AND–OR network (shown using NAND gates) with inputs from the Q output of flip-flops $i-1$ and $i+1$, and an input labelled in_i to which can be connected the i-th output of any other flip-flop; each bit of the register requires an identical AND-OR network. The outputs of all the flip-flops are available in parallel for transfer to another register. Common to the whole register is a *2×4 decoder* by means of which the required register function can be selected, using the four combinations of inputs C_0 and C_1. Four functions are provided: left shift, right shift, parallel load and clear. A decoder is a de-multiplexer (a MUX in reverse) without an input data line — the selected output line has a 1 on it, the other three are set at zero. Alternatively the decoder can be considered as a de-MUX with an input line set permanently at 1.

Note that the decoder outputs act as *enable* inputs to the 2-input NAND gates, allowing the data on the other input through to the 3-input NAND gate if the enable line is at 1, otherwise disabling the output of the 2-input gate. This is illustrated below:

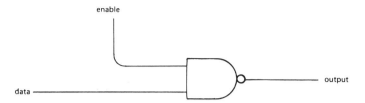

If enable is set to 1, input data is transferred (inverted) to the output; if enable is 0 the output is permanently set at 1 (disabled).

The arithmetic and logic unit (ALU)

Machine-code instructions specify operations to be carried out on data contained in the general-purpose registers of the computer, and in some cases on data held in memory. These operations are of two kinds: arithmetic and logical.

The arithmetic operations are of course addition, subtraction, multiplication and division. Many microprocessors and some minicomputers do not provide multiplication and division, while mainframes have special-purpose logic circuits to provide these functions. In machines without hardware multiply and divide, these functions must be provided by software routines which basically perform a repetitive series of additions or subtractions. The more advanced hardware units feature *floating-point* multiplication and division in which operands and result are represented in a scientific notation with mantissa and exponent. This type of operation is not necessary for many text-handling or simple control applications so a more basic ALU is adequate.

In computers it is usual to represent numbers using the *2s complement* notation. In this system a number is stored in an n-bit register with the least significant $n-1$ bits representing the magnitude of the number and the most significant bit its sign — i.e. whether it is a positive or a negative number:

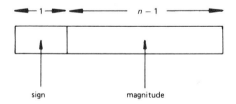

Positive numbers have a sign bit of value 0 and a magnitude in true binary form, for example (considering a 4-bit register for simplicity) the decimal number $+5$ is stored as follows:

0	1	0	1	+5

Negative numbers are derived from positive numbers in the following way:

each bit, including the sign bit, is inverted (complemented) then 1 is added to the least significant end. Thus -5 is represented as:

The magnitude is not in a true binary form for negative numbers. Note that the sign bit automatically becomes 1, indicating that the magnitude is a negative quantity. The advantage of storing numbers in this way is that arithmetic becomes very simple: all numbers are added together, and the signs and magnitudes look after themselves. Consider the operation:

5−3

Using 2s complement arithmetic this is effectively

5+(−3)

where (-3) is the 2s complement negative representation of 3:

The arithmetic operation 5−3 is then an addition process:

giving the result:

which is what we would expect. Notice that positive 2s complement numbers can be derived from their negatives by exactly the same process used in coverting positive forms to negative: invert all the bits and add 1.

The basis for all four arithmetic operations is the binary full-adder (described in Chapter 3). Using 2s complement numbers subtraction is effectively achieved by the addition process. Multiplication is basically a series of repeated additions (and shifts) as illustrated in Fig. 6.3.

The two operands are contained in registers labelled *multiplicand* and *multiplier*. These are to be multiplied together to give a result in the *accumulator* register which is initially cleared to zero. Binary multiplication is basically very simple: if the least significant bit of the multiplier is 1, the multiplicand is added into the accumulator; if it is 0, no addition is performed. Then the multiplier is shifted one place to the right, and the

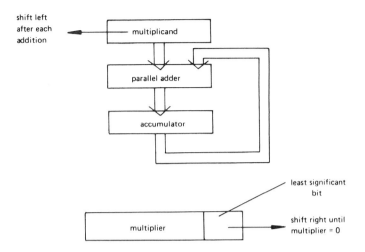

Fig. 6.3 — Illustration of multiplication by repeated additions.

multiplicand one place to the left. If the contents of the multiplier register is now zero the multiplication is complete. Otherwise the process is repeated; the least significant multiplier bit is checked for 1 or 0, and the next addition, if any, performed. This method assumes that the operands have both been converted to a positive form. The sign of the result can be obtained by checking the original signs of the two operands. A slow hardware multiplication unit can be based on the binary adder using the above method. Division can be provided similarly by an iterative method consisting of subtractions and shifts, but the (2s complement) subtractions performed by a binary adder.

Logical operations in computers are required to manipulate the bits held in registers (or in memory). They include shift operations (left, right, rotate) whereby data is moved within a register; NOT, in which all bits of an operand are inverted; and AND, OR, NOT between pairs of registers, the appropriate logical operation being performed between corresponding bits in the two registers. Logical operations, too, can be based on a binary adder, as we shall now see.

Detailed structure of an ALU
In Chapter 3 (Fig. 3.15) the circuit for a binary full-adder was derived. The adder takes two single-bit operands and a carry-in, and provides a sum bit and a carry-out. A simple ALU can be constructed from the basis of a binary full-adder circuit, one circuit for each bit in the word length of the computer. Fig. 6.4 shows a single-bit stage of such an ALU. The binary full-adder circuit is enclosed in dashed lines with the inputs and outputs of Fig. 3.15 in brackets.

The ALU circuit takes inputs A_i and B^i from bit i of the two operand

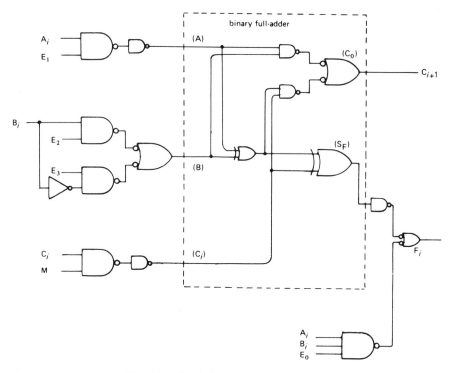

Fig. 6.4 — Single-bit stage of a simple ALU.

registers and a carry-in C_i from the previous (less significant) stage of the ALU. It produces a *function output* F_i and the carry-out C_{i+1} which goes to the next, more significant stage. The full-adder circuit has been extended with extra logic. The *mode control* M and *function selectors* E_0–E_3 are inputs which enable the circuit to produce a number of alternative functions of the operands. When the mode control input is at 1, arithmetic operations are provided at F_i by selecting combinations of the function selectors. The mode control input set to 0 gives a choice of logical functions instead. In the former case, the (2s complement) arithmetic operations add (ADD) and subtract (SUB) make use of the carry input and output bits. For all other operations carry is ignored (except for the least significant carry-in C_1).

Note that for subtraction the least significant carry-in bit (C_1) will be set to 1: together with the inversion of B using input E_3 this has the effect of forming the negative 2s complement of the B operand. Similarly an increment operation (INC) can be implemented by setting $C_1=1$ and selecting only one operand, A or B.

The following table gives some of the possible combinations of mode control and function selectors together with the type of function for each combination. In subtraction (SUB), bits are *borrowed* from rather than carried to successive stages in the operation.

| Mode | Function selectors | | | | Function |
M	E_0	E_1	E_2	E_3	
1	0	1	1	0	ADD A to B (with carry in and out) $(C_1 = 0)$
1	0	1	0	1	SUBtract B from A (with borrow in and out) $(C_1 = 1)$
1	0	1	0	0	INCrement A $(C_1 = 1)$
1	0	0	1	0	INCrement B $(C_1 = 1)$
0	0	1	1	0	EOR of A_i and B_i
0	1	0	0	0	AND of A_i and B_i
0	1	1	1	0	OR of A_i and B_i

The simple ALU in Fig. 6.4 is in turn the basis of an available 4-bit-wide ALU IC. Called the 74181, this chip has the functional appearance shown in Fig. 6.5. Many computers are 8 or 16 bits wide therefore in practice two or four 74181s would be employed in parallel, each dealing with 4 bits of the processor registers. The 74181 ALU is used in the popular PDP-11 range of minicomputers.

Most of the input and output connections in Fig. 6.5 are self-explana-

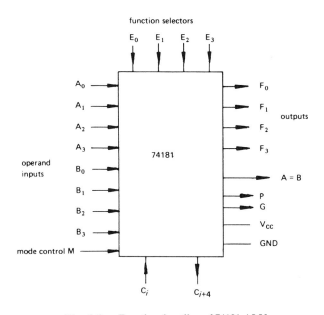

Fig. 6.5 — Functional outline of 74181 ALU.

tory. However, A=B is a *comparator* output giving 1 if each $A_i=B_i$ (otherwise giving 0). P, G, C_i and C_{i+4} are used for linking a 4-bit ALU to neighbouring ALUs (for example in a 16-bit computer) to improve the overall speed of arithmetic operations: they are called *carry look-ahead* connections.

Carry look-ahead

The use of a parallel binary adder in an ALU involves the generation of carry bits for each successive stage of the operation. In effect the addition is not truly a parallel operation because the correct carry-in bit is not available as soon for the more significant end as it is for the less significant end of the adder. At each stage of addition the carry output is produced by a 2-level circuit, indicated by gates 1, 2 and 3 in Fig. 6.6.

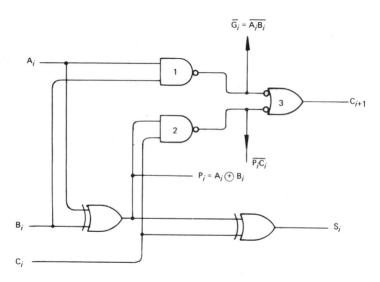

Fig. 6.6 — The *i*th stage of a parallel adder.

Assuming a 10 nanosecond delay per gate, the carry-out is produced for each stage after 20 nanoseconds, once the carry-in from the previous stage is available. For an adder with n stages, the most significant carry-in bit is available after $20\times(n-1)$ nanoseconds, which for a 16-bit addition gives 300 ns in total.

Addition times can be significantly improved by noting that the carry-out from the *i*th stage can be written as:

$$C_{i+1} = G_i + P_iC_i$$

where $G_i = A_iB_i$ and $P_i = A_i \oplus B_i$ as indicated in Fig. 6.6. The carry-out from the first stage is thus

$$C_2 = G_1 + P_1 C_1$$

and from the second

$$C_3 = G_2 + P_2 C_2$$

which can in turn be expressed as

$$C_3 = G_2 + P_2(G_1 + P_1 C_1)$$
$$= G_2 + P_2 G_1 + P_2 P_1 C_1$$

The third-stage carry output is

$$C_4 = G_3 + P_3 C_3$$
$$= G_3 + P_3(G_2 + P_2 G_1 + P_2 P_1 C_1)$$
$$= G_3 + P_3 G_2 + P_3 P_2 G_1 + P_3 P_2 P_1 C_1$$

Each successive carry-out can be expressed in terms of Ps, Gs and C_1 only, in a 2-level sum-of-products form. Each P_i and G_i depend only on A_i and B_i. Therefore every carry-out bit may be produced from values available at the start of the addition process, in a truly parallel operation. P_i and G_i are referred to as *propagate* and *generate* terms respectively. In general the carry-out from stage i can be expressed using propagate and generate terms:

$$C_{i+1} = (G_i + P_i G_{i-1} + P_i P_{i-1} G_{i-2} + \quad \dots \quad + P_i P_{i-1} \ \dots \ P_2 G_1)$$
$$+ P_i P_{i-1} \ \dots \ P_1 C_1$$

This expression becomes more complex the larger the value of i, the complexity being in the number and size of the product terms. In practice, *carry look-ahead* logic circuits based on the above general expression are available for 4-bit groups only. Carry look-ahead is provided in the 74181 ALU as indicated by the P, G, C_i and C_{i+4} connections in Fig. 6.5.

Addition times over groups of 74181s can be improved by the use of an external carry look-ahead generator. Such a generator is available as IC 74182, providing for connection of up to 4 74181s. Its functional appearance is shown in Fig. 6.7.

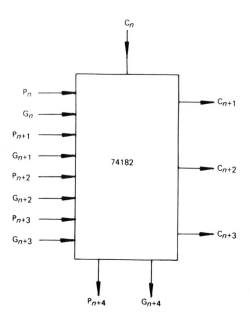

Fig. 6.7 — Functional outline of 74182 carry look-ahead generator.

The use of an external carry generator is illustrated as follows for a 16-bit ALU:

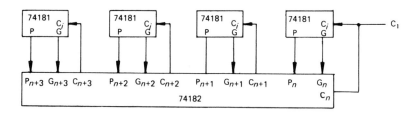

The C_{i+4} output from each 74181 and the P_{n+4}, G_{n+4} outputs from the 74182 are not used in this configuration.

A look-ahead generator typically adds 10 ns to the basic carry-production time of a single stage, but this time is the same for all 4 bits of a 74181. If four 74181s are connected without an external 74182 there are 3 carry production times of 30 ns each before the most significant ALU has the correct carry-in available. This gives a total delay of 90 ns, a significant improvement on the 300 ns of the bare 16-bit adder (without any carry look-ahead logic). With the arrangement shown above, a 74182 linking 4 74181 ALUs, the total time for a 16-bit addition is about 40 ns, a factor of around 8 times better than the bare adder.

6.2 CONTROL STRUCTURE

The fetching and obeying of machine-code instructions corresponds, as we have seen, to sequences of micro-operations within the CPU. The initiation of micro-operations, and their correct sequencing, is the responsibility of the control unit. It derives its basic timing from a clock source and controls the operations by means of a set of control signals. The design of the *control structure* (the control unit and its associated control lines) is of central importance to the architecture of a computer, since it determines the micro-operations which can be provided and consequently the set of machine-code instructions available for use by the programmer.

To give the flavour of a control structure we now consider a simple example based on the outline CPU shown in Fig. 6.1. A more detailed version of the CPU is illustrated in Fig. 6.8 with control signals added, including the ALU mode control M and function selector inputs E_0–E_3. The number of general-purpose registers Rn has been chosen as two: R0 and R1. These are shown with a 1-of-2 MUX connection into the ALU. The MUX goes into the B inputs of the ALU, while the bus is connected to the A inputs and F outputs.

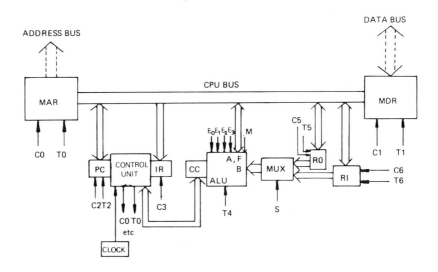

Fig. 6.8 — CPU showing control signals.

Selection of one of the two registers is determined by the value of the control input S: 0, 1 selects R0, R1 respectively. Apart from S, M, and E_0–E_3, all the C_i and T_i are outputs of the control unit (not all shown explicitly in the diagram). Each C_i is connected to the clock input of one of the registers in the ALU. When data is to be transferred into a register the appropriate C_i line is pulsed by the control unit. All transfers are in parallel mode.

The T_i are tri-state enable lines used to control the connection of registers onto the CPU bus. Since IR does not have to output to the bus it has no tri-state enable line. The ALU, being a combinational circuit, has no C_i (clock) line but is connected to the bus by means of a bus buffer which has input T_4 for allowing data to be transferred onto the bus. Although the registers (apart from CC and IR) and ALU have bi-directional communication with the CPU bus, and corresponding direction selection lines which are set/reset by the control unit, these control lines are not shown in the diagram. We shall assume also that each T_i is an active–HI line, in other words when T_i is 1 data can be output; if it is 0 the outputs are in the third (high-impedance) state and are effectively isolated from the bus. When data is to be transferred onto the bus the appropriate T_i is set to 1 (all others will be set at 0) by the control unit.

Thus in a register transfer operation, over the CPU bus, one T_i is set to 1 and one C_i is pulsed. This corresponds to setting up a path between the source and destination, as illustrated below for the transfer

PC $\rightarrow$ MAR

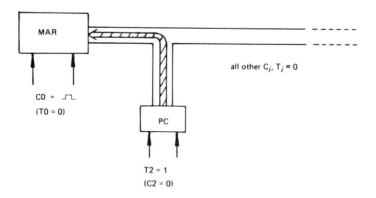

The relative timing of the signals is important. Source data (from PC) must be available on the bus when the destination register (MAR) is pulsed. This is possible as long as T_2 is set to 1 before or during the clock pulse applied to C_0: assuming J–K flip-flops are used to implement the registers, the trailing edge of the pulse must occur after the outputs of the PC register have propagated onto the bus and are available at the MAR inputs. T_2 must be maintained at 1 until after the trailing edge of the pulse. The control unit can sequence these actions in relation to a pulse derived from the clock source as follows:

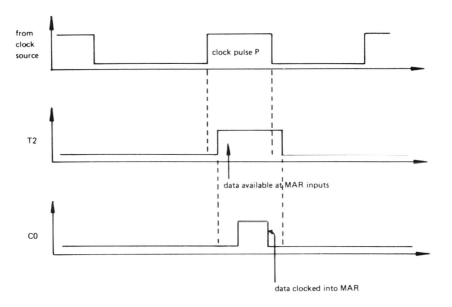

In response to the leading edge of clock pulse P, T_2 is set to 1. After a suitable propagation delay data is available at the MAR inputs. C_0 is pulsed so that the data is clocked into the MAR register, then T_2 is reset to 0.

Let us illustrate the detailed operation of each register transfer in a typical machine-code instruction. We use the example given in Chapter 1, using R0 specifically:

ADD R0, X

('add the contents of memory location X to register R0').

Fig. 6.9 indicates the control line settings appropriate to each register transfer. Control lines for the memory accesses are not shown (using the external address and data buses). 'Decode IR' is an operation internal to the control unit: we shall discuss this operation shortly. Don't care conditions are indicated with Xs, and the pulsing of a C input (while the corresponding T is at 1) by ⎍.

Note that the carry-in to the least significant bit of the ALU is not shown in Figs. 6.8 and 6.9. The operation

Phase	Micro-instruction	Control Signals																			
		C_0	T_0	C_1	T_1	C_2	T_2	C_3	T_3	C_4	T_4	C_5	T_5	C_6	T_6	S	M	E_0	E_1	E_2	E_3
fetch	PC → MAR	⊓	0	0	0	0	1	0	0	0	0	0	0	0	0	X	X	X	X	X	X
	(MAR) → MDR*	0	0	0	0	0	0	0	0	0	0	0	0	0	0	X	X	X	X	X	X
	MDR → IR	0	0	1	0	0	0	⊓	0	0	0	0	0	0	0	X	X	X	X	X	X
decode	decode IR†	0	0	0	0	0	0	0	0	0	0	0	0	0	0	X	X	X	X	X	X
obey	PC + 1 → PC	⊓	0	0	0	⊓	0	0	1	0	0	0	0	0	0	1	1	0	1	0	0
	PC → MAR	0	0	⊓	0	0	1	0	0	0	0	0	0	0	0	X	X	X	X	X	X
	(MAR) → MDR*	0	0	0	1	0	0	0	0	0	0	0	0	0	0	X	X	X	X	X	X
	MDR → MAR	0	0	0	0	0	0	0	0	1	0	0	0	0	0	X	X	X	X	X	X
	(MAR) → MDR*	0	0	0	1	0	0	0	0	0	0	⊓	0	0	0	X	X	X	X	X	X
	MDR + R0 → R0	0	0	0	0	0	0	0	0	1	1	⊓	0	0	0	0	1	0	1	1	1
next	PC + 1 → PC	0	0	0	0	⊓	1	0	1	0	0	0	0	0	0	1	1	0	1	0	0

Fig. 6.9 — Control signal settings for ADD R0, X.

*memory access operations.
†internal to control unit.

$$PC+1 \rightarrow PC$$

is implemented using an INCrement operation in the ALU for which the least significant carry-in would be set to 1.

Both operations

$$PC+1 \rightarrow PC$$

and $$MDR+R0 \rightarrow R0$$

show more than one T line enabled. Within these operations both T_i are not set to 1 at the same time but must be disjointed as shown below for $PC+1 \rightarrow PC$:

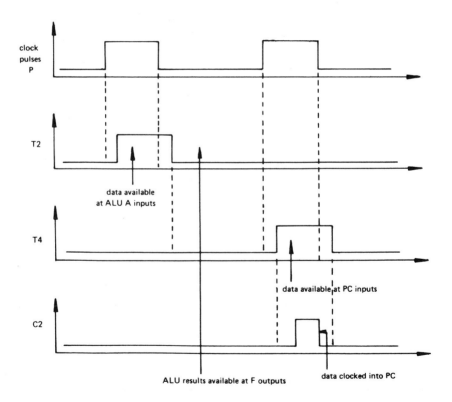

There are effectively two register transfers and this requires two clock pulses P for the operation. The first of the two clock pulses would also initiate the setting of ALU inputs M and E_0–E_3 for the INCrement operation. Similarly for MDR+R0→R0:

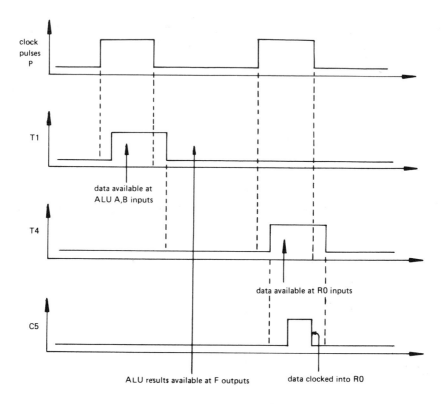

In this case the first clock pulse would initiate the setting of M, E_0–E_3 (for ADDition) and also S, the MUX selector input.

The above register transfers are part of a longer sequence of similar transfers. For a given machine-code instruction the control unit must be able to set/reset each T_i and pulse each C_i in the correct order. To do this it can use a *sequence counter* which has the functional appearance shown in Fig. 6.10(a). The idea of the sequence counter is that the stream of clock pulses is divided into *cycles*, each cycle consisting of a fixed number of clock pulses. The slowest machine-code operation — the one which requires the largest number of micro-operations — determines the cycle length. The sequence counter in the diagram has a cycle length of n and outputs P_1 to P_n which carry separate *phases* of the clock cycle as indicated in Fig. 6.10(b) for $n=8$. Each P_i will initiate the operations of a set of control lines for step i of a machine-code instruction. A sequence counter can be constructed either from a modulo-n counter and an n-output decoder, as shown in Fig. 6.10(c) for $n=8$, or from an n-bit ring counter which requires no decoding logic (but is expensive in flip-flops).

Each machine-code instruction has four basic steps in it, each step

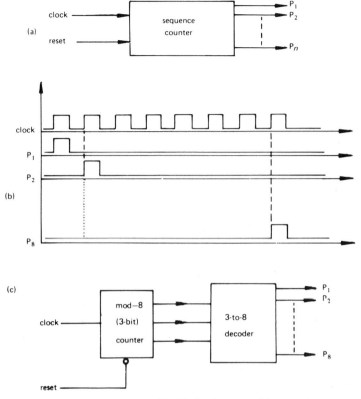

Fig. 6.10 — Sequence counter: (a) block diagram; (b) phased outputs; (c) construction.

consisting of one or more micro-instructions as we have seen: of the four steps for each instruction:

    (1) fetch

    (2) decode

    (3) obey

    (4) next

(1) and (2) are standard for all instructions but (3) and (4) depend on the instruction contents. Therefore the n phases of operation will differ (after (2)) for all instructions and so each P_i will not in general initiate the same set of control lines for one instruction as it does for another. The information which determines the control lines to be initiated by each P_i for a particular machine-code instruction comes from the *instruction decoder*. This is a combinational circuit which decodes the contents of the IR as shown below.

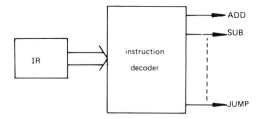

Only one of the outputs is active at any time and distinguishes the current instruction.

The control unit consists, thus far, of a sequence counter and instruction decoder, fed by a clock input and the contents of the instruction register. Its outputs, as we have seen, are the various control lines which allow micro-instructions to be implemented. To implement the entire control structure of the CPU we require further logic in the control unit which maps the instruction decoder outputs and sequence counter phasing signals onto the appropriate control line outputs: we shall call this the *micro-instruction encoder* since the control lines effectively determine the micro-instructions obeyed.

The encoder is basically a multi-input, multi-output combinational logic circuit. In practice a computer may require a few hundred control line outputs, of the order of a hundred machine-code instructions and about ten phases in the instruction cycle, making the design of the control structure a lengthy and expensive process. The general structure of a control unit is outlined in Fig. 6.11.

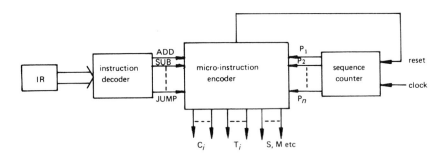

Fig. 6.11 — Outline of a complete control unit.

When a computer is being designed a number of choices will be made before the details of the control structure are tackled. Important dimensions — word length, address bus width, number of registers — would be amongst the first matters to be settled. Ultimately the computer is to support software so the set of machine-code instructions which it will provide is extremely important. These would be specified at an early part of the design process. Using the notation of *register transfers* each machine-code instruction can be expressed as a sequence of micro-instructions (as for the example ADD Rn, X) and thus the required control structure devised. Indeed the overall operation of the CPU can be written in a (pseudo) flow-chart form, specified down to the level of detail of each micro-instruction. A section of such a flow-chart is illustrated in Fig. 6.12 (using our simple example).

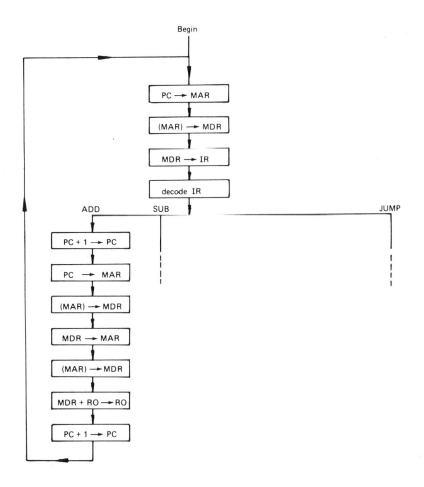

Fig. 6.12 — Micro-instruction flow-chart for overall computer operation.

Once the control signals have been specified and their values written down for each micro-instruction — in a truth-table form similar to that of Fig. 6.9 — the micro-instruction encoder logic can be designed. It could be implemented in discrete combinational logic, using SSI packages, or possibly using ROMs or PLAs. The implementation of the micro-instruction encoder using combinational logic fixes the machine-code instruction set in hardware and is usually referred to as the *hardwired* method of designing computers. A hardwired control unit does not easily allow the modification of machine-code instructions. An alternative method of implementation which allows the flexibility of changing the machine-code instruction set is that of *microprogramming*.

6.3 MICROPROGRAMMING

Microprogramming was first proposed by M. V. Wilkes in 1951 as a methodical way of designing computers. It uses a *control memory* for storing micro-instructions as a series of 1s and 0s. In the same way as a computer program consists of a sequence of machine-code instructions, each machine-code instruction is represented by a sequence of micro-instructions in a control memory called a *microprogram*.

Whereas in a hardwired control unit the setting and unsetting of control lines for each machine code instruction is fixed in a combinational logic circuit and is therefore difficult and expensive to alter, a machine-code instruction in a microprogrammed unit may be changed relatively easily and cheaply by amending a microprogram. Since control memory is implemented by a ROM the amending of a microprogram corresponds to replacing or re-programming a ROM chip.

Microprogramming offers a methodical approach to designing computers in the first instance, but also allows for the possibility that the machine-code instruction set is either not fully specified or has design errors in it when the hardware comes to be constructed. The designer or manufacturer can amend or add machine-code instructions later. Originally control memories were all read-only devices. Some modern computers offer a *writeable control memory* (often called a writeable control store or WCS) whereby the machine-code instruction set can be modified by the user. Such a control memory is termed *dynamically microprogrammable* since it can be altered by a program running on the CPU.

Each machine-code instruction is represented by a microprogram in control memory. When the IR for a particular instruction is decoded, this provides the starting address of the corresponding microprogram. Once a microprogram has started being obeyed the sequencing of micro-instructions is specified within the microprogram itself: each micro-instruction consists of a *control field* and an *address field*. The control field contains the settings of the required control signals. These are read into the *control memory data register* (CMDR) when a micro-instruction is accessed. Its address field bits provide inputs for the *control memory address register* (CMAR). Other inputs to the CMAR come from the IR, effectively locating the start address of the microprogram, while the micro-instruction address field gives the address (within the microprogram) of the next micro-instruction to be obeyed. An outline microprogrammed control unit is shown in Fig. 6.13.

The CMAR and CMDR can be considered to operate much as the MAR and MDR of a conventional memory. Included in the control memory (but not shown in the diagram) is address decoding logic to access the word

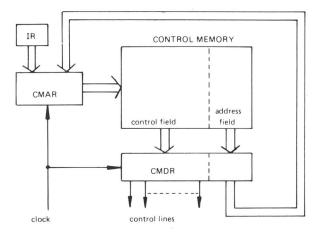

Fig. 6.13 — Outline of a microprogrammed control unit.

specified in the CMAR. Comparing this microprogrammed control unit with the (hardwired) unit of Fig. 6.11, we see that the control memory replaces the micro-instruction encoder logic (and its address decoder is equivalent to the instruction decoder). The sequence counter has disappeared. It is effectively replaced by the ability of the micro-programmed unit to obey a sequence of micro-instructions once a microprogram has been initiated: the microprogram itself does the sequencing. The clock source shown in Fig. 6.13 controls the rate of fetching micro-instructions from control memory. The diagram implies that all control line outputs from the CMDR become valid at the same time. In practice it is possible to reduce the number of micro-instructions required for any machine-code instruction by enabling sub-groups of the control lines at different times within one micro-instruction clock period. This can be achieved by providing several phased clock inputs — using a sequence counter technique — each input controlling a different segment of the CMDR and hence a sub-group of control lines.

Generally the phases within a micro-instruction period will correspond to the phases in which machine-code instructions themselves are fetched and obeyed. It is possible for the fetch and obey phases to be overlapped: the next instruction is fetched while the current one is being obeyed. This can save considerable amounts of time in running a microprogram. Overlapping instructions may necessitate the use of another register between control memory and the CMDR to hold the next instruction while the previous one is still being interpreted in the CMDR.

Branching
Fig. 6.13 does not show any provision for *conditional branching*, which is used in microprogramming in a way familiar to that in machine-code programming. Such branches will be conditional on the value of signals derived from external sources, such as the flip-flops in the CC register

associated with the ALU. In order to provide for this type of branching, the 'next address' generation scheme indicated in Fig. 6.13 must be modified. Just as for machine-code instructions it can be assumed that the next instruction is to be fetched from the next memory location unless the present instruction is either a conditional or an *unconditional* branch (an unconditional branch is equivalent to a JUMP instruction). For both types of branch instruction the next address must be specified; for conditional branches the external condition on which the branch depends must also be specified in the micro-instruction. For all other instructions the next address is generated simply by incrementing the CMAR contents. In the case of conditional branches, if the specified condition is not satisfied, the next address in the instruction is ignored and the CMAR incremented as for other instructions. Unconditional branches always cause the CMAR contents to be altered to the new address specified in the instruction.

The *micro-instruction format* thus has a more complex structure than simply a control field. It will more realistically contain the following fields:

control	mode	next address

where *mode* may for example be a 3-bit field with the possible values:

(0) 000 = no branch (increment CMAR for next address)

(1) 001 = unconditional branch (use specified next address)

(2) 010 = branch if external condition X1 = 1

(3) 011 = branch if external condition X2 = 1

.

.

.

.

(7) 011 = branch if external condition X6 = 1

For the 'no branch' case the next address field is effectively empty. In the 'branch if' cases the specified next address is used if $X_i=1$ otherwise the CMAR is incremented.

This scheme could be implemented by modifying the simple microprogrammed control unit (of Fig. 6.13) as indicated in Fig. 6.14.

The control memory now has three fields. The mode field provides control inputs for a 1-of-8 MUX which in turn initiates logic either to increment the CMAR or to load it with the next address field of the CMDR. MUX data inputs (0) and (1) are wired permanently to 0 (GND) and 1(HI) respectively, the other six to external flip-flops Xi. Either mode (0), or any of the modes (2) to (7) when $Xi=0$, causes the MUX output to be 0, thus the

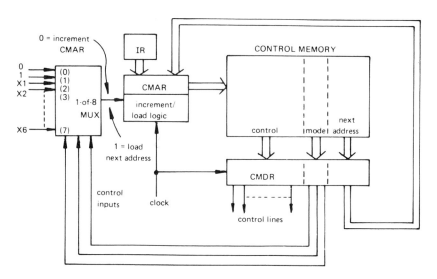

Fig. 6.14 — More detailed microprogrammed control unit.

CMAR is incremented. If the mode field is either (1), or (2) to (7) when $Xi=1$, the MUX output is 1 and then the next address field is loaded into the CMAR.

Horizontal and vertical micro-instructions

The arrangement of the micro-instruction format above implies that all possible control signals are specified in parallel in each micro-instruction. Such an organisation of control bits permits the highest possible degree of concurrency to be achieved: a number of simultaneous operations can be specified within one micro-instruction. This format is called a *horizontal* micro-instruction. It extracts the fastest possible speed of operation for a given architecture and requires no decoding of the control outputs. However, since in practice there are very many control lines — of the order of a hundred or more — the horizontal format leads to very long control memory words which can be impracticable to implement.

At the opposite extreme is a method of encoding control signals within the micro-instruction so that only certain combinations of control outputs can be specified at one time. This reduces the degree of parallelism which can be achieved by one micro-instruction, thus making necessary several micro-instructions to implement a required action using this method, compared to only one using the horizontal format. The width of the control field, and thus of the micro-instruction itself, can be minimised, giving a more manageable control memory word length. However, decoding circuits have to be used to convert the control field contents of the CMDR to suitable control signals. This type of format, the *vertical* micro-instruction, leads to slower speeds of operation because of the lack of parallelism and the need to decode control outputs. It may, on the other hand, be much more efficient in its use of control memory space because very often a relatively few control signal combinations require to be specified together and in such cases the horizontal format uses unnecessarily large amounts of memory.

In practice a scheme somewhere between the two extremes is normally used, and will be chosen to give a compromise between the parallelism (higher speed) of the horizontal format and the control field encoding (smaller control memory) of the vertical arrangement.

7

The hardware/software interface

7.1 INTERDEPENDENCE OF HARDWARE AND SOFTWARE

From the programming point of view, computer hardware is represented by a set of machine-code instructions. The structure of the underlying hardware is otherwise evident in the number and nature of user-programmable registers which are an integral part of the instruction set.

Indeed, it is much more common for the machine-code instruction level to be completely hidden: most programming languages are *high-level*, specifically aimed at removing machine-dependent features from the programmer's province, and most users of a computer see it at a higher level still — as indicated by the levels in Fig. 1.1. Programmers and users are mainly concerned with solving problems and using computers to help them in their everyday tasks, and the details of the machine architecture are of no concern to them. Nevertheless, hardware and software are closely interdependent: software and general user requirements dictate the hardware features, and implicitly the logical structure, of computers; on the other hand their technology and architecture have a very strong bearing on the form and efficiency of the software.

In terms of layers, hardware and software meet at the machine-code instruction level in a hardwired computer, but at the microprogramming level in the more flexible microprogrammed type of machine. Since machine-code instruction sets can be altered easily by microprogramming, it is possible to *emulate* the instruction set of different computers on a microprogrammed computer, effectively giving the programmer (at the machine-code level) a different machine to program. Emulation is not simply a matter of changing the machine-code instruction set but it also depends heavily on the compatibility or otherwise of the registers and the word lengths of the *host* (the machine undergoing the microprogram alterations) and the *target* (the computer being emulated). Emulation permits programs written for one computer to be run on another — perhaps with a loss of efficiency if the host and target are incompatible — and so allows the ideal of *software portability*. Users with a heavy investment in computer programs cannot afford to have to rewrite software on a large scale when upgrading or changing hardware, therefore it is highly desirable to be able to transport all the existing software from the old to the new computer. The availability of microprogrammed machines with an effectively flexible architecture is thus one way in which the structure of computer hardware is influenced by software requirements, in this case by the aim of portability.

Computers are, as we have seen, *multi-level* machines. At the lowest level is the hardware, consisting of the logic circuits in the CPU, memory and input/output units. Hardware and software meet at either the microprogramming or machine-code levels, which are intermediate in level between the hardware and the high-level programming language. Machine code is used for writing operating system software, at least the machine-dependent parts of it. Applications software, and the upper layers of the operating system, tend to be written in high-level languages. A multi-level machine is illustrated in Fig. 7.1, including the uppermost (user) level. Proceeding from

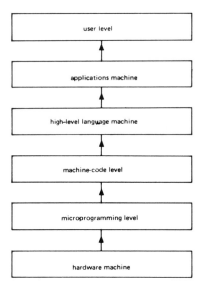

Fig. 7.1 — A multi-level machine.

the second lowest level upwards, each offers a different *virtual machine* interface to the next higher level: below the interface there appears to be a machine with characteristics different from the basic hardware. From the top, the user sees a set of task-oriented commands offered by the applications machine, which in turn has a view of a high-level language machine; supporting the high-level language interface is the underlying operating system, which is built on top of the machine-code instruction level. If the microprogramming level exists it forms a layer between the machine-code level and the basic hardware machine consisting of logic circuits and gates. Otherwise the machine-code level maps directly onto the hardware.

In practice the characteristics of any level may affect not only the next higher one but all those above. In particular the form of the computer architecture — consisting of the hardware machine and its microprogramming level — has an influence on the software and user levels, from the machine-code right up to the user level. The micro-instruction set and machine registers dictate the possible machine-code instructions, which in turn have an effect on the efficiency, or even the implementability, of high-level languages. It is the efficiency (in running time and required memory size) of programs written in high-level languages which determines the suitability of a computer for an application. Choice of computer to do a particular job usually depends on the total machine from the hardware to the high-level machine inclusive.

Conversely, the requirements of each of the software levels, from user down to machine-code, have an influence on the underlying computer architecture. Over the generations of computers, a variety of architectural features has emerged, all a result of higher-level demands. We shall explore some of these to illustrate the dependence of computer design on the software and user levels.

The influence of high-level languages on computer design is evident from a number of factors. The most often quoted of these if the use of the *stack*. In high-level languages arithmetic expressions consist of a series of operands and operators in infix form, for example the product of A and B is written as A * B, that is the multiplication operator is situated in between the two operands. Arbitrarily long expressions may usually be written in a high-level programming statement, and these must be evaluated as the program runs. To evaluate infix expressions the use of a stack is required.

A stack is essentially a last-in, first-out queue, as illustrated in Fig. 7.2.

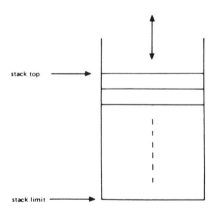

stack top

stack limit

Fig. 7.2 — Outline of a stack.

Items are added at the top of the stack and also removed from the top. The stack grows and diminishes as items are added and removed; it is fixed at one end, called the stack limit. A stack can easily be implemented in a computer memory by setting the stack limit at a fixed address, and allowing the stack to grow away from this address. A stack pointer register is usually implemented in hardware to contain the address of the current top of the stack. Machine-code instructions are provided which automatically adjust the value of the stack pointer when items are added or removed. Computers with such a stack architecture have been built specifically to help the efficient implementation of high-level programming languages.

Stacks are also commonly employed in computers to implement *subroutine* call and return statements. Subroutines are a feature at the machine-code level of the majority of modern computers, and allow the programming of a large task to be split up into a number of small program modules. Generally there would be a main program module and a number of subroutines, each called from the main program. When the subroutine call is obeyed, the value of the PC register, which will be pointing to the instruction after the call, is put onto the stack and the PC register loaded with the address of the subroutine. At the end of the subroutine will be a return instruction; when this is obeyed, it has the effect of removing the address which had been stored on the stack earlier in the process. The address is loaded into the PC, and the main program resumed. Subroutines within subroutines may be implemented since the use of the stack ensures that return addresses are stored in the correct order.

Another use of stacks is in connection with the *interrupt* mechanism which most computers possess. Although not stated in earlier chapters, usually the CPU is capable of being interrupted by external events, in order to implement *multi-programming*. It is extremely important that the resources of the CPU are used as efficiently as possible, and this can be attained by constantly ensuring that the highest priority program runs on the CPU. Originally multiprogramming was introduced to optimise the throughput of work by changing the running program when it requested an input/output operation. I/O generally takes a very long time compared to the time required to obey a machine-code instruction, so a program waiting for completion of I/O would waste CPU time unless replaced by another. Thus multiprogramming ensures full utilisation of processor time. When a program runs on a CPU its *context* consists of the values stored in the machine registers. Removing a program from the CPU involves temporary storage of the register values, which must be subsequently replaced in the registers when that program is reloaded. This storing and reloading may be effected by a succession of stack operations. In modern computers the completion of I/O operations is an external event which causes an interrupt to the processor, and an automatic stacking of the context of the running program. The interrupted program is replaced by an interrupt service routine which determines the cause of the interrupt, and deals with it appropriately. Generally this routine then calls the operating system *scheduler* which may either reload the interrupted program, or load another having higher priority. Other sources of interrupts include timer and fault events: a running program is interrupted if it has run for more than a maximum time-slot or if the computer hardware detects a possible fault condition.

Information is represented in high-level language programming in one of a number of forms: as integers, or real numbers, or characters, in simple cases. Other cases may include Booleans and arrays. The programmer distinguishes between objects not only by name, but also by *type*. Generally speaking operations on mixed types are not permitted. The main reason for having types in languages apart from improving their readability, is to ensure software *reliability*. A programmer is less likely to write incorrect programs where types are used, and likewise it is easy for the *compiler* (the program which translates high-level language into machine-code) to perform type-checks at translation time. However, the likelihood of errors is reduced further if a *tagged* architecture is used. This involves the labelling of each item of information with a tag to indicate its type: this tag is carried about with the value of the item. Thus at run time the hardware can also perform type-checks. Although a tagged architecture may seem a desirable feature, surprisingly few computers have been built in this way. Architectural advances, of which a few are introduced in the present chapter, are more fully discussed in Chapter 8.

High-level programming languages are intended to be *problem-oriented*, and ideally they should disguise the characteristics of the underlying hardware. One of the chief limitations of any computer is its addressing capability, that is the amount of memory which can be addressed by the CPU. The limit is set in the length of the MAR, as explained in Chapter 1. Limiting the amount of memory means that programs of only a certain maximum size can be stored. In a multi-programming machine many programs will concurrently share the main memory, and the amount of space each can occupy can be somewhat restricted. When a programmer writes in a high-level language, nothing should be known of the addressing limitations. Yet the problem exists: the computer must be able to cope with large and small programs alike, invisibly to the programmer. A scheme whereby the main memory and the (much larger) backing store — magnetic discs and tape — may appear to be combined into one substantial memory is implemented on many computers. It is called *virtual memory* (VM). The original idea of VM was developed at Manchester University when the Atlas computer was designed with a *1-level store*, in the early 1960s. It was a decade later when commercial machines incorporating VM became more common. The VM scheme is illustrated in Fig. 7.3.

Addresses generated by the programmer are said to be in *name* space (numerical addresses will be produced by the compiler). These are mapped (as shown in Fig. 7.3) automatically by the hardware into *memory* space, physically consisting of the more immediately accessible main memory and the slower backing store. Such a mapping mechanism is incorporated in the design of the computer. The usual form of implementation of VM is called *paging*, in which main memory, and backing store, are divided into a number of fixed size areas called pages. A program will consist of one or more pages, not all of which are necessarily in the main memory at the same time. The entire program may be scattered over regions of main memory and backing store. It is the VM management mechanism which keeps track

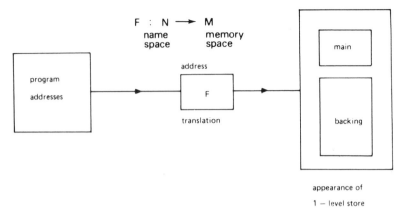

Fig. 7.3 — Outline of virtual memory scheme.

of all the pages belonging to the various programs. The address translation is normally implemented using an *associative memory* which contains a list of all the pages currently in main memory, and their corresponding physical addresses. Pages on backing stores are not represented in this associative memory. When an address is generated within a program at run-time part of the address, the page number, is presented to the associative memory. If the page is present, its physical page address is produced and summed with the word number from the original address. The final effective address is passed to the MAR register, and used to fetch the required word from main memory. This scheme is illustrated in Fig. 7.4.

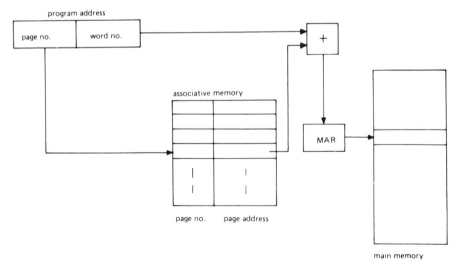

Fig. 7.4 — Operation of a paging system.

If the page number is not present in the associative memory a page fault interrupt is generated and a service routine arranges to fetch the required page from backing store. Obviously this scheme requires a more complex memory management system than the simple MAR, MDR arrangement previously illustrated (Chapter 1). Of central importance is the associative memory itself. This is otherwise called a *content-addressable* memory, which better summarises its operation. Operands are not accessed in the memory by their relative address from the start of the memory but by their contents. Access times using this system are very fast, although the cost of associative memory hardware is high enough to restrict its widespread adoption.

Use of a VM system can help improve the work throughput of a computer since, in the von Neumann machine, memory accesses can cause a bottleneck in its operation, and an automatic memory management system can be tuned to minimise the number of backing store accesses. The *working set model* attributed to P. J. Denning is a strategy used in conjunction with VM which aims to allow each program to keep a minimum number of pages in main memory at once, by monitoring and controlling the pages accessed in a given time interval. Only those pages accessed within this time interval are allowed to remain in memory, while the others are transferred to backing store. This avoids the possibility that too many programs, each with too few pages for their needs, will occupy the memory concurrently: such a state of affairs causes the problem of *thrashing* whereby almost all of the computer's time is spent transferring pages between main memory and backing store. The working set model, too, is a neglected architectural feature despite its apparent attractiveness.

Cache memories are also used to minimise accesses to main memory, and can speed up the operation of a computer typically two or three times. The cache device is situated between the CPU and the main memory, and is a smaller, faster-access memory intended to store the most frequently accessed items of information. A characteristic feature of program operation is that a small percentage of items tend to be accessed for a high percentage of the time. A cache only a few percent of the size of the main memory is capable of a *hit rate* of over 90%, in other words on average 90% of requests to the main memory are satisfied by information contained in the cache. Items found in the cache are (very rapidly) transferred to the CPU and the main memory undisturbed.

The general user requirements for higher speeds of operation also influence computer architecture. Apart from the use of ever-faster integrated circuit technologies, computers can be speeded up by a number of techniques including the cache memory just described. The use of *parallelism* and *pipelining* has been reported for some larger computers, although not in general for smaller, cheaper machines: these architectural features tend to be expensive in hardware. Parallelism effectively aims to use multiple processing elements instead of a single CPU, to take advantage of the inherent parallelism of many computational problems. A typical example of such a problem is matrix arithmetic, which occurs in many computer applications. The idea is that each of the processing elements is given a part of the problem to evaluate, all the operations carried out in parallel. Each processing element usually has its own memory. Fast processors based on this technique are available commercially for applications which require the speed and can justify the cost. Pipelining, on the other hand, attempts to take advantage of the fact that a machine-code instruction consists of several smaller steps (microinstructions) which can often be overlapped in time. In particular the next instruction can be fetched while the present instruction is being obeyed. Since memory fetches take a relatively long time, pipelining — which basically overlaps fetch and obey steps — can significantly improve the running speed of programs. Pipelining is commonly used in the larger mainframes. Parallelism and pipelining are more fully discussed in Chapter 8.

Less obviously, the use of *optimised instruction sets* can be beneficial to the speed of operation of a program. Just as in memory accessing a few items are accessed most of the time, so in practice a relatively few machine-code instructions are used a large percentage of the time. It makes sense to optimise the performance of these machine-code instructions at the expense of all the others: the microprogramming level can be arranged to meet this requirement. User-microprogrammable computers are particularly well suited to producing more efficient operation using this technique: for a particular application it can be found which instructions are most frequently used, and these can be appropriately re-microprogrammed.

7.2   LOOKING AHEAD

Despite the various architectural features described in the previous section, most computers still share the basic von Neumann structure introduced in Chapter 1. The requirements of higher speed and reliability, and the demands of programming languages, have not generally altered the way in which program instructions are fetched and obeyed. Nevertheless it might be appropriate to conclude this introduction to the subject of computer structure by speculating briefly on likely advances in design and construction in the immediate future.

One key point concerns the relationship of technology to computer architecture. Over the years since integrated circuits first appeared the number of components on a chip has increased very rapidly. At the same time speeds have increased and costs decreased. These advances in technology mean that more and more powerful CPUs and larger and larger memories can be fabricated at minimal cost on a single chip. Developments of this kind have significantly increased the number of application areas in which computers are used, most notably those in industrial and domestic control, and in entertainment. However, they have not of themselves brought advances in computer architecture.

On the other hand, LSI and VLSI technologies have had a notable impact on the logic design techniques of computer systems. Large-scale design is carried out as explained in Chapter 5: complex devices such as microprocessors may still be conceived in terms of gates and flip-flops, but are implemented by implanting layers on a silicon chip. The traditional minimisation aims no longer apply, but are replaced by other criteria such as component packing density, the size of silicon chips which can be made without flaws and by the requirements for encapsulating the product in an integrated circuit package. The application designer may now think in terms of much higher level building blocks, and in some cases the way they are connected to implement the application can be specified without resorting to traditional logic design techniques.

Advances in IC technology will initially continue at the same pace as before. In the foreseeable future the trends will continue: larger packing densities will be achieved, and the rate of increase of operating speeds may be maintained (although this rate will decrease as the limiting factor of the speed of light is realised), but the problem of chip reliability will inevitably grow.

Advances in computer architecture are beginning to be the result of the requirements of new forms of programming language. The present high-level languages, although independent of the features of a particular machine hardware, nevertheless reflect the conventional von Neumann computer structure. The next, and final, chapter describes advances and new directions in computer architecture.

8

New directions in computer architecture

8.1 INTRODUCTION

In this book we have been concerned with the theory and practice of computer logic. Boolean algebra, combinational and sequential logic circuits, and their design and implementation have been studied in some detail with respect to the von Neumann computer architecture.

Although almost all present-day computers are still von Neumann machines, there are developments towards new architectures which in the long run may provide a better vehicle for running users' applications. Much of the initiative in new computer architectures comes from the desire to provide users with programming languages better suited to their needs.

Higher-level building blocks including ALUs, registers and memory are being used in the emerging architectures, which are increasingly being designed directly into VLSI technology. The major difference in these new architectures is predominantly in the way control of the machine is exercised: the von Neumann type of control unit giving way to radically different control structures.

In this chapter we explore new directions in computer architecture, describing the main types of new feature and explaining how they came about. The structure of the chapter is as follows.

First we review the von Neumann characteristics and the incremental changes which have taken place in this fundamental architecture over the past few decades. In this way the shortcomings of the von Neumann machine are exposed. Next we explore approaches to improving the performance of computers, an important first step in explaining the divergence of designs from the traditional structure. This leads in turn to a description of the major new architectural directions.

Finally, a case study is presented of the Flagship project, a British endeavour combining the Manchester University dataflow machine, one of the newest class of non-von Neumann computers, and the ALICE language-driven architecture from Imperial College, London.

8.2 THE VON NEUMANN ARCHITECTURE (REVISITED)

In this section we review the characteristics of the von Neumann computer and its historical developments. Then we discuss the deficiencies of this architecture, and outline the motivations for improving upon it.

We begin by recalling that the von Neumann computer is a 'stored program' machine: the memory holds not just data for processing but also the instructions to do the processing. To obey a program the computer fetches and decodes each instruction in turn, the sequence of instructions being ordered by the program itself. Memory consists of a linear array of cells, each being numbered consecutively: this number is called the memory 'address'.

In addition, there is a low-level 'machine code' onto which users' programs, written in so-called 'high-level' languages, are mapped by means of a language compiler. This machine code directly reflects the machine's architecture.

8.2.1   A computer classification

The classical von Neumann computer contains a single computing element consisting of a processor, memory and input/output facilities. In the 1960s, when computer systems with more than one processor were being developed, the following classification of computers became accepted:

SISD   – single instruction, single data stream
SIMD   – single instruction, multiple data stream
MIMD   – multiple instruction, multiple data stream

The SISD corresponds to the conventional von Neumann machine, where a single instruction stream is operating on a single stream of data. The SIMD is essentially an array or parallel processor, where a number of processing elements are operating in parallel, using the same sequence of instructions, on different streams of data. A MIMD system is one in which there are different data streams being processed, but in this case by different sets of instructions: this class is otherwise known as a multiprocessor system.

Even though the SIMD and MIMD configurations contain several processors, these can individually be SISD machines, each processor with its own memory and input/output units. The main difference between these and a single SISD is that the individual SISDs are interconnected in some way, typically by a matrix switch or by a linear bus communications system. The SISD elements would typically, however, be von Neumann machines. This multiplicity of computing elements is an obvious step towards improving the performance of computer systems, but at large cost. It is perhaps not the most obvious way of obtaining higher speeds of computation: the advance of chip technology has meant a steady increase in processor clock frequencies and memory access times, and these have increased computing power with dramatic reductions in cost. In Section 8.3 we look further at performance improvement strategies.

8.2.2   Some developments

Many of the improvements of present-day machine architectures over the earliest EDSAC and EDVAC were developed during the 1950s. These included:

University of Manchester, England:
  index registers
  virtual store (Atlas computer)

Ferranti Ltd, England:
  general-purpose registers (Pegasus computer)

IBM, USA:
  indirect addressing (IBM 709)
  floating-point numbers (IBM 704)
  asynchronous input/output (IBM 709)

Univac, USA:
  program interrupts (Univac 1103).

During the 1960s multiprocessing became a common feature of computers, with batch-processing operating systems to handle the multiplicity of concurrent jobs. As time went on, multi-access computers were developed so that input and output could be by means of teletype (later VDU) terminals rather than by punched card and line printer. Several computer companies are attributed with the development of shared computers and suitable operating system software.

The 1970s saw the rise of the microprocessor CPU and the new chip technologies, including rapidly increasing semiconductor memory densities with very large access speed improvements. If anything, the microprocessor tended to halt the advance of machine architecture: ten years later, at the beginning of the 1980s, we had 16-bit microprocessor CPUs with the architecture and capabilities (at vastly reduced cost) of the board-level minicomputers of ten to fifteen years earlier. The 1970s can perhaps be remembered as the decade when the computer industry concentrated on squeezing the logic of a 16-bit minicomputer onto a single chip.

8.2.3 The semantic gap

In many ways the architecture of present-day computers is satisfactory. Their price/performance ratio is constantly becoming smaller, as it has been doing for the last decade: users are getting cheaper computing power to solve their problems. However, this user satisfaction derives almost entirely from advances in technology which have produced faster, smaller, cheaper building blocks. Disguised inside the new technology packages is the same basic von Neumann architecture: its limitations will surely be recognised as a problem once the price/performance ratio is no longer improving.

Despite the fact that computer users, and vendors to some extent, are happy enough for the present, the research community at least are aware of the severe shortcomings of the von Neumann architecture, and have begun to look ahead towards radically new designs. The main cause of these shortcomings is the *semantic gap*, the difference between the high-level programming language concepts and those inherent in the computer architecture. Alternatively the semantic gap can be seen as the divide between the programming environment and the representation of the programming concepts in the machine.

Consequences of the semantic gap include large and complex language compilers which produce programs which are generally larger than necessary, with consequent inefficiency when the resulting machine code runs on the target computer.

The obvious way of closing the gap is to program computers entirely in their machine language, but this is quite unsatisfactory if it involves lowering the level of the programming language concepts towards the machine (programming in von Neumann machine code in other words). On the other hand, raising the machine code concepts towards the problem-oriented high-level language is exactly what is required. A difficulty here is that not every type of problem could be satisfied by a common high-level machine language: even if this were possible, there would be those who would disagree with the choice of language.

An issue rather aside from that of the semantic gap is that of the nature of the high-level programming language. There is no doubt that 'conventional' programming languages were developed with the von Neumann architecture clearly in mind—Fortran, which appeared in the early 1950s, was the first successful high-level language and was strongly reminiscent of the machine code into it would be translated. High-level languages have never really broken away from this mould, apart from early ventures into Lisp (list processing language) and, somewhat more recently, significant work in artificial intelligence producing languages such as Prolog and Hope.

The relationship between language and architecture has therefore tended to be driven from the machine end, but perhaps it would be better if directions in computer architecture were driven by the programming language. This is indeed the way computer architecture researchers are moving now, as we shall see in Section 8.4. There is a precedent, however, dating back fifteen years or more: the language Algol influenced the Burroughs Corporation in particular to design and build their B5500 and other computers with stack-oriented features to enable Algol to run more efficiently on the processor (and to reduce the semantic gap for the compiler). Various experimental machines have also been built over the years, including ones influenced by Cobol, Lisp, Pascal, APL, and more recently (in Intel's iAPX 432 chip set) Ada.

8.3 IMPROVING THE PERFORMANCE OF VON NEUMANN MACHINES

How can we do our computing faster, more cheaply, more reliably than before?

Technology has largely taken care of the first two of these: VLSI and microprocessor technology have made huge strides in the past several years. Where reliability of a very high order is required, duplication (replication) of components is employed—triple modular redundancy (TMR) techniques for example—but in this case cost is not a primary factor. In general, goals are conflicting and one or more must usually be sacrificed to obtain the most important criteria for a particular application.

In addition to the increases in speed brought about by new technology, two main techniques have been developed to make conventional computers operate faster. These are the techniques of

> pipelining, and
> parallelism

8.3.1 Pipelining

Recall (see Section 8.2) that in a von Neumann computer each instruction is fetched from memory, decoded in the control unit, and obeyed before the program counter is adjusted to point to the next instruction held in memory.

When the present instruction execution is complete, the new value of the program counter is used to fetch the next instruction: the control unit and the rest of the CPU are idle until the next instruction is held in the instruction register ready to be decoded.

CPUs are very much faster than memory: machine instruction execution times are therefore dominated by the memory accesses required during the phases of the instruction. On average (typically) a machine code instruction takes three or four memory access times to complete:

> 1 for fetch of instruction
> 1 for fetch of operand/address
> 1 or 2 for further fetches and for storing results.

If, as soon as the previous instruction is complete, the instruction register already held the next instruction, the average instruction time would be reduced to two or three memory access times—a saving of between a quarter and a third of the time: programs would run 25–33% faster on average.

Pre-fetching the next instruction while the CPU obeys the current instruction is basically what pipelining is all about. In more general terms, the idea is to avoid unnecessary delays by always having instructions (and possibly also operands) available in the CPU. Pipelining is an attempt to overcome the limitations of the von Neumann architecture by improving on the narrow sequential pipe between CPU and memory: the so-called von Neumann bottleneck.

Pipelining was first introduced in the 1960s in very large computers, where instructions go through several sub-stages.

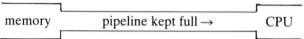

memory   pipeline kept full →   CPU

The main problem with pipelining is obvious: if the current instruction alters the nature of the program counter (a jump or branch instruction) then prefetching the adjacent instruction in memory serves no useful purpose.

Nevertheless, on the safe assumption that a large percentage of the time the program will be linear (no jumps or branches) then pipelining will achieve substantial run-time savings.

8.3.2 Parallelism

Also in the 1960s there was a strong interest in speeding up computations by providing several processing units. The problem in doing this is that parallelism in the program has to be evident.

There is a class of computing problems to which the technique is ideally suited: matrix manipulation problems found in physics, for example; meteorological problems; mathematical solutions of equations; in these problems the same set of instructions is applied to different sets of data in parallel.

Of course array processors are very expensive—but for the sorts of applications for which they were developed, cost was no barrier.

General computing problems lack such obvious parallelism as the class of problems listed above. Nevertheless, it is precisely this implicit parallelism which new programming languages hope to exploit.

For multi-user machines developed in the 1960s the problem was not to find parallelism in a single user's application but to run them on a sequential time-sliced basis: so-called multiprogramming. A natural, if expensive, extension of this is to run users' programs in parallel on several processors rather than multiprogramming them.

Interest in multiprocessors became very strong in the 1970s and many systems were built: these were (as array computers) expensive in hardware. Technical problems in building multiprocessor systems include the provision of shared memory between the processors using a common communications bus.

An alternative to this, developed more recently, is for each processor to possess only its own local memory but to pass information in the form of messages across a common communications network. Such a message passing strategy is seen in the Cosmic Cube designed by C. L. Seitz at the California Institute of Technology. The largest configuration currently in use is a 64-processor system which, it is claimed, can perform various scientific calculations up to ten times faster than middle-range popular minicomputers, at a reasonable cost. However, it is feasible to build systems consisting of more than a thousand processors. To illustrate the potential performance/price ratio: it should be possible to provide a tenth of the power of a large supercomputer at a hundredth of the cost.

Another example of a message passing architecture is the INMOS transputer, which is basically a simple but fast processing element having its own local memory and physical links to allow it to be connected to up to four other transputers. In other words it can be regarded as a building block for a variable configuration multiple processor system. A vitally important part of the transputer programme was the parallel development of its own high-level programming language called occam.

The name occam is derived from a Latin quotation written by William of Occam in the fourteenth century: it says that things should be kept simple. Occam is indeed a simple language, inspired by the work of C. A. R. Hoare on Communicating Sequential Processes (CSP). It is a process-based language and contains primitive constructions SEQ and PAR the first of which causes processes to be run sequentially, the second allowing processes to be run in parallel.

Communication between processes is achieved by the use of channels for input or output: these are simple to use within an occam program. The value of the combination of occam and the transputer is that they allow parallel programs to be written and run quickly and efficiently. They are a valuable contribution to the development of parallel computing.

8.4   IMPROVEMENTS IN ARCHITECTURE

Several architectural advances have been made over the years, including:

—Tagged storage
—Capabilities
—Associative memory
—Reduced instruction sets
—Reduction
—Dataflow

Each of these ideas has been slow to develop, and none has made an immediate impact on the computer industry. In the sections that follow each is introduced and briefly described.

8.4.1   Tagged storage

The idea of tagged (or typed) storage is to help close the semantic gap by labelling data with semantic information, most simply with the type of the data. This tag is stored with the data value in the data storage cell, and requires extra bits of storage per value.

Tagging complements the notion of strong typing in programming languages and enables illegal operations between cells of different type to be detected at run time. Furthermore it allows computer instruction sets to be designed using a minimum of generic operations, since the tag identity can tell the CPU which variety of operation is required at run time (thus for example only one generic ADD instruction need be provided—integer or real additions will be distinguished by the tag). This architectural feature will make for less complex compilers because they require to do less semantic analysis, and probably also less work at the code generation stage.

Tagging has not become a feature of commonly produced computers and remains, meantime, an experimental architectural advance.

8.4.2   Capability-based addressing

A *capability* is a means of limiting access to a computing resource. An authorised user will possess the appropriate capability to use the resource, whereas an unauthorised user will be denied access. Examples of resources are peripheral devices, sets of data, or particular programs. In hardware terms all resources will be represented by areas in the memory map of the computer, and all access to a specific resource can be controlled by giving or denying permission to the appropriate memory region.

The idea of a capability dates back to work published in 1966 by J. B. Dennis and E. C. van Horn on programming semantics; its employment in computer hardware began with R. S. Fabry's work on capability-based addressing reported in 1974. The aim is that programs and data should be compartmentalised into domains, access to which is controlled by the use of appropriate permissions. The initial idea was to close the semantic gap between the structures used by the programmer and those found within the hardware machine. In order to access a particular piece of program or data on behalf of a user, the CPU would have to own a capability for that resource. Every capability would be an unforgeable ticket of permission, issued by some central authority.

In hardware terms the capability is a base-limit register pair that also includes a bit pattern containing the permitted access rights (usually one or more of 'read', 'write', 'execute'). It is an indirect addressing scheme which imposes extra overheads on access to data. In other words, every time a program reads or writes a data item in memory it does so through a so-called capability register which gives (and checks) the appropriate permission to use the resource. Moreover, capability registers have to be loaded and reloaded as necessary to give access to the resources that the program needs as it progresses.

However, extra benefits result, particularly the limitation of failures to within the domain defined by the capability: thus we have a 'domain of protection' or a 'firewall' which traps the effect of hardware or software faults. It is this feature perhaps which has attracted the attention of computer designers, and a number of experimental and commercial machines have been built on the basis of capabilities, including:

> Plessey System 250 (1974)
> Cambridge CAP (1977)
> IBM System /38 (1978)
> IBM SWARD (1980)
> Intel iAPX 432 (1981)

The Plessey machine was built primarily for the telecommunications switching market which imposes extremely high reliability requirements on equipment. It was a multiprocessor system with an operating system designed to tolerate faults and recover from hardware or software failures at several levels of severity. Although it is no longer manufactured, it was the first commercially produced capability computer and was sold in several countries in the 1970s.

At Cambridge University much of the research work involving the experimental CAP computer was related to the design of operating systems and protection mechanisms as well as to the capability hardware itself.

The IBM SWARD (meaning 'SoftWAre oRienteD') was an experimental machine incorporating tagged storage as well as a capability mechanism. The idea was to explore the possibility of designing a computer from the software end as it were— to attempt to answer the growing need for the production of software more reliable and cheaply.

IBM's commercial capability machine, the System/38, has a single-level store. This attribute, seen also in the Plessey 250, merges the main and various backing storage models into one unified store presented to the programmer. It is rather like virtual memory but has the additional features of uniformity and also retention of run-time data values across the different underlying storage types.

More recently the Intel iAPX 432 has been produced as a microprocessor chip set (two chips implemented in VLSI logic) that embodies capabilities, but is also a so-called object-oriented machine. An object consists of a set of data together with the operations that can be applied to the object. It gives the high-level programmer an abstraction mechanism by which to represent objects in the problem or application space, and since the object is directly supported in the hardware this is clearly a way of closing down the semantic gap between application and computer.

In the same way as for SWARD, the principal design objective of the iAPX 432 was to reduce the cost and increase the reliability of the software production process. In fact the machine was designed with Ada strongly in mind as its system programming language. It is claimed that the iAPX 432 gives good encouragement for software design practices, that it indeed can simplify the software task by the easy provision of toolsets and debuggers, and that it allows the complexity of both operating system and compilers to be reduced. As in the other capability machines, the consequences of failures in hardware or software are limited by small protection domains.

8.4.3   Database processors

The use of associative (content-addressable) memory for fast lookup helps improve the speed of commercial applications involving databases. The key to this improvement is the parallel nature of the memory access: basically the contents of the cell to be located are presented to the memory and a pattern matching operation is carried out in parallel on all the cells involved in the search. Thus the location time for a single lookup is independent of the number of memory cells being searched.

Some special-purpose database processors including associative memory have been developed, for example the RAP (relational associative processor) developed at the University of Toronto, Canada. This is a so-called 'backend' processor intended to complement a traditional host by providing specialised database operations requested by the host.

8.4.4   RISC architectures

Reduced Instruction Set Computers (RISCs) have been developed in an attempt to produce faster program execution through the use of a carefully designed, simple machine instruction set. Much of the research and development has taken place at IBM Research, at the University of California at Berkeley, and at Stanford University. IBM's PC/RT, for example, is a commercial product of their research on RISC machines. A commercial

RISC called the ARM (Acorn RISC Machine) has also recently been produced by Acorn in the UK.

RISC developments involve a rethink of the architectural principles of the 1970s, which were firmly rooted in a belief in memory-to-memory and stack-based architectures, with microprogramming and caches universally used. Writeable control stores (WCSs) were provided as a user option (and still are) on many computers to facilitate the writing of user code at the microprogramming level where efficiency of programs was vital.

In trying to close the semantic gap these principles led to a performance gap which WCSs were intended to close up. Unfortunately WCS is difficult to use. Additionally, the architecture of computers was getting too complex for compiler writers to exploit efficiently, and was producing hardware which was too expensive for the resulting performance.

RISC designers aim to produce a good price/performance ratio by building a machine with a *reduced* set of instructions where each instruction is simple (operating in one machine cycle—*reduced* instructions). A key factor is to base the architecture on a register-to-register model of operation, keeping variable values in registers instead of in memory, thus avoiding the overhead of accessing memory frequently. Furthermore, only LOAD and STORE operations access memory (when necessary): arithmetic and logical operations are done on values held in registers.

A new set of architectural principles, for RISC machines, appears:

(1) keep machine operations simple
(2) simple instructions should be as fast as microinstructions
(3) simple decoding and pipelined operation are more important than program size
(4) compilers should try to simplify high-level instructions rather than generate sequences of complex machine code.

The common factors in the RISC machines at present built are:

(1) operations are register-to-register, with only LOAD and STORE accessing memory
(2) operations and addressing modes are reduced in number and complexity:
> register-to-register operations take 1 cycle times for floating-point operations use a co-processor;
> only 2 addressing modes are provided —indexed and PC-relative
(3) none uses microprogramming
(4) all are heavily pipelined
(5) the use of delayed branching avoids pipeline penalties or 'bubbles'.

These factors tend to produce a machine with a better performance/price ratio than conventional computers.

8.4.5   Reduction machines

A reduction machine is an example of a class of architecture called 'demand-driven'. The principle is that the need for the result of an operation causes that operation to be obeyed. This is totally different from the way that a von Neumann computer operates, and needs further explanation.

In a von Neumann machine a program consists of a sequence of machine-code instructions which are fetched and obeyed one after the other; this occurs in a linear fashion until a jump or branch instruction causes control to be transferred to another part of the instruction sequence.

In a reduction machine things are quite different: a program is organised not as a linear sequence of instructions but instead as a mathematical function which is defined in terms of more basic functions. Each more basic function is itself defined in terms of still more elementary functions: this recursive form of definition can continue to an arbitrary depth, until a so-called atom (i.e. a fixed value) is reached. A simple example of a recursive definition is one for factorial n, namely:

$$n! = n*(n\text{-}1)!$$

where $0! = 1$

In this case the depth of recursion is the value of n, and the atom has the value 1.

Obeying a program is equivalent to evaluating the highest-level mathematical function. This causes a recursive evaluation of the functions defined at successively lower levels.

The program in reduction machines, then, is represented in quite a different way. It takes the form of a nested expression, for example:

$$((a*b) + (c-d))$$

where each of $(a*b)$ and $(c-d)$ are evaluated first: their results are needed in order to produce values, say e and f respectively, to form:

$$(e+f)$$

If the result of $(e+f)$ is needed to give a value to a higher-level expression then it in turn is evaluated. Functions and arguments other than arithmetical ones can form expressions and will be reduced in the same way.

There is no notion of 'variable' in this approach: the result of an expression, once evaluated, has a label (for example e above) but this has a permanent value associated with it. This property, known as referential transparency, makes it more natural to program a reduction architecture in a declarative form of programming language (such as Prolog or Hope) rather than a conventional imperative language such as Ada. The development of suitable programming languages for advanced computer architectures is clearly important: ideally, research into both architecture and language should go hand in hand.

The principal design objective of reduction architectures is to take advantage of the inherent parallelism in programs. This is done by assigning pieces of work to processing elements in parallel whenever this is possible and thereby to speed up computations. Declarative programming languages offer more scope for expressing the natural parallelism in problem solutions than imperative languages and are therefore the primary vehicle in language-driven computer architecture research.

8.4.6 Dataflow architectures

The most promising new architectural approach is that of dataflow. This belongs to a class of computer architecture known as 'data-driven'. The design motivation for dataflow machines is the same as for reduction systems, that of exploiting to the full the natural concurrency in programs.

Whereas a reduction machine evaluates expressions only on demand, dataflow computers cause operations to be obeyed whenever all their operands are available: thus the availability or flow of data within a program is the means by which sequencing of operations is achieved.

Programs in this approach are represented by a two-dimensional directed graph structure which shows the instructions at the nodes, and the flow of data between instructions as directed arcs joining nodes together. An example is shown in Fig. 8.1 for the evaluation of

$$z = (x\text{-}3)*(x+y)$$

There are three instructions and therefore three corresponding nodes:

inst1: $x\text{-}3$ producing result p, say
inst2: $x+y$ producing q
inst3: $p*q$

In Fig. 8.1, the value of x (coming from a previous instruction) is given as 6,

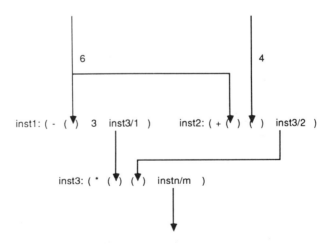

Fig. 8.1 — Dataflow instruction evaluation.

and the value of y as 4. Each data value passes along an arc from the instruction that produced the data to the instruction that will use it next. Only when all the input data values for an instruction are available can the instruction be obeyed. In the graph representation of a program, instructions that can potentially be obeyed in parallel are written side by side along a horizontal line. Those which must be obeyed sequentially are written vertically under each other.

Thus in the example, inst1 and inst2 can be evaluated at the same time, but inst3 only when the results of inst1 and inst2 have both been passed to it. Within each instruction node is the identity of the next instruction/parameter pair to which the result is to be passed. So in Fig. 8.1 inst1 identifies inst3 and parameter position 1 as the place to send its result. Finally the result of inst3 will be passed to instruction n at parameter position m.

A realistic application program will be very much larger than this simple example and may contain in its program graph many instructions which can potentially be obeyed in parallel. There must be several, or many, processing elements in a dataflow machine in order to take advantage of this potential for parallelism and so speed up the overall program execution time.

The pioneering dataflow work was done mainly by J. B. Dennis and others at MIT in the USA in the early 1970s, but developments since then have been made in France, Japan and Great Britain, notably at Manchester University by the work of J. R. Gurd and I. Watson.

In Fig. 8.2 a generalised structure of a dataflow machine is shown. There

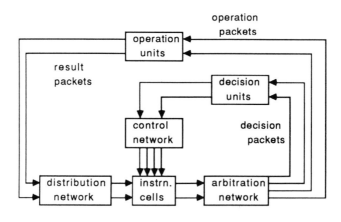

Fig. 8.2 — A dataflow machine structure.

is no CPU or memory in the sense of the von Neumann architecture. Instead a dataflow computer contains three main sections:

—the instruction cell memory
—the operation and decision units
—the arbitration, distribution and control networks

The instruction cell memory contains instructions like the ones in Fig. 8.1, consisting of an operation code (such as +), one or more input ports (shown as ( ) in the diagram) and the identity of the next instruction/parameter pair (such as inst3/2).

The operation and decision units section does the computations: operation units deal with instructions which produce data values, such as arithmetic operations, while the decision units look after instructions producing Boolean results.

When an instruction is enabled, that is all its operands are available, the distribution network packages it up and sends this *instruction packet* to an operation or decision unit as appropriate. The distribution and control networks respectively take data or Boolean *result packets* and send them to the specified instruction cell.

Dataflow computer programming languages can be at either high, intermediate or low level. High level corresponds to the familiar programming language level, for example Pascal, except that dataflow versions tend to be *single assignment* languages which have the property that 'variables' are assigned only once in a program. This makes it easier for the compiler to generate parallel (or potentially parallel) machine code statements for running on the dataflow hardware.

Low level corresponds to the machine code level of the dataflow computer, while an intermediate level may additionally be provided in the same way as a macro-assembler is for conventional systems.

8.5 CASE STUDY

In Japan, Europe and the USA there are large research and development programmes to produce the so-called fifth-generation computer system. A key part of these programmes of work is the development of suitable hardware and software architectures to support the advanced applications envisaged.

In Great Britain 'Flagship' is the largest computer architecture project supported under the five-year Alvey programme. Managed by a consortium involving the industrial companies ICL and Plessey, Flagship derives much of its direction from the merging of the Manchester University dataflow work and that of the ALICE architecture originated by J. Darlington at Imperial College, London.

8.5.1   The Manchester dataflow project

The basic dataflow structure introduced in the previous section has been refined and developed by various research groups, including that of Gurd and Watson at Manchester University. They have built what is called a dynamic tagging machine, one which can support code recursion or concurrent activation of the same code copy: this helps towards one of the principal aims of the group, to produce a very high performance machine.

In this scheme, the result of an instruction is packaged up in a data *token* which also contains the address of the instruction to which the data is being directed (tokens correspond to the result packets previously described). The values 6 and 4 in Fig. 8.1, travelling along input arcs to instructions 2 and 1 respectively, would be carried in the data value fields of token packets.

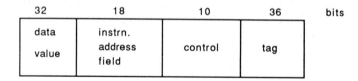

32	18	10	36	bits
data value	instrn. address field	control	tag	

Fig. 8.3 — Manchester data token format.

The format of a token in the Manchester schem is shown in Fig. 8.3. The tag (together with control) field holds context information about the particular activation of the instruction to which the token is directed: an instruction will be obeyed only when the tags in the input data tokens match exactly. Included in the tag are the iteration level, the activation name (which identifies different uses of the same code section), and the index (allowing different parts of an array to be processed by the same code concurrently).

In Fig. 8.4 the structure of the Manchester machine is outlined. It

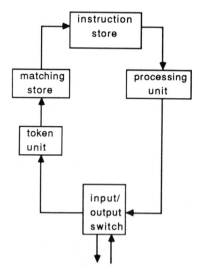

Fig. 8.4 — Manchester dataflow machine structure.

consists of five main units: the instruction and matching stores, the processing unit, the token queue and the input/output switch.

The input/output switch deals with the transfer of tokens and programs between the dataflow machine and an attached host computer: the dataflow machine can be connected to a conventional computer for test purposes.

Next in the ring configuration comes the token queue, which acts as temporary storage for tokens lying on the arcs of the active dataflow programs.

The matching store attempts to match pairs of tokens from the token queue that have the same tag and instruction address field (any token without a matching partner continues to wait in the token queue store). This associative matching is carried out in a random access memory (RAM) using special hardware hashing techniques, and is the most crucial part of the Manchester machine because it determines the maximum data rate round the ring.

Pairs of matched tokens next arrive at the instruction store, which contains the dataflow programs in the form of instruction cells. The store is addressed by the contents of the instruction address field in order to locate the instruction cell to be obeyed.

Executable instructions are generated and sent on to the processing unit. This contains up to 20 individual processing elements which can be processing instructions in parallel. Output tokens are produced and these travel round to the token queue and matching unit to enable further instructions in the active dataflow programs. Eventually output tokens will leave the ring via the input/output switch and arrive at the host.

One of the chief aims of dataflow machine design is to achieve a linear increase in machine power as hardware resources are added. In the case of the Manchester dataflow machine the ring shown in Fig. 8.4 is treated as a single building block and multiple ring configurations put together using a packet-switched network for inter-ring communications. Investigations have shown that a 16-ring system will produce a 14 times speed increase, quite close to the desired linear relationship between power and resources.

However, the hardware employed in this dataflow machine is very expensive, particularly the associative matching hardware. One of the main aims is to reduce this cost considerably and show that dataflow computers can become cost-effective in the future.

8.5.2   ALICE

The other University component of the flagship work is based on the ALICE project at Imperial College, London. In contrast to the Manchester work, this is a language-driven attempt to design a parallel computer architecture, starting from a declarative language. As we have already said in Section 8.4, declarative languages are better at expressing parallelism than the conventional imperative type and are therefore considered the best starting point. The prototype ALICE work is based on Hope, a functional language developed at Edinburgh University, but there is also interest within Flagship in logic languages such as Prolog, and in Lisp.

A program written in a declarative language consists of a set of statements (or declarations) which are in the form of functional expressions. In order that a machine can obey the program and evaluate the functions with real arguments, the expressions are treated as *rewrite rules* which tell how to replace the argument parts of expressions successively until a final function value is obtained. This is similar to the process of reducing nested expressions (see Section 8.4 on reduction machines): ALICE is essentially a reduction machine.

The best way of representing the program is in a two-dimensional directed graph as for dataflow computers. In this form the natural parallelism of the program is evident. From the graph can be extracted sets of expressions for (potential) parallel rewriting in the form of 'packets'. Each packet contains information corresponding to a node of the graph and its output arcs, independently representing part of the program's graph structure.

Thus the ALICE machine is described as a packet-rewrite graph reduction machine. A prototype has been built, consisting of a set of processing elements (up to 18 at present) and a set of storage elements (up to 20 of these) interconnected by a network such that any processor can access any store. The processors are basically packet-rewrite units which access available packets in store. INMOS transputers at present form the basis of the processing elements.

8.5.3   Flagship

The Flagship hardware will reflect the experience of both the Manchester dataflow machine and the ALICE prototype. It will be built using semi-custom-integrated circuit technology with the intention of producing a very high performance machine. It is envisaged that custom VLSI parts will be the eventual commercial extension of the Flagship project.

Also part of the Flagship programme is the development of a standard intermediate language called DACTL (Declarative Alvey Compiler Target Language). Each high-level language to be used will have a first stage compiler to produce DACTL code. Each hardware variant will have its own second stage compiler to generate machine code from DACTL. If the goal of reducing the semantic gap is achieved, by closely matching hardware with programming language, then these compilers should be relatively simple to implement.

It remains to be seen, however, whether the declarative style of programming language is indeed the right one for the future generations of computer architecture.

Reading list

The following list gives recommendations for further reading on a chapter-by-chapter basis.

Chapter 1 — The structure of computers

1. Goldschlager, L. and Lister, A., *Computer science: a modern introduction*, Prentice-Hall, 1982.

   A good brief introduction to the subject of computer science, including both hardware and software aspects.

2. Brookshear, J. G., Computer science: an overview, Benjamin/Cummings, 1985.

   An alternative introduction to computer hardware and software.

3. Bowden, B. V. (Ed.), *Faster than thought*, Pitman, 1953; paperback edition, 1971.

   A series of papers published in the early days of computing, on the history, structure and applications of computers.

4. Randell, B. (Ed.), *The origins of digital computers: selected papers*, Springer Verlag, 1973.

   Traces the history of computers from before Babbage up to the first generation of stored-program electronic machines. The story is told by a set of carefully selected papers, each reporting significant steps in computer developments, and each prefaced by a commentary by the editor.

5. Burks, A. W., Goldstine, H. H. and von Neumann, J., *Preliminary discussion of the logical design of an electronic computing instrument*, U.S. Army Ordnance Report, 1946; reprinted in Bell, C. G. and Newell, A., *Computer structures: readings and examples*, McGraw-Hill, 1971.

   This two-part report describes the features of the so-called von Neumann machine, a description which still applies to today's computers.

6. Bardeen, J. and Brattain, W. H., The transistor, a semiconductor triode, *Phys. Rev.*, vol. 74, pp. 230–231, 1948.
>   Report of the development of the transistor.

7. Denning, P. J., Third generation computer systems, *A.C.M. Computing Surveys*, vol. 3, pp. 175–216, 1971.
>   Excellent review of computers of the third generation, describing both hardware and software developments of the previous two generations.

8. Langdon, G. G., *Logic design: a review of theory and practice*, Academic Press, 1974.
>   Useful historical review of developments in logic design applied to computers.

Chapter 2 — Logic building blocks

1. *Microelectronics, Scientific American*, September 1977; republished by W. H. Freeman, 1978.
>   An issue devoted to the structure and applications of microelectronic circuits — how integrated circuits, particularly microprocessors and memories, are fabricated and incorporated in computer systems.

2. Mazda, F. F., *Integrated circuits: technology and applications*, Cambridge University Press, 1978.
>   A short description of integrated circuit fabrication, logic families and the use of integrated circuits in practical applications.

3. Morris, R. L. and Miller, J. R. (Eds) *Designing with TTL integrated circuits*, McGraw-Hill, 1971.
>   Written by the staff of Texas Instruments, this book is particularly valuable for its description of the TTL family.

4. *IC Master*, United Technical Publications Inc.
>   A publication from the USA containing a full list of available integrated circuits, produced independently of any semiconductor manufacturer. The broad IC categories are digital, linear, interface, memory and microprocessor.

5. Boole, G., *An investigation of the laws of thought*, Macmillan 1854; reprinted by Dover, 1958.
>   Boole's work is the foundation of the modern techniques of logic design, although the form in which its results are expressed is unpalatable to the modern reader.

6. Huntington, E. V., Sets of independent postulates for the algebra of logic, *Trans. American Mathematical Society*, vol. 5, pp. 288–309, 1904.

> This paper re-express the basic rules of Boolean algebra in a more modern form.

7. Shannon, C. E., A symbolic analysis of relay and switching circuits, *Trans. AIEE*, vol. 57, pp. 713–723, 1938.

> In this paper Shannon shows how relay and switching circuits can be described consistently with the rules of Boolean algebra. The techniques presented are used in modern digital logic design.

Chapter 3 — Combinational and sequential logic

1. Hill, F. J. and Peterson, G. R., *Introduction to switching theory and logical design*, Wiley, 2nd edition, 1974.

> A well-established text on logic design. Gives a full account of the theory of design techniques.

2. Lewin, D., *Logical design of switching circuits*, Nelson, 2nd edition, 1974.

> Recommended for its sections on synchronous and asynchronous sequential circuit design, and on logic design using MSI components.

3. Mowle, F. J., *A systematic approach to digital logic design*, Addison-Wesley, 1976.

> Contains an excellent description of the theory of Boolean algebra, and has many useful logic design examples throughout the text.

4. Karnaugh, M., The map method for synthesis of combinational logic circuits, *Trans. AIEE*, vol. 72, pp. 593–599, 1953.

> Original description of the K-map method for representing (and synthesising) combinational circuits.

5. Quine, W. V., The problem of simplifying truth functions, *Am. Math. Mon.*, vol. 59, pp. 521–531, 1952.

> This paper presents the original ideas for the tabular method of minimisation of logic functions.

6. McCluskey, E., *Minimization of Boolean functions, Bell Syst. Tech. Journal*, vol. 35, pp. 1417–1444, 1956.

> Developing Quine's ideas, describes the tabular minimisation method now known as the Quine–McCluskey method.

7. Moore, E. F., *Gedanken experiments on sequential machines, Automation Studies (Ann. Math. Studies* No. 34), Princeton University Press, 1956.

> Describes a theoretical model of a sequential logic circuit which has proved extremely useful to designers.

8. Mealy, G. H., A method of synthesizing sequential circuits, *Bell Syst. Tech. Journal*, vol. 34, pp. 1045–1079, 1955.

> Describes an alternative model of a sequential logic circuit. The ideas in this paper and Moore's are frequently combined into the collective Moore/Mealy model.

9. Minsky, M., *Computation: finite and infinite machines*, Prentice-Hall, 1972.

> An excellent text on the theory of computation. Recommended for further reading on finite-state machines.

Chapter 4 — Logic circuits in practice

1. Zissos, D., *Problems and solutions in logic design*, Oxford University Press, 1976.

> An excellent collection of problems with worked solutions in both combinational and sequential logic.

2. Lewin, D., *Logical design of switching circuits*, Nelson, 2nd edition, 1974.

> Contains useful additional reading on circuit hazards.

3. Morris, R. L. and Miller, J. R. (Eds) *Designing with TTL integrated circuits*, McGraw-Hill, 1971.

> Contains a full explanation of the fanout capabilities of TTL circuits.

4. Tocci, R., *Digital systems: principles and applications*, Prentice-Hall, revised edition, 1980.

> Contains useful and well-illustrated sections on circuit problems in practice.

5. Peatman, J. B., *Microcomputer-based design*, McGraw-Hill, 1977.

> Despite the title, includes valuable sections of the practical uses of integrated circuits. The use of microprocessors (as universal logic elements) in control applications makes interesting, and relevant, reading.

6. Fletcher, W. I., *Engineering approach to digital design*, Prentice-Hall, 1980.

> Links theory to design, introducing modern design practice with the aim of producing realisable, reliable hardware.

7. McCluskey, E. J., *Logic design principles: with emphasis on testable semicustom circuits*, Prentice-Hall, 1986.

> A comprehensive account of good logic design practice with many examples.

8. Weste, N. and Esraghian, K., *Principles of CMOS VLSI Design*, Prentice-Hall, 1985.

> A thorough account including many practical circuits of the most important integrated circuit design process of the 1980s.

Chapter 5 — Very large-scale integrated circuits

1. Mead, C. and Conway, L., *Introduction to VLSI Systems*, Addison-Wesley, 1980.

> Since its publication, this book has come to be regarded by many as the 'bible' of VLSI system design. Concentrating on NMOS devices, some of the material is already dated (such is the pace of change in the subject) but it must still be regarded as essential reading.

2. Hicks, P. J. (Ed.), *Semi-custom IC design and VLSI*, Peter Peregrinus Ltd, on behalf of the Institution of Electrical Engineers, 1983.

> An excellent collection of chapters by many different authors providing a comprehensive account of all aspects of semi-custom system design from programmable logic devices to gate-arrays and standard cells.

3. Weste, N. and Eshraghian, K., *Principles of CMOS VLSI design*, Addison-Wesley, 1985).

> Destined to become to CMOS design what Mead and Conway is to NMOS. Essential reading for anyone considering full-custom CMOS design.

4. Mukherjee, A., *Introduction to NMOS & CMOS VLSI systems design*, Prentice-Hall, 1986.

> A useful account of designing with the two major MOS technologies giving readers the opportunity of comparing their uses in a single text.

5. Sze, S. M. (Ed.), *VLSI design processes*, McGraw-Hill, 1983.

> Comprising chapters from many different authors, the book provides a detailed account of the physics and manufacture of VLSI chips. Copious references are given with each chapter.

6. Russell, G., Kinniment, D. J., Chester, E. G. and McLauchlan, M. R., *CAD for VLSI*, Van Nostrand Reinhold (UK), 1985.

> An overview, in a single volume, of the use of computers in the different phases of the VLSI design process.

7. Read, J. W. (Ed.), *Gate arrays — design and applications,* Collins, 1985.

> This book covers all kinds of gate-array circuits including those with both analogue and digital elements on the same chip.

8. Bennetts, R. G., *Design of testable logic circuits,* Addison-Wesley, 1984.

> Emphasising the point that 'testability' should be part of the design process, this book suggests some of the ways in which this may be achieved.

9. Wilkins, B. R., *Testing digital circuits,* Van Nostrand Reinhold (UK), 1986.

> Whilst not specifically about VLSI devices, this book deals very clearly with the general problems of testing digital systems. It is intended primarily as an undergraduate text and is written in a tutorial style with many useful examples.

10. Kenyon, J. (Ed.), *Electronic Design Automation.* Electronic Design Automation Ltd.

> A monthly newspaper-style journal providing a very useful regular update of the state of the art in VLSI and associated fields.

Chapter 6 — von Neumann computer architecture

1. Hayes, J. P., *Computer architecture and organization,* McGraw-Hill, ISE, 1978.

> Contains an excellent description of computer design methodology. The uses of logic circuits are well illustrated. Recommended also for its full section on the overall organisation of computer systems.

2. Boulaye, G. G., *Microprogramming,* Macmillan, 1975.

> A good brief account of the principles and techniques of microprogramming.

3. Langdon, G. G., *Logic design: a review of theory and practice,* Academic Press, 1974.

> Gives historical account of the techniques of computer design. Of particular relevance is the discussion of the use of timing signals within computers.

4. Siewiorek, D. P., Bell, C. G. and Newell, A., *Computer structures: principles and examples,* McGraw-Hill, 1982.

> Contains a wealth of information about the detailed structure of various different computers. Shows the variety of computer architectures which have been devised.

5. Tanenbaum, A. S., *Structured computer organization*, Prentice-Hall, 2nd edition, 1984.
> The notion of levels within a computer system is strongly emphasised. The microprogramming level is particularly well described.

6. Wilkes, M. V., *The best way to design an automatic calculating machine, Rept. Manchester University Computer Inaugural Conf.*, pp. 16–18, 1951; reprinted in Swartzlander, E. E. (Ed.), *Computer design development: principal papers*, pp. 266–270, Hayden, 1976.
> The original paper on microprogramming.

Chapter 7 — The hardware/software interface

1. Donovan, J. J., *Systems programming*, McGraw-Hill, ISE, 1972.
> A fairly complete text on system software. Particularly recommended are the sections on machine language and assemblers. Relates software and computer architecture clearly, despite being based on a specific mainframe.

2. Lister, A. M., *Fundamentals of operating systems*, Macmillan, 3rd edition, 1984.
> The best available brief account of operating systems structure.

3. Brown, P. J., *Macro processors and techniques for portable software*, Wiley, 1974.
> A good introduction to macros and more specifically to their use in implementing virtual machine architectures.

4. Tanenbaum, A. S., *Structured computer organization*, Prentice-Hall, 2nd edition, 1984.
> The account of multi-level machines is strongly recommended.

5. Wilkes, M. V., *Time-sharing computer systems*, Macdonald & Jane's 3rd edition, 1975.
> The subjects of virtual memory and protection are briefly, and well, described.

6. Denning, P. J., Fault tolerant operating systems, *A.C.M. Computing Surveys*, vol. 8, pp. 359–389, 1976.
> A review paper which describes the implications for computer architecture of implementing fault-tolerant systems.

7. Anderson, T. and Randell, B. (Eds), *Computing systems reliability*, Cambridge University Press, 1978.
> A collection of papers covering all aspects of hardware and software reliability.

8. Meijer, A. and Peeters, P., *Computer network architectures*, Pitman, 1982.

> A highly recommended description of the architectures of computer networks, strongly based on the ISO's Open Systems Interconnection reference model of networks.

9. Tanenbaum, A. S., *Computer networks*, Prentice-Hall, 1981.

> An excellent textbook covering the technical issues in computer networks and protocols.

10. Myers, G. J., *Advances in computer architecture*, Wiley, 2nd edition, 1982.

> Highlights the need for new architectures which are more suitable for implementing software requirements.

11. Denning, P. J., Why not innovations in computer architecture?, *A.C.M. Computer Architecture News*, vol. 8, pp. 4–7, 1980.

> A short discussion of the reasons why conventional computer architectures predominate. Includes useful further references.

Chapter 8 — New directions in computer architecture

1. Myers, G. J., *Advances in Computer Architecture*, Wiley, 2nd edition, 1982.

> An excellent coverage of the problems inherent in the von Neumann architecture, and of the major architectural advances. Includes an extended case study of an experimental IBM machine called SWARD.

2. Siewiorek, D. P., Bell, C. G. and Newell, A., *Computer Structures: Principles and Examples*, McGraw-Hill, 1982.

> A massive collection of information on specific computer systems describing the main manufacturers' major projects over the decades of the computer industry, including the 'maxicomputers' built by CDC and Cray.

3. Flynn, M. J., Very high-speed computing systems, *Proc. IEEE*, vol. 1901–1909, 1966.

> The original categorisation of computers into SISD, SIMD and MIMD types: whether single or multiple instruction/data streams are supported.

4. Vegdahl, S. R., A survey of proposed architectures for the execution of functional languages, *IEEE Transactions on Computers* C-33, vol. 12, 1050–1071, 1984.

> Starting with the requirements of functional programming languages identifies the key design issues for functional machine architectures and describes some specific machines.

5. Special section on computer architecture, *Communications of the ACM*, January 1985.

This special issue contains papers which give good descriptive details of research activities in the important areas of dataflow, highly concurrent machines, and RISC architectures.

(a) Patterson, D. A. Reduced instruction set computers, *CACM* 28, vol. 1, 8–21, 1985.

(b) Seitz, C. L., The cosmic cube, *CACM* 28, vol. 1, 22–23, 1985.

(c) Gurd, J. R., Kirkham, C. C. and Watson, I., The Manchester prototype dataflow computer, *CACM* 28, vol. 1, 34–52, 1985.

6. Dettmer, R., Flagship: a fifth-generation machine, *IEE Electronics & Power*, March, 203–208, 1986.

An overview of the research directions of Flagship, a British Alvey project which combines the Manchester dataflow work and that of the Imperial College ALICE reduction machine.

7. Jeffery, T., The μPD7281 processor, *Byte*, November, 237–246, 1985.

Describes the development and characteristics of a NEC Electronics chip designed for high-speed image processing work: its architecture is based on pipelining and dataflow.

8. Treleaven, P. C., Brownbridge, D. R. and Hopkins, R. P., Data-driven and demand-driven computer architecture, *ACM Computing Surveys*, vol. 14, 1, 93–143, 1982.

An extensive survey article on dataflow (data-driven) and reduction (demand-driven) architectures, with a large number of useful references to previous work.

9. Backus, J., Can programming be liberated from the von Neumann style, *CACM*, vol. 21,8, 613–641, 1978.

A highly recommended paper on the fundamental question of the nature of programming languages.

10. Morris, D. and Ibbett, R. N., *The MU5 Computer System*, Macmillan, 1979.

A detailed and well organised description of the architecture of the experimental MU5 computer system built at Manchester University between 1968 and 1973. The reader will gain a valuable insight into the work of computer designers seeking to implement a new architecture.

Appendix 1: transistor–transistor logic data sheets

The following pages are reprinted, by kind permission of Texas Instruments Limited[†], from *The TTL data book for design engineers* (2nd edition). The material is representative of digital semiconductor product information and comprises:

(1) an index to selection guide information for SSI and MSI/LSI functions;

(2) five sample selection guide pages, two for SSI and three for MSI/LSI products;

(3) two pages from the TTL integrated circuits mechanical data section, the first giving general ordering information, the second showing specifications of a 14-pin plastic dual-in/line integrated circuit package;

(4) five sample data sheet pages showing the pin configurations and functions of a number of integrated circuits — these pages are each referenced in one of the selection guide pages in (2) above.

Texas Instruments Limited is a semiconductor *manufacturer*. Their products and literature, in common with those of other manufacturers, are available mainly through a number of appointed *distributors*, such as Quarndon Electronics (Semiconductors) Limited of Derby, or Celdis of Reading.

†Texas Instruments Limited,
 Northern European Semiconductor Division
 Manton Lane
 Bedford MK41 7PA
 England

FUNCTIONAL INDEX/SELECTION GUIDE

The following pages contain functional indexes and selection guides designed to simplify the choice of a particular function to fit a specific application. Essential characteristics of similar or like functions are grouped for comparative analysis, and the electrical specifications are referenced by page number. The following categories of functions are covered:

SSI FUNCTIONS
FUNCTIONAL INDEX/SELECTION GUIDE

POSITIVE-NAND GATES AND INVERTERS WITH TOTEM-POLE OUTPUTS
ELECTRICAL TABLES — PAGE 6-2

DESCRIPTION	TYPICAL PROPAGATION DELAY TIME	TYP POWER DISSIPATION PER GATE	DEVICE TYPE AND PACKAGE				PIN ASSIGNMENTS PAGE NO.
			−55°C to 125°C		0°C to 70°C		
HEX INVERTERS	3 ns	19 mW	SN54S04	J, W	SN74S04	J, N	5-7
	6 ns	22 mW	SN54H04	J, W	SN74H04	J, N	
	9.5 ns	2 mW	SN54LS04	J, W	SN74LS04	J, N	
	10 ns	10 mW	SN5404	J, W	SN7404	J, N	
	33 ns	1 mW	SN54L04	J, T	SN74L04	J, N	
QUADRUPLE 2-INPUT POSITIVE-NAND GATES	3 ns	19 mW	SN54S00	J, W	SN74S00	J, N	5-6
	6 ns	22 mW	SN54H00	J, W	SN74H00	J, N	
	9.5 ns	2 mW	SN54LS00	J, W	SN74LS00	J, N	
	10 ns	10 mW	SN5400	J, W	SN7400	J, N	
	33 ns	1 mW	SN54L00	J, T	SN74L00	J, N	
TRIPLE 3-INPUT POSITIVE-NAND GATES	3 ns	19 mW	SN54S10	J, W	SN74S10	J, N	
	6 ns	22 mW	SN54H10	J, W	SN74H10	J, N	
	9.5 ns	2 mW	SN54LS10	J, W	SN74LS10	J, N	
	10 ns	10 mW	SN5410	J, W	SN7410	J, N	
	33 ns	1 mW	SN54L10	J, T	SN74L10	J, N	
DUAL 4-INPUT POSITIVE-NAND GATES	3 ns	19 mW	SN54S20	J, W	SN74S20	J, N	5-10
	6 ns	22 mW	SN54H20	J, W	SN74H20	J, N	
	9.5 ns	2 mW	SN54LS20	J, W	SN74LS20	J, N	
	10 ns	10 mW	SN5420	J, W	SN7420	J, N	
	33 ns	1 mW	SN54L20	J, T	SN74L20	J, N	
8-INPUT POSITIVE-NAND GATES	3 ns	19 mW	SN54S30	J, W	SN74S30	J, N	5-12
	6 ns	22 mW	SN54H30	J, W	SN74H30	J, N	
	17 ns	2.4 mW	SN54LS30	J, W	SN74LS30	J, N	
	10 ns	10 mW	SN5430	J, W	SN7430	J, N	
	33 ns	1 mW	SN54L30	J, T	SN74L30	J, N	
13-INPUT POSITIVE-NAND GATES	3 ns	19 mW	SN54S133	J, W	SN74S133	J, N	5-38

POSITIVE-NAND GATES AND INVERTERS WITH OPEN-COLLECTOR OUTPUTS
ELECTRICAL TABLES — PAGE 6-4

DESCRIPTION	TYPICAL PROPAGATION DELAY TIME	TYP POWER DISSIPATION PER GATE	DEVICE TYPE AND PACKAGE				PIN ASSIGNMENTS PAGE NO.
			−55°C to 125°C		0°C to 70°C		
HEX INVERTERS	5 ns	17.5 mW	SN54S05	J, W	SN74S05	J, N	5-7
	8 ns	22 mW	SN54H05	J, W	SN74H05	J, N	
	16 ns	2 mW	SN54LS05	J, W	SN74LS05	J, N	
	24 ns	10 mW	SN5405	J, W	SN7405	J, N	
QUADRUPLE 2-INPUT POSITIVE-NAND GATES	5 ns	17.5 mW	SN54S03	J, W	SN74S03	J, N	5-7
	8 ns	22 mW	SN54H01	J, W	SN74H01	J, N	5-6
	16 ns	2 mW	SN54LS01	J, W	SN74LS01	J, N	5-6
	16 ns	2 mW	SN54LS03	J, W	SN74LS03	J, N	5-7
	22 ns	10 mW	SN5401	J, W	SN7401	J, N	5-6
	22 ns	10 mW	SN5403	J	SN7403	J, N	5-7
	46 ns	1 mW	SN54L01	T			5-6
	46 ns	1 mW	SN54L03	J	SN74L03	J, N	5-7
TRIPLE 3-INPUT POSITIVE-NAND GATES	16 ns	2 mW	SN54LS12	J, W	SN74LS12	J, N	5-9
	22 ns	10 mW	SN5412	J, W	SN7412	J, N	
DUAL 4-INPUT POSITIVE-NAND GATES	5 ns	17.5 mW	SN54S22	J, W	SN74S22	J, N	5-11
	8 ns	22 mW	SN54H22	J, W	SN74H22	J, N	
	16 ns	2 mW	SN54LS22	J, W	SN74LS22	J, N	
	22 ns	10 mW	SN5422	J, W	SN7422	J, N	

TEXAS INSTRUMENTS

SSI FUNCTIONS
FUNCTIONAL INDEX/SELECTION GUIDE

PULSE-TRIGGERED DUAL FLIP-FLOPS

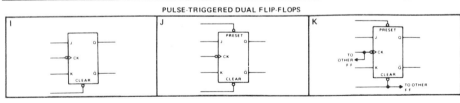

PULSE-TRIGGERED SINGLE FLIP-FLOPS

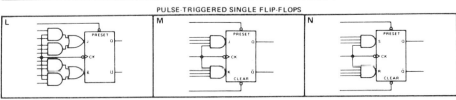

DWG. REF.	TYPICAL CHARACTERISTICS		DATA TIMES		DEVICE TYPE AND PACKAGE				PAGE REFERENCES	
	f_{max} (MHz)	Pwr/F·F (mW)	SETUP (ns)	HOLD (ns)	–55°C to 125°C		0°C to 70°C		PIN ASSIGNMENTS	ELECTRICAL
I	30	80	0†	0.	SN54H73	J, W	SN74H73	J, N	5-22	6-50
	20	50	0†	0.	SN5473	J, W	SN7473	J, N	5-22	6-46
	20.	50	0†	0.	SN54107	J	SN74107	J, N	5-32	6-46
	3	3.8	0†	0.	SN54L73	J, T	SN74L73	J, N	5-22	6-54
J	30	80	0†	0.	SN54H76	J, W	SN74H76	J, N	5-23	6-50
	20	50	0†	0.	SN5476	J, W	SN7476	J, N	5-23	6-46
K	30	80	0†	0.	SN54H78	J, W	SN74H78	J, N	5-24	6-50
	3	3.8	0†	0.	SN54L78	J, T	SN74L78	J, N	5-24	6-54
L	30	80	0†	0.	SN54H71	J, W	SN74H71	J, N	5-21	6-50
M	30	80	0†	0.	SN54H72	J, W	SN74H72	J, N	5-22	6-50
	20	50	0†	0.	SN5472	J, W	SN7472	J, N	5-22	6-46
	3	3.8	0†	0.	SN54L72	J, T	SN74L72	J, N	5-22	6-54
N	3	3.8	0†	0.	SN54L71	J, T	SN74L71	J, N	5-21	6-54

J-K FLIP-FLOPS WITH DATA LOCKOUT
DUAL   SINGLE   D-TYPE FLIP-FLOPS DUAL

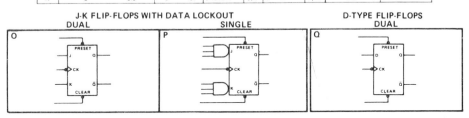

DWG. REF.	TYPICAL CHARACTERISTICS		DATA TIMES		DEVICE TYPE AND PACKAGE				PAGE REFERENCES	
	f_{max} (MHz)	Pwr/F·F (mW)	SETUP (ns)	HOLD (ns)	–55°C to 125°C		0°C to 70°C		PIN ASSIGNMENTS	ELECTRICAL
O	25	70	0†	30†	SN54111	J, W	SN74111	J, N	5-33	6-46
P	25	100	20†	5†	SN54110	J, W	SN74110	J, N	5-33	6-46
Q	110	75	3†	2†	SN54S74	J, W	SN74S74	J, N	5-22	6-58
	43	75	15†	5†	SN54H74	J, W	SN74H74	J, N	5-22	6-50
	33	10	25†	5†	SN54LS74A	J, W	SN74LS74A	J, N	5-22	6-56
	25	43	20†	5†	SN5474	J, W	SN7474	J, N	5-22	6-46
	3	4	50†	15†	SN54L74	J, T	SN74L74	J, N	5-22	6-54

†↓The arrow indicates the edge of the clock pulse used for reference: ↑ for the rising edge, ↓ for the falling edge.

TEXAS INSTRUMENTS

MSI/LSI FUNCTIONS
FUNCTIONAL INDEX/SELECTION GUIDE

ADDERS

DESCRIPTION	TYPICAL CARRY TIME	TYPICAL ADD TIME	TYP POWER DISSIPATION PER BIT	DEVICE TYPE AND PACKAGE				PAGE NO.
				−55°C to 125°C		0°C to 70°C		
SINGLE 1-BIT GATED FULL ADDERS	10.5 ns	52 ns	105 mW	SN5480	J, W	SN7480	J, N	7-41
SINGLE 2-BIT FULL ADDERS	14.5 ns	25 ns	87 mW	SN5482	J, W	SN7482	J, N	7-49
SINGLE 4-BIT FULL ADDERS	10 ns	15 ns	24 mW	SN54LS83A	J, W	SN74LS83A	J, N	7-53
	10 ns	15 ns	24 mW	SN54LS283	J, W	SN74LS283	J, N	7-415
	11 ns	7 ns	124 mW	SN54S283	J	SN74S283	J, N	7-415
	10 ns	16 ns	76 mW	SN5483A	J, W	SN7483A	J, N	7-53
	10 ns	16 ns	76 mW	SN54283	J, W	SN74283	J, N	7-415
DUAL 1-BIT CARRY-SAVE FULL ADDERS	11 ns	11 ns	110 mW	SN54H183	J, W	SN74H183	J, N	7-287
	15 ns	15 ns	23 mW	SN54LS183*	J, W	SN74LS183*	J, N	7-287

ACCUMULATORS, ARITHMETIC LOGIC UNITS, LOOK-AHEAD CARRY GENERATORS

DESCRIPTION	TYPICAL CARRY TIME	TYPICAL ADD TIME	TYP TOTAL POWER DISSIPATION	DEVICE TYPE AND PACKAGE				PAGE NO.
				−55°C to 125°C		0°C to 70°C		
4-BIT PARALLEL BINARY ACCUMULATORS	10 ns	20 ns	720 mW	SN54S281	J, W	SN74S281	J, N	7-410
4-BIT ARITHMETIC LOGIC UNITS/ FUNCTION GENERATORS	11 ns	20 ns	525 mW			SN74S381	N	7-484
	7 ns	11 ns	600 mW	SN54S181	J, W	SN74S181	J, N	7-271
	12.5 ns	24 ns	455 mW	SN54181	J, W	SN74181	J, N	7-271
	16 ns	24 ns	102 mW	SN54LS181	J, W	SN74LS181	J, N	7-271
LOOK-AHEAD CARRY GENERATORS	7 ns		260 mW	SN54S182	J, W	SN74S182	J, N	7-282
	13 ns		180 mW	SN54182	J, W	SN74182	J, N	

MULTIPLIERS

DESCRIPTION	DEVICE TYPE AND PACKAGE				PAGE NO.
	−55°C to 125°C		0°C to 70°C		
2-BIT-BY-4-BIT PARALLEL BINARY MULTIPLIERS	SN54LS261	J, W	SN74LS261	J, N	7-380
4-BIT-BY-4-BIT PARALLEL BINARY MULTIPLIERS	SN54284, SN54285	J, W	SN74284, SN74285	J, N	7-420
	SN54S274	J	SN74S274	J, N	7-391
7-BIT-SLICE WALLACE TREES	SN54LS275	J	SN74LS275	J, N	7-391
	SN54S275	J	SN74S275	J, N	
25-MHz 6-BIT-BINARY RATE MULTIPLIERS	SN5497	J, W	SN7497	J, N	7-102
25-MHz DECADE RATE MULTIPLIERS	SN54167	J, W	SN74167	J, N	7-222

COMPARATORS

DESCRIPTION	TYPICAL COMPARE TIME	TYP TOTAL POWER DISSIPATION	DEVICE TYPE AND PACKAGE				PAGE NO.
			−55°C to 125°C		0°C to 70°C		
4-BIT MAGNITUDE COMPARATORS	11.5 ns	365 mW	SN54S85	J, W	SN74S85	J, N	7-57
	21 ns	275 mW	SN5485	J, W	SN7485	J, N	
	23.5 ns	52 mW	SN54LS85	J, W	SN74LS85	J, N	
	82 ns	20 mW	SN54L85	J	SN74L85	J, N	

*New product in development as of October 1976.

TEXAS INSTRUMENTS

MSI/LSI FUNCTIONS
FUNCTIONAL INDEX/SELECTION GUIDE

DECODERS/DEMULTIPLEXERS

DESCRIPTION	TYPE OF OUTPUT	TYPICAL SELECT TIME	TYPICAL ENABLE TIME	TYP TOTAL POWER DISSIPATION	DEVICE TYPE AND PACKAGE −55°C to 125°C		DEVICE TYPE AND PACKAGE 0°C to 70°C		PAGE NO.
4-LINE-TO-16-LINE	Totem-Pole	23 ns	19 ns	170 mW	SN54154	J, W	SN74154	J, N	7-171
	Totem-Pole	46 ns	38 ns	85 mW	SN54L154	J	SN74L154	J, N	7-171
	Open-Collector	24 ns	19 ns	170 mW	SN54159	J, W	SN74159	J, N	7-188
4-LINE-TO-10-LINE, BCD-TO-DECIMAL	Totem-Pole	17 ns		35 mW	SN54LS42	J, W	SN54LS42	J, N	
	Totem-Pole	17 ns		140 mW	SN5442A	J, W	SN7442A	J, N	7-15
	Totem-Pole	34 ns		70 mW	SN54L42	J	SN74L42	J, N	
4-LINE-TO-10-LINE, EXCESS-3-TO-DECIMAL	Totem-Pole	17 ns		140 mW	SN5443A	J, W	SN7443A	J, N	7-15
	Totem-Pole	34 ns		70 mW	SN54L43	J	SN74L43	J, N	
4-LINE-TO-10-LINE EXCESS-3-GRAY-TO-DECIMAL	Totem-Pole	17 ns		140 mW	SN5444A	J, W	SN7444A	J, N	7-15
	Totem-Pole	34 ns		70 mW	SN54L44	J	SN74L44	J, N	
3-LINE-TO-8-LINE	Totem-Pole	8 ns	7 ns	245 mW	SN54S138	J, W	SN74S138	J, N	7-134
	Totem-Pole	22 ns	21 ns	31 mW	SN54LS138	J, W	SN74LS138	J, N	7-134
DUAL 2-LINE-TO-4-LINE	Totem-Pole	7.5 ns	6 ns	300 mW	SN54S139	J, W	SN74S139	J, N	7-134
	Totem-Pole	22 ns	19 ns	34 mW	SN54LS139	J, W	SN74LS139	J, N	7-134
	Totem-Pole	18 ns	15 ns	30 mW	SN54LS155	J, W	SN74LS155	J, N	7-175
	Totem-Pole	21 ns	16 ns	125 mW	SN54155	J, W	SN74155	J, N	7-175
	Open-Collector	23 ns	18 ns	125 mW	SN54156	J, W	SN74156	J, N	7-175
	Open-Collector	33 ns	26 ns	31 mW	SN54LS156	J, W	SN74LS156	J, N	7-175

OPEN-COLLECTOR DISPLAY DECODERS/DRIVERS WITH COUNTERS/LATCHES

DESCRIPTION	OUTPUT SINK CURRENT	OFF-STATE OUTPUT VOLTAGE	TYP TOTAL POWER DISSIPATION	BLANKING	DEVICE TYPE AND PACKAGE −55°C to 125°C		DEVICE TYPE AND PACKAGE 0°C to 70°C		PAGE NO.
BCD COUNTER/ 4-BIT LATCH/ BCD-TO-DECIMAL DECODER/DRIVER	7 mA	55 V	340 mW				SN74142	J, N	7-140
BCD COUNTER/ 4-BIT LATCH/ BCD-TO-SEVEN-SEGMENT DECODER/ LED DRIVER	Constant Current 15 mA	7 V	280 mW	Ripple	SN54143	J, W	SN74143	J, N	7-143
BCD COUNTER/ 4-BIT LATCH/ BCD-TO-SEVEN-SEGMENT DECODER/ LAMP DRIVER	20 mA	15 V	280 mW	Ripple	SN54144	J, W			7-143
	25 mA	15 V	280 mW	Ripple			SN74144	J, N	

RESULTANT DISPLAYS USING '143, '144

0   1   2   3   4   5   6   7   8   9

TEXAS INSTRUMENTS

MSI/LSI FUNCTIONS
FUNCTIONAL INDEX/SELECTION GUIDE

PROGRAMMABLE READ-ONLY MEMORIES (PROM'S)[†]

DESCRIPTION	ORGANI-ZATION	TYPE OF OUTPUT	TYPICAL ADDRESS TIME	TYPICAL ENABLE TIME	TYP POWER DISSIPATION PER BIT	DEVICE TYPE AND PACKAGE		
						−55°C to 125°C		0°C to 70°C
4096-BIT ARRAYS	512 X 8	3-State	55 ns	20 ns	0.14 mW	SN54S472	J	SN74S472	J, N
	512 X 8	O-C	55 ns	20 ns	0.14 mW	SN54S473	J	SN74S473	J, N
	512 X 8	3-State	55 ns	20 ns	0.14 mW	SN54S474	J, W	SN74S474	J, N
	512 X 8	O-C	55 ns	20 ns	0.14 mW	SN54S475	J, W	SN74S475	J, N
2048-BIT ARRAYS	256 X 8	O-C	50 ns	20 ns	0.24 mW	SN54S470	J	SN74S470	J, N
	256 X 8	3-State	50 ns	20 ns	0.27 mW	SN54S471	J	SN74S471	J, N
1024-BIT ARRAYS	256 X 4	3-State	40 ns	15 ns	0.49 mW	SN54S287	J, W	SN74S287	J, N
	256 X 4	O-C	40 ns	15 ns	0.49 mW	SN54S387	J, W	SN74S387	J, N
512-BIT ARRAYS	64 X 8	O-C	50 ns	47 ns	0.6 mW	SN54186	J, W	SN74186	J, N
256-BIT ARRAYS	32 X 8	O-C	29 ns	28 ns	1.3 mW	SN54188A	J, W	SN74188A	J, N
	32 X 8	O-C	25 ns	12 ns	1.56 mW	SN54S188	J, W	SN74S188	J, N
	32 X 8	3-State	25 ns	12 ns	1.56 mW	SN54S288	J, W	SN74S288	J, N

MICROPROCESSOR CONTROLLERS AND SUPPORT FUNCTIONS

DESCRIPTION	SYSTEM APPLICATION	TYP TOTAL POWER DISSIPATION	DEVICE TYPE AND PACKAGE				PAGE NO.
			−55°C to 125°C		0°C to 70°C		
SYSTEM CONTROLLERS	8080A	700 mW			SN74S428 (TIM8228)	N	7-514
	8080A	700 mW			SN74S438 (TIM8238)	N	7-514
	Universal	450 mW	SN54S482	J	SN74S482	J, N	†
REGISTERS	TMS 9900	110 mW	SN54LS259	J, W	SN74LS259 (TIM9906)	J, N	7-376
	MOS	210 mW	SN54LS363*	J	SN74LS363*	J, N	7-467
		210 mW	SN54LS364*	J	SN74LS364*	J, N	7-467
MULTI-MODE LATCHES	8080A	410 mW	SN54S412	J, W	SN74S412 (TIM8212)	J, N	7-502
TRANSCEIVERS AND BUS DRIVERS		625 mW	SN54S226*	J, W	SN74S226*	J, N	7-345
		207 mW	SN54LS245*	J	SN74LS245*	J, N	7-349
TRANSCEIVERS AND BUS DRIVERS (SSI)		98 mW	SN54LS240	J	SN74LS240	J, N	6-83
		450 mW	SN54S240	J	SN74S240	J, N	6-83
		100 mW	SN54LS241	J	SN74LS241	J, N	6-83
		538 mW	SN54S241	J	SN74S241	J, N	6-83
		128 mW	SN54LS242	J, W	SN74LS242	J, N	6-87
		128 mW	SN54LS243	J, W	SN74LS243	J, N	6-87
		100 mW	SN54LS244	J	SN74LS244	J, N	6-83
CLOCK ELEMENTS	TMS 9900	669 mW			SN74LS362 (TIM9904)*	J, N	7-460
	8080A	719 mW			SN74LS424 (TIM8224)	J, N	7-507
LOGIC ELEMENTS	TMS 9900	190 mW	SN54148	J, W	SN74148 (TIM9907)	J, N	7-151
	TMS 9900	35 mW	SN54LS251	J, W	SN74LS251 (TIM9905)	J, N	7-362
	TMS 9900	63 mW	SN54LS348*	J, W	SN74LS348* (TIM9908)	J, N	7-448

*New product in development as of October 1976.

†See Bipolar Microcomputer Components Data Book, LCC4270.

TEXAS INSTRUMENTS

TTL INTEGRATED CIRCUITS MECHANICAL DATA

ORDERING INSTRUCTIONS

Electrical characteristics presented in this data book, unless otherwise noted, apply for circuit type(s) listed in the page heading regardless of package. The availability of a circuit function in a particular package is denoted by an alphabetical reference above the pin-connection diagram(s). These alphabetical references refer to mechanical outline drawings shown in this section.

Factory orders for circuits described in this catalog should include a four-part type number as explained in the following example.

EXAMPLE: SN 54LS75 J –00

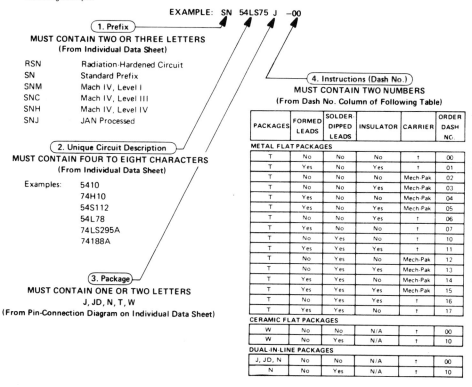

1. Prefix

MUST CONTAIN TWO OR THREE LETTERS
(From Individual Data Sheet)

RSN   Radiation-Hardened Circuit
SN   Standard Prefix
SNM   Mach IV, Level I
SNC   Mach IV, Level III
SNH   Mach IV, Level IV
SNJ   JAN Processed

2. Unique Circuit Description

MUST CONTAIN FOUR TO EIGHT CHARACTERS
(From Individual Data Sheet)

Examples: 5410
            74H10
            54S112
            54L78
            74LS295A
            74188A

3. Package

MUST CONTAIN ONE OR TWO LETTERS
J, JD, N, T, W
(From Pin-Connection Diagram on Individual Data Sheet)

4. Instructions (Dash No.)

MUST CONTAIN TWO NUMBERS
(From Dash No. Column of Following Table)

PACKAGES	FORMED LEADS	SOLDER-DIPPED LEADS	INSULATOR	CARRIER	ORDER DASH NO.
METAL FLAT PACKAGES					
T	No	No	No	†	00
T	Yes	No	Yes	†	01
T	No	No	No	Mech-Pak	02
T	No	No	Yes	Mech-Pak	03
T	Yes	No	No	Mech-Pak	04
T	Yes	No	Yes	Mech-Pak	05
T	No	No	Yes	†	06
T	Yes	No	No	†	07
T	No	Yes	No	†	10
T	Yes	Yes	Yes	†	11
T	No	Yes	No	Mech-Pak	12
T	No	Yes	Yes	Mech-Pak	13
T	Yes	Yes	No	Mech-Pak	14
T	Yes	Yes	Yes	Mech-Pak	15
T	No	Yes	Yes	†	16
T	Yes	Yes	No	†	17
CERAMIC FLAT PACKAGES					
W	No	No	N/A	†	00
W	No	Yes	N/A	†	10
DUAL-IN-LINE PACKAGES					
J, JD, N	No	No	N/A	†	00
N	No	Yes	N/A	†	10

†These circuits are shipped in one of the carriers shown below. Unless a specific method of shipment is specified by the customer (with possible additional posts), circuits will be shipped in the most practical carrier. Please contact your TI sales representative for the method that will best suit your particular needs.

Flat (T, W)
—Barnes Carrier
—Milton Ross Carrier

Dual-in-line ((J, JD, N)
—Slide Magazines
—A-Channel Plastic Tubing
—Barnes Carrier (N only)
—Sectioned Cardboard Box
—Individual Plastic Box

TEXAS INSTRUMENTS

TTL INTEGRATED CIRCUITS MECHANICAL DATA

N plastic dual-in-line packages

These dual-in-line packages consist of a circuit mounted on a 14-, 16-, 20-, or 28-lead frame and encapsulated within an electrically nonconductive plastic compound. The compound will withstand soldering temperature with no deformation and circuit performance characteristics remain stable when operated in high-humidity conditions. The packages are intended for insertion in mounting hole rows on 0.300 (7,62) or 0.600 (15,24) centers. Once the leads are compressed and inserted, sufficient tension is provided to secure the package in the board during soldering. Leads require no additional cleaning or processing when used in soldered assembly.

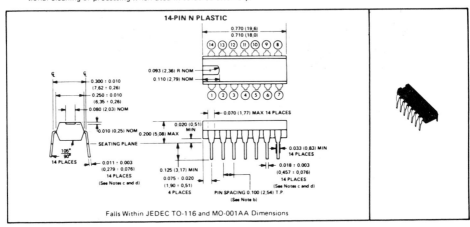

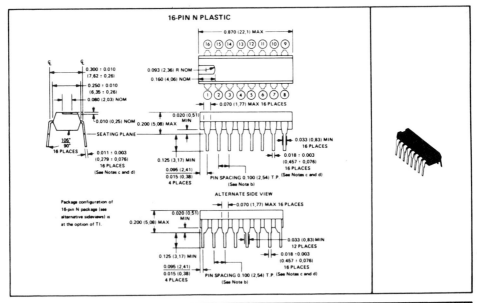

TEXAS INSTRUMENTS

54/74 FAMILIES OF COMPATIBLE TTL CIRCUITS

PIN ASSIGNMENTS (TOP VIEWS)

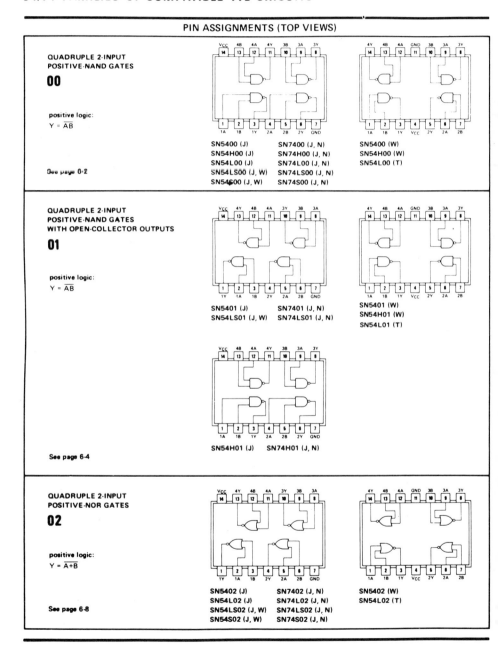

QUADRUPLE 2-INPUT
POSITIVE-NAND GATES

00

positive logic:
$Y = \overline{AB}$

See page 6-2

SN5400 (J)   SN7400 (J, N)   SN5400 (W)
SN54H00 (J)   SN74H00 (J, N)   SN54H00 (W)
SN54L00 (J)   SN74L00 (J, N)   SN54L00 (T)
SN54LS00 (J, W)   SN74LS00 (J, N)
SN54S00 (J, W)   SN74S00 (J, N)

QUADRUPLE 2-INPUT
POSITIVE-NAND GATES
WITH OPEN-COLLECTOR OUTPUTS

01

positive logic:
$Y = \overline{AB}$

SN5401 (J)   SN7401 (J, N)   SN5401 (W)
SN54LS01 (J, W)   SN74LS01 (J, N)   SN54H01 (W)
                                         SN54L01 (T)

SN54H01 (J)   SN74H01 (J, N)

See page 6-4

QUADRUPLE 2-INPUT
POSITIVE-NOR GATES

02

positive logic:
$Y = \overline{A+B}$

See page 6-8

SN5402 (J)   SN7402 (J, N)   SN5402 (W)
SN54L02 (J)   SN74L02 (J, N)   SN54L02 (T)
SN54LS02 (J, W)   SN74LS02 (J, N)
SN54S02 (J, W)   SN74S02 (J, N)

TEXAS INSTRUMENTS

54/74 FAMILIES OF COMPATIBLE TTL CIRCUITS

PIN ASSIGNMENTS (TOP VIEWS)

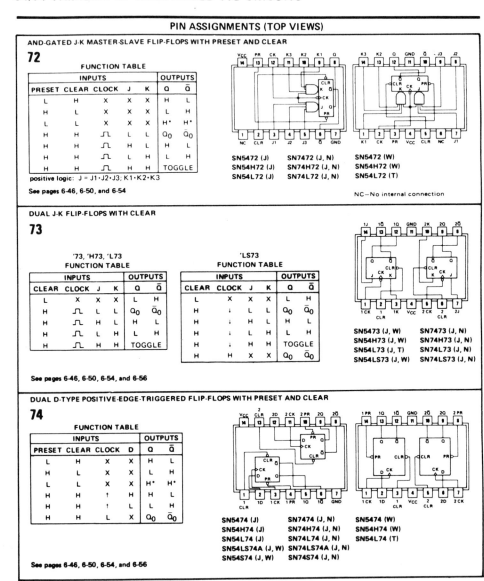

AND-GATED J-K MASTER-SLAVE FLIP-FLOPS WITH PRESET AND CLEAR

72

FUNCTION TABLE

INPUTS					OUTPUTS	
PRESET	CLEAR	CLOCK	J	K	Q	Q̄
L	H	X	X	X	H	L
H	L	X	X	X	L	H
L	L	X	X	X	H*	H*
H	H	⊓	L	L	Q₀	Q̄₀
H	H	⊓	H	L	H	L
H	H	⊓	L	H	L	H
H	H	⊓	H	H	TOGGLE	

positive logic: J = J1·J2·J3; K1·K2·K3

See pages 6-46, 6-50, and 6-54

SN5472 (J)   SN7472 (J, N)   SN5472 (W)
SN54H72 (J)   SN74H72 (J, N)   SN54H72 (W)
SN54L72 (J)   SN74L72 (J, N)   SN54L72 (T)

NC—No internal connection

DUAL J-K FLIP-FLOPS WITH CLEAR

73

'73, 'H73, 'L73
FUNCTION TABLE

INPUTS			OUTPUTS	
CLEAR	CLOCK	J	K	Q	Q̄
L	X	X	X	L	H
H	⊓	L	L	Q₀	Q̄₀
H	⊓	H	L	H	L
H	⊓	L	H	L	H
H	⊓	H	H	TOGGLE	

'LS73
FUNCTION TABLE

INPUTS			OUTPUTS	
CLEAR	CLOCK	J	K	Q	Q̄
L	X	X	X	L	H
H	↓	L	L	Q₀	Q̄₀
H	↓	H	L	H	L
H	↓	L	H	L	H
H	↓	H	H	TOGGLE	
H	H	X	X	Q₀	Q̄₀

See pages 6-46, 6-50, 6-54, and 6-56

SN5473 (J, W)   SN7473 (J, N)
SN54H73 (J, W)   SN74H73 (J, N)
SN54L73 (J, T)   SN74L73 (J, N)
SN54LS73 (J, W)   SN74LS73 (J, N)

DUAL D-TYPE POSITIVE-EDGE-TRIGGERED FLIP-FLOPS WITH PRESET AND CLEAR

74

FUNCTION TABLE

INPUTS				OUTPUTS	
PRESET	CLEAR	CLOCK	D	Q	Q̄
L	H	X	X	H	L
H	L	X	X	L	H
L	L	X	X	H*	H*
H	H	↑	H	H	L
H	H	↑	L	L	H
H	H	L	X	Q₀	Q̄₀

See pages 6-46, 6-50, 6-54, and 6-56

SN5474 (J)   SN7474 (J, N)   SN5474 (W)
SN54H74 (J)   SN74H74 (J, N)   SN54H74 (W)
SN54L74 (J)   SN74L74 (J, N)   SN54L74 (T)
SN54LS74A (J, W)   SN74LS74A (J, N)
SN54S74 (J, W)   SN74S74 (J, N)

See explanation of function tables on page 3-8.
*This configuration is nonstable; that is, it will not persist when preset and clear inputs return to their inactive (high) level.

TEXAS INSTRUMENTS

TTL MSI

TYPES SN54LS138, SN54LS139, SN54S138, SN54S139, SN74LS138, SN74LS139, SN74S138, SN74S139 DECODERS/DEMULTIPLEXERS

BULLETIN NO. DL-S 7611804, DECEMBER 1972–REVISED OCTOBER 1976

- Designed Specifically for High-Speed:
  Memory Decoders
  Data Transmission Systems

- 'S138 and 'LS138 3-to-8-Line Decoders Incorporate 3 Enable Inputs to Simplify Cascading and/or Data Reception

- 'S139 and 'LS139 Contain Two Fully Independent 2-to-4-Line Decoders/ Demultiplexers

- Schottky Clamped for High Performance

TYPE	TYPICAL PROPAGATION DELAY (3 LEVELS OF LOGIC)	TYPICAL POWER DISSIPATION
'LS138	22 ns	32 mW
'S138	8 ns	245 mW
'LS139	22 ns	34 mW
'S139	7.5 ns	300 mW

SN54LS138, SN54S138 . . . J OR W PACKAGE
SN74LS138, SN74S138 . . . J OR N PACKAGE
(TOP VIEW)

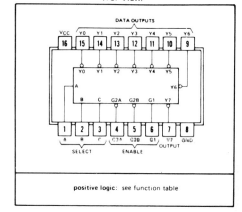

positive logic: see function table

SN54LS139, SN54S139 . . . J OR W PACKAGE
SN74LS139, SN74S139 . . . J OR N PACKAGE
(TOP VIEW)

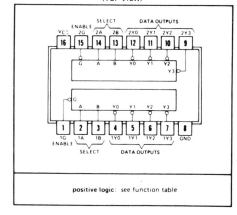

positive logic: see function table

description

These Schottky-clamped TTL MSI circuits are designed to be used in high-performance memory-decoding or data-routing applications requiring very short propagation delay times. In high-performance memory systems these decoders can be used to minimize the effects of system decoding. When employed with high-speed memories utilizing a fast-enable circuit the delay times of these decoders and the enable time of the memory are usually less than the typical access time of the memory. This means that the effective system delay introduced by the Schottky-clamped system decoder is negligible.

The 'LS138 and 'S138 decode one-of-eight lines dependent on the conditions at the three binary select inputs and the three enable inputs. Two active-low and one active-high enable inputs reduce the need for external gates or inverters when expanding. A 24-line decoder can be implemented without external inverters and a 32-line decoder requires only one inverter. An enable input can be used as a data input for demultiplexing applications.

The 'LS139 and 'S139 comprise two individual two-line-to-four-line decoders in a single package. The active-low enable input can be used as a data line in demultiplexing applications.

All of these decoders/demultiplexers feature fully buffered inputs each of which represents only one normalized Series 54LS/74LS load ('LS138, 'LS139) or one normalized Series 54S/74S load ('S138, 'S139) to its driving circuit. All inputs are clamped with high-performance Schottky diodes to suppress line-ringing and simplify system design. Series 54LS and 54S devices are characterized for operation over the full military temperature range of −55°C to 125°C; Series 74LS and 74S devices are characterized for 0°C to 70°C industrial systems.

TEXAS INSTRUMENTS

TTL
MSI

TYPES SN54181, SN54LS181, SN54S181, SN74181, SN74LS181, SN74S181
ARITHMETIC LOGIC UNITS/FUNCTION GENERATORS
BULLETIN NO. DL-S 7611831, DECEMBER 1972 — REVISED OCTOBER 1976

- Full Look-Ahead for High-Speed Operations on Long Words

- Input Clamping Diodes Minimize Transmission-Line Effects

- Darlington Outputs Reduce Turn-Off Time

- Arithmetic Operating Modes:
    Addition
    Subtraction
    Shift Operand A One Position
    Magnitude Comparison
    Plus Twelve Other Arithmetic
        Operations

- Logic Function Modes:
    Exclusive-OR
    Comparator
    AND, NAND, OR, NOR
    Plus Ten Other Logic Operations

SN54181, SN54LS181, SN54S181 . . . J OR W PACKAGE
SN74181, SN74LS181, SN74S181 . . . J OR N PACKAGE
(TOP VIEW)

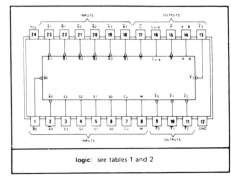

logic: see tables 1 and 2

TYPICAL ADDITION TIMES

NUMBER OF BITS	ADDITION TIMES			PACKAGE COUNT		CARRY METHOD BETWEEN ALU's
	USING '181 AND '182	USING 'LS181 AND '182	USING 'S181 AND 'S182	ARITHMETIC/ LOGIC UNITS	LOOK-AHEAD CARRY GENERATORS	
1 to 4	24 ns	24 ns	11 ns	1		NONE
5 to 8	36 ns	40 ns	18 ns	2		RIPPLE
9 to 16	36 ns	44 ns	19 ns	3 or 4	1	FULL LOOK-AHEAD
17 to 64	60 ns	68 ns	28 ns	5 to 16	2 to 5	FULL LOOK-AHEAD

description

The '181, 'LS181, and 'S181 are arithmetic logic units (ALU)/function generators that have a complexity of 75 equivalent gates on a monolithic chip. These circuits perform 16 binary arithmetic operations on two 4-bit words as shown in Tables 1 and 2. These operations are selected by the four function-select lines (S0, S1, S2, S3) and include addition, subtraction, decrement, and straight transfer. When performing arithmetic manipulations, the internal carries must be enabled by applying a low-level voltage to the mode control input (M). A full carry look-ahead scheme is made available in these devices for fast, simultaneous carry generation by means of two cascade-outputs (pins 15 and 17) for the four bits in the package. When used in conjunction with the SN54182, SN54S182, SN74182, or SN74S182, full carry look-ahead circuits, high-speed arithmetic operations can be performed. The typical addition times shown above illustrate the little additional time required for addition of longer words when full carry look-ahead is employed. The method of cascading '182 or 'S182 circuits with these ALU's to provide multi-level full carry look-ahead is illustrated under typical applications data for the '182 and 'S182.

If high speed is not of importance, a ripple-carry input (C_n) and a ripple-carry output (C_{n+4}) are available. However, the ripple-carry delay has also been minimized so that arithmetic manipulations for small word lengths can be performed without external circuitry.

TEXAS INSTRUMENTS

TTL
MSI

TYPES SN54LS245, SN74LS245
OCTAL BUS TRANSCEIVERS WITH 3-STATE OUTPUTS

BULLETIN NO. DL-S 7612471, OCTOBER 1976

- Bi-directional Bus Transceiver in a High-Density 20-Pin Package
- 3-State Outputs Drive Bus Lines Directly
- P-N-P Inputs Reduce D-C Loading on Bus Lines
- Hysteresis at Bus Inputs Improve Noise Margins
- Typical Propagation Delay Times, Port-to-Port . . . 12 ns
- Typical Enable/Disable Times . . . 17 ns

TYPE	I_{OL} (SINK CURRENT)	I_{OH} (SOURCE CURRENT)
SN54LS245	12 mA	−12 mA
SN74LS245	24 mA	−15 mA

SN54LS245 . . . J PACKAGE
SN74LS245 . . . J OR N PACKAGE
(TOP VIEW)

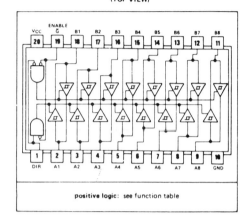

positive logic: see function table

description

These octal bus transceivers are designed for asynchronous two-way communication between data buses. The control function implementation minimizes external timing requirements.

The device allows data transmission from the A bus to the B bus or from the B bus to the A bus depending upon the logic level at the direction control (DIR) input. The enable input ($\overline{G}$) can be used to disable the device so that the buses are effectively isolated.

The SN54LS245 is characterized for operation over the full military temperature range of −55°C to 125°C. The SN74LS245 is characterized for operation from 0°C to 70°C.

schematics of inputs and outputs

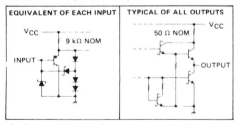

FUNCTION TABLE

ENABLE $\overline{G}$	DIRECTION CONTROL DIR	OPERATION
L	L	B data to A bus
L	H	A data to B bus
H	X	Isolation

H = high level, L = low level, X = irrelevant

absolute maximum ratings over operating free-air temperature range (unless otherwise noted)

Supply voltage, V_{CC} (see Note 1)	7 V
Input voltage	7 V
Operating free-air temperature range: SN54LS245	−55°C to 125°C
SN74LS245	0°C to 70°C
Storage temperature range	−65°C to 150°C

NOTE 1: Voltage values are with respect to network ground terminal.

TEXAS INSTRUMENTS

Appendix 2: programmable logic device data sheets

The following pages are reprinted, by kind permission of the Altera Corporation, from the *Altera Data Book* (1987 edition). The information given is typical of that available to designers working with programmable logic devices. The company also produces a range of application notes and briefs describing the technology of programmable logic devices and showing some of the many ways in which they may be used. Several of these notes and briefs are collected together in the company's EPLD handbook.

The device illustrated, the EP600, is one of a range of erasable programmable logic devices (EPLDs) produced by Altera. It is essentially a PAL as defined in Chapter 5, the AND array being user-programmable and the OR array being pre-programmed. The logical power of the device is enhanced, however, by the provision of an output register whose architecture may be configured by the programmer. Examples of how this can be done are given in the data sheet. This register, together with the provision of selectable internal feedback, allows the construction of both synchronous and asynchronous circuits from this device.

As suggested in the data sheet, the development of programming information for the device may be accomplished with the company's own A+PLUS development software, one feature of which is the provision of a TTL macro-function library. A designer may thus translate TTL designs directly into PAL form, using graphical entry and the logic structures he is already familiar with. He does not need to bother with a detailed understanding of the way in which these structures are realised inside the EPLD if he does not wish to do so. There are several software design aids of this kind available, some of which are not tailored to a particular supplier's devices but allow designs to be made for most devices on the market. They are designed to be 'upgradable' so that, as new devices are made available, the software can be enhanced to allow designs to be produced for them.

Once a design has been produced and tested — a simulator is usually provided as part of the software design environment — a JEDEC file of programming information can be generated to be transmitted to a hardware-programming device. The EPLD can then be programmed or 'blown' ready for use.

EP600

ERASABLE PROGRAMMABLE LOGIC DEVICE

FEATURES

- High density (over 600 gates) replacement for TTL and 74HC.
- Advanced CHMOS EPROM technology, allows erase and reprogram.
- High speed, $t_{pd} = 25$ ns.
- "Zero Power" typically $10\mu A$ standby.
- **Asynchronous clocking of all registers or banked register operation from 2 synchronous clocks.**
- Sixteen Macrocells with configurable I/O architecture allowing 20 inputs and 16 outputs.
- **Programmable registers providing D, T, SR or JK flipflops with individual Clear control.**
- 100% generically testable—provides 100% programming yield.
- Programmable "Security Bit" allows total protection of proprietary designs.
- Advanced software support featuring Schematic Capture, Interactive Netlist, Boolean Equation and State Machine design entry.
- Space saving 24 pin, 300 mil, dual in-line package and 28 pin J-leaded chip carrier.

GENERAL DESCRIPTION

The ALTERA EP600 Programmable Logic Device is capable of implementing over 600 equivalent gates of SSI and MSI logic functions all in a space saving 24 pin, DIP, 300 mil package or a 28 pin J-leaded chip carrier.

The EP600 uses familiar sum-of-products logic providing a programmable AND with fixed OR structure. The device accommodates both combinatorial and sequential logic functions with up to 20 inputs and 16 outputs. The EP600 includes an ALTERA proprietary programmable I/O architecture providing individual selection of either combinatorial or registered output and feedback signals, active high or low.

A unique feature of the EP600 is the ability to program D, T, SR, or JK flipflop operation individually for each output without sacrificing product terms. In addition, each register can be individually clocked from any of the input or feedback paths available in the AND array. These features allow a variety of logic functions to be simultaneously implemented.

The CHMOS EPROM technology reduces the power consumption to less than 20% of equivalent bipolar devices without sacrificing speed performance. Other advantages include: 100% generic testing (all devices are 100% tested at the factory). The device can be erased with ultraviolet light. Design changes are no longer costly, nor is there a need for post programming testing.

CONNECTION DIAGRAM

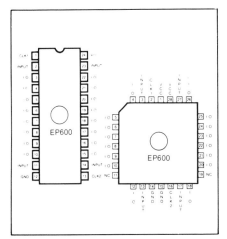

REV. 3.0

Programming the EP600 is accomplished with the use of Altera's A+PLUS development software which supports four different design entry methods. Once the circuit has been entered, the A+PLUS software performs automatic translation into logical equations, boolean minimization, and design fitting directly into an EP600.

FUNCTIONAL DESCRIPTION

The EP600 is an Erasable Programmable Logic Device (EPLD) which uses a CMOS EPROM technology to configure connections in a programmable AND logic array. The device also contains a revolutionary programmable I/O architecture which provides advanced functional capability for user programmable logic.

Externally, the EP600 provides 4 dedicated data inputs, 2 synchronous clock inputs, and 16 I/O pins which may be configured for input, output, or bidirectional operation.

Figure 1 and 2 shows the EP600 basic Macrocell and the complete block diagram. The internal architecture is organized with familiar sum-of-products (AND-OR) structure. Inputs to the programmable AND array come from true and complement signals of the four dedicated data inputs and sixteen I/O architecture control blocks. The 40 input AND array encompasses 160 product terms which are distributed among 16 available Macrocells. Each EP600 product term represents a 40 input AND gate.

Each Macrocell contains ten product terms. Eight product terms are dedicated for logic implementation. One product term is used for Clear control of the Macrocell internal register. The remaining product term is used for Output Enable/Asynchronous Clock implementation.

At the intersection point of an input signal and a product term there exists an EPROM connection. In the erased state, all connections are made. This means both the true and complement of all inputs are connected to each product term. Connections are opened during the programming process. Therefore, any product term may be connected to the true or complement of any array input signal. When both the true and complement of any signal is left intact, a logical false results on the output of the AND gate. If both the true and complement connections are open, then a logical "don't care" results for that input. If all inputs for the product term are programmed open, then a logical true results on the output of the AND gate.

Two dedicated clock inputs provide synchronous clock signals to the EP600 internal registers. Each of the clock signals controls a bank of eight registers. CLK1 controls registers associated with Macrocells 9-16. CLK2 controls registers associated with Macrocells 1-8. The EP600 advanced I/O architecture allows the number of synchronous registers to be user defined, from one to sixteen. Both dedicated clock inputs are positive edge triggered.

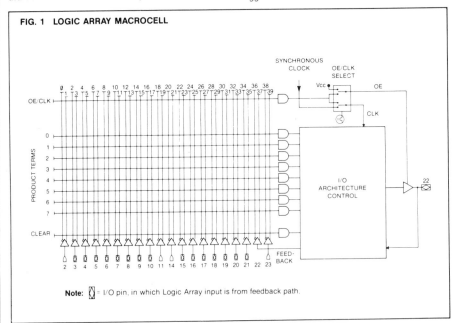

FIG. 1   LOGIC ARRAY MACROCELL

Note: ▯ = I/O pin, in which Logic Array input is from feedback path.

ALTERA

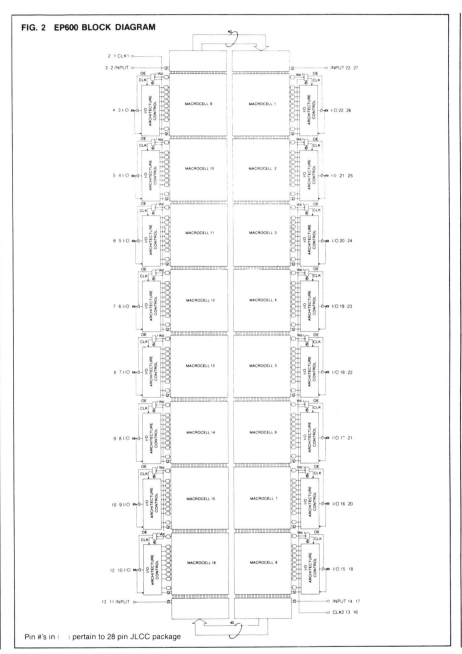

FIG. 2   EP600 BLOCK DIAGRAM

Pin #'s in ( ) pertain to 28 pin JLCC package

ALTERA

I/O ARCHITECTURE

The EP600 Input/Output Architecture provides each Macrocell with over 50 possible I/O configurations. Each I/O can be configured for combinatorial or registered output, with programmable output polarity. Four different types of registers (D, T, JK, SR), can be implemented into every I/O without any additional logic requirements. I/O feedback selection can also be programmed for registered or input (pin) feedback. Another benefit of the EP600 I/O architecture is its ability to individually clock each internal register from asynchronous clock signals.

OE/CLK Selection

Figure 3 shows the two modes of operation which are provided by the OE/CLK Select Multiplexer. The operation of this multiplexer is controlled by a single EPROM bit and may be individually configured for each EP600 I/O pin. In Mode 0, the three-state output buffer is controlled by a single product term. If the output of the AND gate is a logical true then the output buffer is enabled. If a logical false resides on the output of the AND gate then the output buffer is seen as high impedance. In this mode the Macrocell flipflop may be clocked by its respective synchronous clock input. After erasure, OE/CLK Select Mux is configured as Mode 0.

In Mode 1, the Output Enable buffer is always enabled. The Macrocell flipflop now may be triggered from an asynchronous clock signal generated by the OE/CLK multiplexable product term. This mode allows individual clocking of flipflops from any available signal in the AND array. Because both true and complement

signals reside in the AND array, the flipflop may be configured for positive or negative edge trigger operation. With the clock now controlled by a product term, gated clock structures are also possible.

OUTPUT/FEEDBACK Selection

Figure 4 shows the EP600 basic output configurations. Along with combinatorial output, four register types are available. Each Macrocell I/O may be independently configured. All registers have individual Asynchronous Clear control from a dedicated product term. When the product term is asserted to a logical one, the Macrocell register will immediately be loaded with a logical zero independently of the clock. On power up, the EP600 performs the Clear function automatically.

When the D or T register is selected, eight product terms are ORed together and made available to the register input. The Invert Select EPROM bit determines output polarity. The Feedback Select Multiplexer enables registered, I/O (pin) or no feedback to the AND array.

If the JK or SR registers are selected, the eight product terms are shared among two OR gates. The allocation of product terms for each register input is optimized by the A+PLUS development software. The Invert Select EPROM bits configures output polarity. The Feedback Select Multiplexer enables registered or no feedback to the AND array.

Any I/O pin may be configured as a dedicated input by selecting no output and pin feedback. No output is obtained by disabling the Macrocell output buffer.

In the erased state, the I/O is configured for combinatorial active low output with input (pin) feedback.

FIG. 3   OE/CLK SELECT MUX

MODE Ø
OE = P-Term Controlled
CLK = Synchronous

MODE 1
OE = Enabled
CLK = Asynchronous

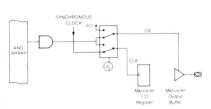

The register is clocked by the synchronous clock signal which is common to 7 other Macrocells. The output is enabled by the logic from the product term.

The output is permanently enabled and the register is clocked via the product term. This allows for gated clocks that may be generated from elsewhere in the EP600.

FIG. 4   I/O CONFIGURATIONS

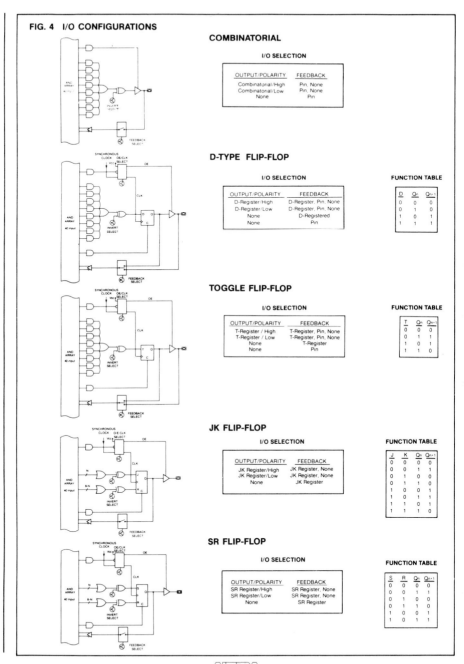

COMBINATORIAL

I/O SELECTION

OUTPUT/POLARITY	FEEDBACK
Combinatorial/High	Pin, None
Combinatorial/Low	Pin, None
None	Pin

D-TYPE FLIP-FLOP

I/O SELECTION

OUTPUT/POLARITY	FEEDBACK
D-Register/High	D-Register, Pin, None
D-Register/Low	D-Register, Pin, None
None	D-Registered
None	Pin

FUNCTION TABLE

D	Q_n	Q_{n+1}
0	0	0
0	1	0
1	0	1
1	1	1

TOGGLE FLIP-FLOP

I/O SELECTION

OUTPUT/POLARITY	FEEDBACK
T-Register / High	T-Register, Pin, None
T-Register / Low	T-Register, Pin, None
None	T-Register
None	Pin

FUNCTION TABLE

T	Q_n	Q_{n+1}
0	0	0
0	1	1
1	0	1
1	1	0

JK FLIP-FLOP

I/O SELECTION

OUTPUT/POLARITY	FEEDBACK
JK Register/High	JK Register, None
JK Register/Low	JK Register, None
None	JK Register

FUNCTION TABLE

J	K	Q_n	Q_{n+1}
0	0	0	0
0	0	1	1
0	1	0	0
0	1	1	0
1	0	0	1
1	0	1	1
1	1	0	1
1	1	1	0

SR FLIP-FLOP

I/O SELECTION

OUTPUT/POLARITY	FEEDBACK
SR Register/High	SR Register, None
SR Register/Low	SR Register, None
None	SR Register

FUNCTION TABLE

S	R	Q_n	Q_{n+1}
0	0	0	0
0	0	1	1
0	1	0	0
0	1	1	0
1	0	0	1
1	0	1	1

ALTERA

ABSOLUTE MAXIMUM RATINGS

COMMERCIAL, INDUSTRIAL, MILITARY

Note: See Design Recommendations

SYMBOL	PARAMETER	CONDITIONS	MIN	MAX	UNIT
V_{CC}	Supply voltage	With respect to GND note (3)	–2.0	7.0	V
V_{PP}	Programming supply voltage		–2.0	13.5	V
V_I	DC INPUT voltage		–2.0	7.0	V
I_{MAX}	DC V_{CC} or GND current		–100	+100	mA
I_{OUT}	DC OUTPUT current, per pin		–25	+25	mA
P_D	Power dissipation			250	mW
T_{STG}	Storage temperature	No bias	–65	+150	°C
T_{AMB}	Ambient temperature	Under bias, note (6)	–65	+135	°C
ESD	ElectroStatic Discharge Voltage		±2100		V

RECOMMENDED OPERATING CONDITIONS

SYMBOL	PARAMETER	CONDITIONS	MIN	MAX	UNIT
V_{CC}	Supply Voltage	note (6)	4.75 (4.5)	5.25 (5.5)	V
V_I	INPUT voltage		0	V_{CC}	V
V_O	OUTPUT voltage		0	V_{CC}	V
T_A	Operating temperature	For Commercial	0	70	°C
T_A	Operating temperature	For Industrial	–40	85	°C
T_A	Operating temperature	For Military	–55	125	°C
T_R	INPUT rise time	note (9)		500	ns
T_F	INPUT fall time	note (9)		500	ns

DC OPERATING CHARACTERISTICS

(V_{CC} = 5V ±5%, T_A = 0°C to 70°C for Commercial)
(V_{CC} = 5V ± 10%, T_A = –40°C to 85°C for Industrial)
(V_{CC} = 5V ±10%, T_A = –55°C to 125°C for Military)
Note (1) and (6)

SYMBOL	PARAMETER	CONDITIONS	MIN	TYP	MAX	UNIT
V_{IH}	HIGH level input voltage		2.0		V_{CC} + 0.3	V
V_{IL}	LOW level input voltage		–0.3		0.8	V
V_{OH}	HIGH level TTL output voltage	I_{OH} = –4mA DC	2.4			V
V_{OH}	HIGH level CMOS output voltage	I_{OH} = –2mA DC	3.84			V
V_{OL}	LOW level output voltage	I_{OL} = 4mA DC			0.45	V
I_I	Input leakage current	V_I = V_{CC} or GND note (6)	–10 (–20)		+10 (+20)	µA
I_{OZ}	3-state output off-state current	V_O = V_{CC} or GND note (6)	–10 (–20)		+10 (+20)	µA
I_{CC1}	V_{CC} supply current (standby)	V_I = V_{CC} or GND No load note (8)		10	150	µA
I_{CC2}	V_{CC} supply current (active)	V_I = V_{CC} or GND No load, f = 1.0 MHz note (7)		3	10 (15)	mA

CAPACITANCE

Note (4)

SYMBOL	PARAMETER	CONDITIONS	MIN	MAX	UNIT
C_{IN}	Input Capacitance	V_{IN} = 0V f = 1.0 MHz		20	pF
C_{OUT}	Output Capacitance	V_{OUT} = 0V f = 1.0 MHz		20	pF
C_{CLK}	Clock Pin Capacitance	V_{IN} = 0V f = 1.0 MHz		20	pF

ALTERA

AC CHARACTERISTICS Note (5)

EP600, EP600-1, EP600-2, EP600-3

(V_{CC} = 5V ± 5%, T_A = 0°C to 70°C for Commercial)
(V_{CC} = 5V ± 10%, T_A = –40°C to 85°C for Industrial)
(V_{CC} = 5V ± 10%, T_A = –55°C to 125°C for Military)

SYMBOL	PARAMETER	CONDITIONS	EP600-1 MIN	EP600-1 MAX	EP600-2 MIN	EP600-2 MAX	EP600-3 MIN	EP600-3 MAX	EP600 MIN	EP600 MAX	UNIT
t_{PD}	Input to non-registered output	C_1 = 50pF		25		35		45		55	ns
t_{PZX}	Input to output enable			25		35		45		55	ns
t_{PXZ}	Input to output disable	C_1 = 5pF note (2)		25		35		45		55	ns
t_{CLR}	Asynchronous output clear time	C_1 = 50pF		30		40		50		60	ns
t_{IO}	I/O input buffer delay			5		5		5		5	ns

SYNCHRONOUS CLOCK MODE

SYMBOL	PARAMETER	CONDITIONS	EP600-1 MIN	EP600-1 MAX	EP600-2 MIN	EP600-2 MAX	EP600-3 MIN	EP600-3 MAX	EP600 MIN	EP600 MAX	UNIT
f_{MAX}	Maximum frequency		45.5		33.3		26.3		22.2		MHz
t_{SU}	Input setup time		22		30		38		45		ns
t_H	Input hold time		0		0		0		0		ns
t_{CH}	Clock high time		11		15		17.5		22.5		ns
t_{CL}	Clock low time		11		15		17.5		22.5		ns
t_{CO1}	Clock to output delay			15		22		25		30	ns
t_{CNT}	Minimum clock period (register output feedback to register input - internal path)	note (7)		33		45		55		65	ns
f_{CNT}	Internal maximum frequency ($1/t_{CNT}$)	note (7)	30.3		22.2		18.2		15.4		MHz

ASYNCHRONOUS CLOCK MODE

SYMBOL	PARAMETER	CONDITIONS	EP600-1 MIN	EP600-1 MAX	EP600-2 MIN	EP600-2 MAX	EP600-3 MIN	EP600-3 MAX	EP600 MIN	EP600 MAX	UNIT
f_{MAX}	Maximum frequency		45.5		33.3		26.3		22.2		MHz
t_{ASU}	Input setup time		10		10		10		10		ns
t_{AH}	Input hold time		15		15		15		15		ns
t_{ACH}	Clock high time		11		15		17.5		22.5		ns
t_{ACL}	Clock low time		11		15		17.5		22.5		ns
t_{ACO1}	Clock to output delay			27		42		53		65	ns
t_{ACNT}	Minimum clock period (register output feedback to register input - internal path)			33		45		55		65	ns
f_{ACNT}	Internal maximum frequency ($1/t_{ACNT}$)		30.3		22.2		18.2		15.4		MHz

Notes:
1. Typical values are for T_A = 25°C, V_{CC} = 5V
2. Sample tested only for an output change of 500mV.
3. Minimum DC input is –0.3V. During transitions, the inputs may undershoot to –2.0V for periods less than 20ns.
4. Capacitance measured at 25°C. Sample tested only. Clock pin capacitance for dedicated clock inputs only. Pin 13, (high voltage pin during programming), has capacitance of 50 pF max.
5. All AC values tested with TURBO-BIT™ programmed.
6. Figures in ( ) pertain to military and industrial temperature versions.
7. Measured with device programmed as a 16 bit counter.
8. EPLD automatically goes into standby mode if logic transitions do not occur when in non-turbo mode (approximately 100 ns after last transition).
9. Clock t_R, t_F = 250ns (100ns).
10. The f_{MAX} values shown represent the highest frequency for pipelined data.

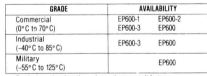

GRADE	AVAILABILITY	
Commercial (0°C to 70°C)	EP600-1 EP600-3	EP600-2 EP600
Industrial (–40°C to 85°C)	EP600-3	EP600
Military (–55°C to 125°C)		EP600

For devices other than those shown please consult factory.

FIG. 5   SWITCHING WAVEFORMS

COMBINATORIAL MODE

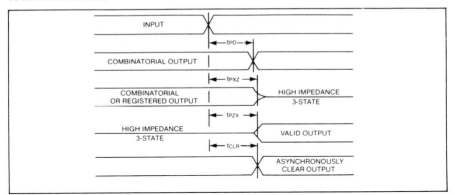

SYNCHRONOUS CLOCK MODE

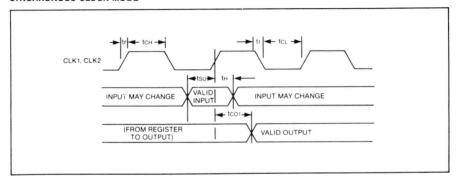

ASYNCHRONOUS CLOCK MODE

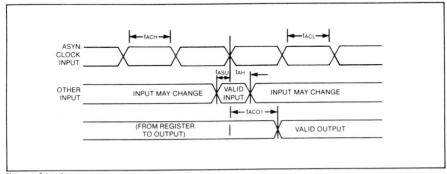

Notes: t_r & t_f < 6ns
        t_{CL} & t_{CH} measured at 0.3V and 2.7V
        all other timing at 1.5V
        Input voltage levels at 0V and 3V

ALTERA

FUNCTIONAL TESTING

The EP600 is fully functionally tested and guaranteed through complete testing of each programmable EPROM bit and all internal logic elements thus ensuring 100% programming yield.

As a result, traditional problems associated with fuse-programmed circuits are eliminated. The erasable nature of the EP600 allows test program patterns to be used and then erased. This facility to use application-independent, general purpose tests is called generic testing and is unique among user-defined LSI logic devices.

FIG. 6   AC TEST CONDITIONS

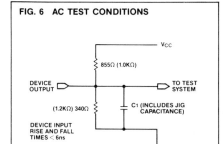

( ) — CMOS LEVEL TEST CONDITIONS

Power supply transients can affect AC measurements, simultaneous transitions of multiple outputs should be avoided for accurate measurement. Do not attempt to perform threshold tests under AC conditions. Large amplitude, fast ground current transients normally occur as the device outputs discharge the load capacitances. These transients flowing through the parasitic inductance between the device ground pin and the test system ground can create significant reductions in observable input noise immunity.

DESIGN SECURITY

The EP600 contains a programmable design security feature that controls the access to the data programmed into the device. If this programmable feature is used, a proprietary design implemented in the device cannot be copied nor retrieved. This enables a high level of design control to be obtained since programmed data within EPROM cells is invisible. The bit that controls this function, along with all other program data, may be reset simply by erasing the device.

FIG. 7 I_{CC} VS F_{MAX}

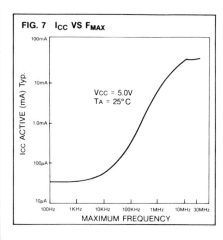

FIG. 8   OUTPUT DRIVE CURRENTS

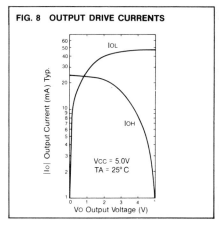

Appendix 3: some commercial VLSI design systems (available as at January 1987)

There are now many systems available for designing VLSI chips. Following arangements made in 1985 between a number of commercial companies and a consortium of British universities and polytechnics, the systems described here are those most likely to be met by students studying in these institutions. This is not to say that they are useful only as educational training systems. With one exception, which is specifically intended as such, they are all capable of producing designs for full-scale commercial chips equivalent to several thousand gates. Two are based on gate-array technology, one is a very wide-ranging system encompassing gate-array, standard-cell and full-custom designs, and the fourth is primarily intended as a very powerful full-custom design system.

QUDOS

QUDOS, which stands for 'quick designs on silicon', offers a design and manufacturing facility based on electron-beam lithography. The company provides the hardware and software design tools and, once a design is fully checked, simulated and tested, will produce finished chips using its own in-house processing facility based on Ferranti or Texas-Intruments gate-arrays. Users are thus able to follow the complete 'route to silicon' with a single manufacturer for prototypes or low-volume production. If a design goes into high-volume production, it can be transferred to the wafer manufacturer.

The present scheme is at two distinct levels. The company has strong links with Acorn Computers Ltd and QUDOS have produced an educational design package which runs on a BBC Microcomputer with a 6502 second processor. Chip designs are entered using a hardware description language written in BBC Basic. A simulator and manual routing layout package capable of handling 300 to 400 gates are then used to produce the design files for an E-beam machine. Because E-beam technology is used, multi-project chips and multi-chip wafers may be produced, making the system very economical for educational purposes.

The professional level software runs on a VAX, an Acorn workstation or similar systems and allows the design of 3000-gate chips A mouse-driven hardware description language is used for chip design entry. The simulator allows track capacitance effects to be included when layout is complete and both manual and auto-layout programs are provided. All the advantages of the use of E-beam technology are again available.

Turn-round times from a few days to a few weeks are quoted and prices for prototype quantities can be as low as a hundred pounds.

MICRO CIRCUIT ENGINEERING (MCE)

MCE offer a suite of software design tools based on their own Falcon range of logic arrays and designed to run on VAX computers, Apollo workstations or IBM/PCs. The Falcon range essentially employs the gate-array philosophy, each chip being fully preprocessed except for a metallisation layer. The software, however, uses the standard cell approach which is made possible because of the chip layout. Each chip consists of an array of 'logic cells' laid out in a row–cell configuration with input/output connections at the top and bottom of the cells and interconnection highways between the rows of cells. The basic CMOS logic cell consists of four polysilicon-gate MOS transistors: two N-channel and two P-channel. A comprehensive software and hardware library of standard cells is provided based on this configuration. When designing a system, a designer simply has to call up standard cells from the library and, at the layout stage, these will automatically be converted into fully internally connected areas of silicon with inputs and outputs leading directly onto the interconnection highways. Interconnection of these standard cells is then directly comparable with laying out a printed circuit board. Peripheral cells are available to buffer signals into and out of the chip.

Chip designs may be entered using either a mouse-driven schematic capture package or a hardware description language, both of which are hierarchical in nature. Designs are implemented in the form of 'modules', each module consisting of a collection of the standard cells available from the library and/or modules already created. Completed designs are then simulated and tested using the simulator and test waveform generation software. Layout, which involves the use of extensive placing and routing software, can be done by the customer or may be left to MCE and is followed by another simulation and test run taking account of track loading effects. When a mutually acceptable device detail specification has been achieved, MCE produce masks, process and test wafers, and package and test chips.

Prices of a few hundred pounds per processed chip and turn-round times of a few weeks are offered.

SILVAR-LISCO

Founded in 1981 by the merging together of the American Silicon Valley Research Company and the Belgian Leuven Industrial Software Company, Silvar-Lisco provide what is arguably the most comprehensive range of IC and p.c.b. CAE tools in the industry. Designated the SL-2000 software family, the design suite offers modules for all levels of the design process from schematic capture at the input level to simulation and layout. The company's stated policy is one of integration and flexibility. To back this claim they have ensured that, not only will all their modules run together, but interfaces are provided to other manufacturers' software packages as well. Several well-established simulators, for example, can be used from within the suite. They have also aimed for software portability, intending to provide a CAE base for existing general-purpose hardware installations, such as VAX or Apollo, rather than require the use of specially designed hardware.

The first part of the design process is to create a circuit database via the schematic design system (SDS), a fully hierarchical data capture package offering a very flexible window facility. This then provides the input for whichever simulator and layout modules are chosen. The system provides several different simulators and allows interfaces to industry standards such as HILO and SPICE. Layout modules are provided at component level (to allow for full-custom design), standard cell, gate array and p.c.b. levels. For the latter three, both interactive-manual and automatic layout routines can be supported.

Being so wide-ranging, the system is not tied to any particular manufacturer's IC production process but can produce mask artwork or E-beam information for many different chip technologies.

It should, of course, be borne in mind that, being so comprehensive, the system does demand a large investment of time from a user before he can hope to become skilled in all aspects of its use.

RACAL REDAC'S ISIS

Originally developed by INMOS as a full-custom design tool to produce the Transputer, the ISIS design system is now marketed by Racal-Redac to provide both full-custom and standard-cell design facilities for all digital MOS processes. The software covers all aspects of VLSI design, from logic capture and simulation, through layout and design rule checking to mask generation and E-beam output. Interfaces are available to other suppliers' software packages, e.g. SPICE. The software runs on VAX or Apollo systems with the addition of Racal-Redac's own V800 graphics workstation for the layout and schematic capture packages.

When used for full-custom design, the system employs techniques which allow remarkably rapid design even for very large circuits. As indicated in Chapter 5, design of a full-custom chip is a task requiring several different designers. The ISIS system is based on a floor-plan approach in which a designer can 'claim' a particular part of the floor-plan which is then barred to other designers who may observe what he is doing but not alter it themselves. All parts of the floor-plan may, however, be worked on in parallel. At the lowest level — specifying transistors (or so-called leaf cells) — interactive design rule checking is provided. If two devices are placed next to each other in a way which would violate the design rules, the offending ones are highlighted on the screen so that an immediate alteration can be made. At all stages of design a system of 'isomorphic hierarchies' is employed. Firstly, the design structure is truly hierarchical from the overall chip specification right the way down to the device structures. The particular form the design structure takes has to correspond, at each level of the hierarchy, on a one-to-one basis with the silicon layout. Any mismatches will result in error detection. This does impose some restrictions on a designer (all modules must be rectangular, for example) but the benefits of a chip which is 'correct by design' are claimed to outweigh these.

The advantage of the ISIS suite as a standard cell design system is that many of the full-custom design procedures are available to the user as well as the usual standard cell facilities. Automatic placement and routing procedures may thus be run but these may be interrupted at any time by the designer to optimise layout.

The system is not tied to any particular manufacturer's chip technology, but may be used in full-custom mode for any MOS process whose detail design rules can be specified in the required form. 3-micron and 5-micron CMOS standard cell libraries are also currently available, both intended to fit envelope design rules suitable for a number of manufacturers' processes.

FURTHER INFORMATION

Full details of these systems may be obtained from the suppliers at the following addresses:

Qudos Ltd
Cambridge Science Park
Milton Road
Cambridge
CB4 4FD

Micro Circuit Engineering
Alexandra Way
Ashchurch
Tewkesbury
Gloucestershire
GL20 8TB

Silvar-Lisco Ltd
Alpha House
London Road
Bracknell
Berkshire
RG12 2TJ

Racal-Redac Ltd
Newtown
Tewkesbury
Gloucestershire
GL20 8HE

Index

ELLIS HORWOOD BOOKS IN COMPUTING SCIENCE
General Editors: Professor JOHN CAMPBELL, University College London, and
BRIAN L. MEEK, King's College London (KQC), University of London
Series in Computers and Their Applications
Series Editor: BRIAN L. MEEK, Computer Centre, King's College London
(KQC), University of London

Peter, R.	Recursive Functions in Computer Theory
Phillips, C. & Cornelius, B.J.	Computational Numerical Methods
Rahtz, S.P.Q.	Information Technology and the Humanities
Ramsden, E.	Microcomputers in Education 2
Rubin, T.	Human Factors in the Design of User Interfaces
Schirmer, C.	Programming in C for UNIX
Sharp, J.A.	Data Flow Computing
Sherif, M.A.	Effective Management of Database Projects
Smith, I.C.H.	Microcomputers in Education
Smith, J.M. & Stutely, R.	Reader's Aids to ISO 8879 SGML
Späth, H.	Cluster Analysis Algorithms
Späth, H.	Cluster Dissection and Analysis
Stratford-Collins, M.J.	ADA: A Programmer's Conversion Course
Teskey, F.N.	Principles of Text Processing
Tizzard, K.	C for Professional Programmers
Turner, S.J.	An Introduction to Compiler Design
Whiddett, R.J.	UNIX: A Practical Guide
Whiddett, R.J.	Concurrent Programming for Software Engineers
Yannakoudakis, E.J. & Hutton, P.J.	Speech Synthesis and Recognition Systems
Young, S.J.	An Introduction to ADA, 2nd (Revised) Edition
Young, S.J.	Real Time Languages
Zech, R.	FORTH

Computer Communitcations and Networking

Currie, W.S.	Local Area Networks Explained
Deasington, R.J.	A Practical Guide to Computer Communications and Networking, 2nd edition
Deasington, R.J.	X.25 Explained: Protocols for Packet Switching Networks, 2nd edition
Henshall, J. & Shaw, A.	ISO/OSI Explained: End to End Computer Communications Systems
Kauffels, F.-J.	Local Networks